Questions & Answers

Criminal Procedure—
Police Investigation

Carolina Academic Press
Questions & Answers Series

Questions & Answers: Administrative Law,
Third Edition
Linda D. Jellum, Karen A. Jordan

Questions & Answers: Antitrust
Shubha Ghosh

Questions & Answers: Bankruptcy, Second Edition
Mary Jo Wiggins

Questions & Answers: Business Associations,
Second Edition
Douglas M. Branson

Questions & Answers: Civil Procedure,
Fourth Edition
William V. Dorsaneo, III, Elizabeth Thornburg

Questions & Answers: Constitutional Law,
Third Edition
Paul E. McGreal, Linda S. Eads, Charles W. Rhodes

Questions & Answers: Contracts,
Third Edition
Scott J. Burnham

Questions & Answers: Copyright Law,
Second Edition
Dave Fagundes, Robert C. Lind

Questions & Answers: Criminal Law,
Fourth Edition
Emily Marcus Levine, Paul Marcus

Questions & Answers: Criminal Procedure—
Police Investigation, Fourth Edition
Wayne A. Logan

Questions & Answers: Criminal Procedure—
Prosecution and Adjudication, Third Edition
Neil P. Cohen, Michael J. Benza, Wayne A. Logan

Questions & Answers: Environmental Law
Dru Stevenson

Questions & Answers: Evidence, Fourth Edition
Paul C. Giannelli

Questions & Answers: Family Law, Third Edition
Mark Strasser

Questions & Answers: Federal Estate & Gift
Taxation, Third Edition
James M. Delaney, Elaine Hightower Gagliardi

Questions & Answers: Federal Income Tax,
Second Edition
James M. Delaney

Questions & Answers: Intellectual Property,
Third Edition
Gary Myers, Lee Ann Wheelis Lockridge

Questions & Answers: International Law
Rebecca Bratspies

Questions & Answers: Patent Law
Cynthia M. Ho

Questions & Answers: Payment Systems,
Second Edition
Timothy R. Zinnecker

Questions & Answers: Professional Responsibility,
Fourth Edition
Patrick Emery Longan

Questions & Answers: Property,
Second Edition
John Copeland Nagle

Questions & Answers: Remedies
Rachel M. Janutis, Tracy A. Thomas

Questions & Answers: Secured Transactions,
Third Edition
Bruce A. Markell, Timothy R. Zinnecker

Questions & Answers: The First Amendment,
Third Edition
Russell L. Weaver, William D. Araiza

Questions & Answers: Torts,
Fourth Edition
Anita Bernstein

Questions & Answers: Trademark and
Unfair Competition
Vince F. Chiappetta

Questions & Answers: Wills, Trusts, and Estates,
Third Edition
Thomas M. Featherston, Jr.

Questions & Answers
Criminal Procedure— Police Investigation

Multiple Choice and Short Answer
Questions and Answers

FOURTH EDITION

Wayne A. Logan
STEVEN M. GOLDSTEIN PROFESSOR OF LAW
FLORIDA STATE UNIVERSITY COLLEGE OF LAW

CAROLINA ACADEMIC PRESS
Durham, North Carolina

ISBN 978-1-5310-2114-6
e-ISBN 978-1-5310-2115-3
LCCN 2021938778

Carolina Academic Press, LLC
700 Kent Street
Durham, North Carolina 27701
(919) 489-7486
www.cap-press.com

Printed in the United States of America

Contents

Preface   ix

About the Author   xi

Questions   1

Topic 1: Incorporation   3

Topic 2: State Constitutional Protections   5

Topic 3: Fourth Amendment Right of Privacy   7

Topic 4: Private Searches   11

Topic 5: Motion to Dismiss   13

Topic 6: Search Warrants   15

Topic 7: Searches without Warrants   19

Topic 8: Probable Cause: Police Truthfulness   23

Topic 9: Search Warrants: Particularization   25

Topic 10: Execution of a Search Warrant   27

Topic 11: Plain View   29

Topic 12: Custodial Arrest for Petty Offenses   31

Topic 13: Arrest   33

Topic 14: Judicial Review of an Arrest   37

Topic 15: Pretextual Stops and Arrests   39

Topic 16: Protective Sweep of a Home   41

Topic 17: Search of a Person or Item Incident to Arrest   43

Topic 18: Search of a Home Incident to Arrest   45

Topic 19: Exigent Circumstances   47

Topic 20: Community Caretaking Function   51

Topic 21: Search of an Automobile Incident to an Arrest   53

Topic 22: Automobile Exception   55

Topic 23: Search of Containers   59

Topic 24: Impoundment and Inventory Search of a Vehicle   61

Topic 25: Comparing Different Justifications for the Search of an Automobile   63

Topic 26: Stop and Frisk   65

Topic 27: Checkpoint Stops   69

Topic 28: Traffic Stops: Duration and Scope of Inquiry   71

Topic 29: Administrative Searches   73

Topic 30: Special Needs Searches   75

Topic 31: Consent Searches   77

Topic 32: Electronic Eavesdropping   81

Topic 33: Exclusionary Rule   83

Topic 34: Good Faith Exception   85

Topic 35: Interrogation and Confession: Custody   87

Topic 36: Interrogation and Confession: Public Safety Exception   89

Topic 37: Interrogation   91

Topic 38: *Miranda* Warnings   95

Topic 39: Waiver of *Miranda* Rights   97

Topic 40: First Confession without Warnings   99

Topic 41: Exercising *Miranda* Rights   101

Topic 42: Invoking the Right to Remain Silent   103

Topic 43: Resumpton of Interrogation   105

Topic 44: Sixth Amendment Rights   107

Topic 45: Interrogation and Confessions: Due Process (Voluntariness)   109

Topic 46: Eyewitness Identification   111

Topic 47: Standing   115

Topic 48: Appellate Review of a Motion to Suppress   117

Topic 49: Derivative Evidence   119

Topic 50: Derivative Evidence: *Miranda* Violation   121

Topic 51: Derivative Evidence: Causal Connection   123

Topic 52: Derivative Evidence: What May be Suppressed   125

Topic 53: Derivative Evidence: Exceptions   127

Topic 54: Impeachment   129

Practice Final Exam: Questions   133

Part I: Questions   133

Part II: Questions   140

Answers 143

Topic 1: Incorporation 145

Topic 2: State Constitutional Protections 147

Topic 3: Fourth Amendment Right of Privacy 149   5/5

Topic 4: Private Searches 155

Topic 5: Motion to Dismiss 157

Topic 6: Search Warrants 159

Topic 7: Searches without Warrants 163

Topic 8: Probable Cause: Police Truthfulness 169

Topic 9: Search Warrants: Particularization 171

Topic 10: Execution of a Search Warrant 173

Topic 11: Plain View 175

Topic 12: Custodial Arrest for Petty Offenses 177

Topic 13: Arrest 179

Topic 14: Judicial Review of an Arrest 181

Topic 15: Pretextual Stops and Arrests 183

Topic 16: Protective Sweep of a Home 185

Topic 17: Search of a Person or Item Incident to Arrest 187

Topic 18: Search of a Home Incident to Arrest 189

Topic 19: Exigent Circumstances 193

Topic 20: Community Caretaking Function 197

Topic 21: Search of an Automobile Incident to an Arrest 199

Topic 22: Automobile Exception 201

Topic 23: Search of Containers 205

Topic 24: Impound and Inventory Search of a Vehicle 207

Topic 25: Comparing Different Justifications for the Search of an Automobile 209

Topic 26: Stop and Frisk 211

Topic 27: Checkpoint Stops 217

Topic 28: Traffic Stops: Duration and Scope of Inquiry 219

Topic 29: Administrative Searches 221

Topic 30: Special Needs Searches 223

Topic 31: Consent Searches 225

Topic 32: Electronic Eavesdropping 229

Topic 33: Exclusionary Rule 231

Topic 34: Good Faith Exception   233

Topic 35: Interrogation and Confession: Custody   237

Topic 36: Interrogaton and Confession: Public Safety Exception   239

Topic 37: Interrogation   241

Topic 38: *Miranda* Warnings   245

Topic 39: Waiver of *Miranda* Rights   247

Topic 40: First Confession without Warnings   249

Topic 41: Exercising *Miranda* Rights   251

Topic 42: Invoking the Right to Remain Silent   253

Topic 43: Resumpton of Interrogation   255

Topic 44: Sixth Amendment Rights   257

Topic 45: Interrogation and Confessions: Due Process (Voluntariness)   259

Topic 46: Eyewitness Identification   261

Topic 47: Standing   265

Topic 48: Appellate Review of a Motion to Suppress   269

Topic 49: Derivative Evidence   273

Topic 50: Derivative Evidence: *Miranda* Violation   275

Topic 51: Derivative Evidence: Causal Connection   277

Topic 52: Derivative Evidence: What May be Supressed   279

Topic 53: Derivative Evidence Exceptions   281

Topic 54: Impeachment   285

Practice Final Exam: Answers   289

Part I: Answers   289

Part II: Answers   300

Index   303

Preface

This book will assist your learning and exam preparation for the criminal procedure-police investigation course and the bar exam. The book contains both multiple choice questions and answers and short essay questions and answers.

As the Table of Contents reflects, the book addresses the broad gamut of issues concerning the Fourth Amendment, which regulates searches and seizures by law enforcement; constitutional doctrine limiting the securing and use of confessions; limits on techniques used to identify suspects; and the extent to which unlawfully secured evidence is barred from government use at trial (the exclusionary rule).

Ideally, you should try to answer each question before consulting the corresponding answer. This approach will facilitate your learning and alert you to any areas perhaps requiring further study and understanding.

The book seeks to balance brevity with the need to provide realistic, useful questions. The answers to short essay questions vary in length, none being more than a few paragraphs. Do not worry if your answer is slightly longer or shorter than that suggested. As long as the substance is adequate, your answer is just fine. If your answer is longer, you may want to consider whether you could have provided a shorter response. On some law school exams, where time is limited, brevity may be a valuable asset.

This Q & A benefits from the work of former contributing authors Professors Neil Cohen and Michael Benza, especially Professor Cohen, who was a driving force behind the project and whose dedication to teaching and scholarship remains an inspiration.

Professor Wayne A. Logan
Florida State University
College of Law
April 2021

About the Author

Wayne A. Logan, Steven M. Goldstein Professor at the Florida State University College of Law, teaches and writes in the areas of Criminal Law, Criminal Procedure, and Sentencing. He is the recipient of a university-wide teaching award and the author of several dozen law review articles, with work appearing in such publications as the *Georgetown Law Journal,* the *Michigan Law Review,* the *Pennsylvania Law Review,* the *Vanderbilt Law Review,* and the *Texas Law Review.* His books include *Knowledge as Power: Criminal Registration and Community Notification Laws in America* (Stanford University Press, 2009), *Florida Search and Seizure* (LexisNexis, 2020 & 2021), the *Ex Post Facto Clause: Its History and Role in a Punitive Society* (Oxford Univ. Press, forthcoming 2022), and *Sentencing Law, Policy, and Practice* (Foundation Press, forthcoming 2022) (with Professor Michael O'Hear). Professor Logan is an elected member of the American Law Institute and a past chair of the Criminal Justice Section of the Association of American Law Schools.

Questions

Incorporation

Herb Simmons, alleged member of a gang suspected of engaging in multiple frauds, was the target of local prosecutors as well as the local U.S. Attorney. A federal grand jury investigated Simmons for two years but did not return an indictment. State prosecutors filed a multi-count Information charging Simmons with conspiracy to commit fraud. Simmons sought to have the Information dismissed, asserting that he had a right under the Fifth Amendment right to a grand jury indictment. The trial judge denied the motion to dismiss, pointing to a state statute that authorized charges to be initiated by Indictment or Information. Simmons was convicted of all charges and appealed, challenging the state's failure to accord him his Fifth Amendment right to indictment.

1. The Court of Appeals will:

   (A) reverse the conviction because all of the rights contained in the Bill of Rights have been applied to the states through the Fourteenth Amendment, and Simmons was denied the right to a grand jury indictment.

   (B) reverse the conviction because charges involving infamous crimes such as fraud must originate with a grand jury.

   (C) affirm the conviction because the Fifth Amendment right to grand jury indictment has not been incorporated into the Fourteenth Amendment.

   (D) affirm the conviction because the failure to secure a grand jury indictment is harmless error.

Jane Donaldson photographed a police officer arresting her son at a political demonstration. She was ordered to step back from the arrest; she not only refused to comply with this command but actually struck the officer on the shoulder with her fist. She was then arrested and charged in state court with simple assault on a police officer, a low-level felony carrying a potential one-year jail or prison term. Donaldson's lawyer demanded a jury trial because of the political nature of the incident. The request was denied because state law guaranteed a right to trial by jury only for offenses carrying a penalty of more than a year of incarceration. Donaldson was tried by the court, convicted and sentenced to one year in jail. Donaldson appealed, claiming that her Sixth Amendment right to trial by jury was violated.

2. How should the court of appeals rule?

   (A) The court will reverse the conviction because the Sixth Amendment right to a jury trial is fundamental to the nation's justice system.

(B) The court will reverse the conviction because the Sixth Amendment guarantees a right to a jury trial in all cases.

(C) The court will affirm the conviction because the Sixth Amendment right applies only to trials in federal courts, and the states are free to institute their own procedures.

(D) The court will affirm the conviction because the Sixth Amendment guarantee does not seek to ensure fair outcomes in politically charged cases.

State Constitutional Protections

While on routine traffic patrol, Officer Krupansky spotted Terry Tesler driving his 1977 Chevy Chevette. Officer Krupansky knew Tesler was a drug addict and decided to follow him. Tesler eventually drove through a stop sign without coming to a complete and full stop. Officer Krupansky pulled Tesler over and arrested Tesler for failing to stop. Incident to the arrest, Officer Krupansky searched Tesler and found a small quantity of marijuana in his shirt pocket. The trial court rejected the defense motion to suppress the marijuana, holding that the Fourth Amendment does not bar a custodial arrest for such a minor offense. On appeal, the State Supreme Court reversed the conviction on the grounds that state statutory law mandates that a police officer issue a summons for a minor traffic offense and does not, then, allow the officer to conduct a search of a person incident to an arrest. The State Supreme Court held that the officer violated both the United States Constitution's Fourth Amendment and the state constitution when she arrested the defendant. The state has appealed to the U.S. Supreme Court.

3. Will the U.S. Supreme Court reverse the State Supreme Court?

   ANSWER:

Change the facts in Question 3 and ask what if the State Supreme Court ignored the state's prohibition against custodial arrests for minor traffic offenses and upheld the conviction under the authority of *Atwater v. City of Lago Vista*, 532 U.S. 318 (2001), that an arrest for a minor offense does not violate the Fourth Amendment. The defendant appealed to the U.S. Supreme Court.

4. Will the U.S. Supreme Court reverse the state conviction for failing to hold that the arrest was unreasonable under state law?

   (A) The Supreme Court will reverse the conviction because the state's interpretation violated the state provision.

   (B) The Supreme Court will reverse the conviction because the State Supreme Court violated the Fourth Amendment command against unreasonable searches and seizures.

   (C) The Supreme Court will affirm the conviction and reject the defense argument that the state constitution bars such arrests.

   (D) The Supreme Court will affirm the conviction because the action of police did not violate the Fourth Amendment.

Fourth Amendment Right of Privacy

[handwritten: no warrant PC? RS?]

Randall Ollie, a City of Orange policeman, is walking the beat on Paul Muster's street. A neighbor approaches Ollie and tells him that Muster has been playing loud music and disturbing the peace. Officer Ollie walks up the driveway of Muster's house listening for music. At the rear of Muster's house is a small plastic shed. The shed is windowless and its door is closed but not locked. The shed is located five feet from the rear door of the house and is visible from the driveway. Officer Ollie opens Muster's shed and sees hundreds of empty cold tablet packages and antifreeze containers. Knowing that these materials are used to make crystal methamphetamine, Officer Ollie returns to the police station and obtains a warrant for Muster's arrest.

Prior to trial, Muster asserts a Fourth Amendment challenge to the Ollie's conduct.

5. Should the court grant the motion to suppress?

[handwritten: ✓] (A) The court should grant the motion because the shed is within the curtilage of the house. *[handwritten: warrant]*

(B) The court should deny the motion because the shed is outside the curtilage of the house. *[handwritten: if outside curtilage then right answer]*

(C) The court should deny the motion because Officer Ollie was allowed to walk up the driveway and look around.

(D) The court should grant the motion because Officer Ollie was not allowed to walk up the driveway and look around. *[handwritten: complaint led to RS so ok? home? home privacy well protected]*

A police officer and a drug detection dog were patrolling in front of a bus terminal. The officer observed the defendant in the bus station change directions when the defendant saw the officer and her dog enter the bus station. The officer walked quickly up to the defendant and said, "Excuse me. May I speak with you?" The defendant stopped and the officer then directed her drug dog to sniff the luggage situated at the defendant's feet. The drug dog sniffed the luggage and then sat down, indicating the presence of drugs. After the positive indication from the dog, the officer arrested and searched the defendant and found drugs on his person and in the luggage. The defendant was charged with illegal possession of drugs and sought to exclude all evidence seized from his person as the fruit of an illegal search and seizure.

6. How should the court rule?

[handwritten: SiA sniff aroused RS enough for arrest → SiA revealed drugs SiA are exceptions to warrant → search luggage allowed? inventory]

(A) The defendant was seized illegally prior to the dog sniff and the drugs are the fruit of the illegal seizure.

(B) The defendant was legally seized prior to the dog sniff and the drugs were seized incident
to the lawful seizure.

(C) The drugs were seized incident to the lawful arrest of the defendant following the dog sniff.

(D) The drugs were seized incident to a legitimate *Terry* stop.

Police had Tony Soprano's home under surveillance. Soprano was suspected of being involved
in a bank robbery scheme. At night, the police used night vision binoculars to maintain their surveillance. On the night in question, agents situated on a public sidewalk across the street from the
front of Tony's home, with their binoculars trained on a slight gap in the curtains of the home's
darkened front family room, saw a bag with "Wells Fargo Bank" emblazoned on it being delivered
to Tony in the family room. It was a dark night: no moon, no stars. Without the night vision binoculars, the police would not have been able to see the delivery of the bag. After observing Tony receiving the bag, the officers learned that the bag deliveryman was the suspect in a bank robbery
of a Wells Fargo branch bank in Monmouth earlier that day.

Based upon their observations, the police secured a search warrant for Tony's home and seized
the bag, which contained thousands of dollars. Tony's lawyers claim that the search warrant was
invalid because the probable cause was based upon a Fourth Amendment violation. (For this question, do not consider any possible exceptions to the federal exclusionary rule.)

7. Is the evidence secured by the police admissible?

(A) No, because the police violated Tony's Fourth Amendment rights by using the night vision binoculars.

(B) Yes, because just as criminal suspects use sense-enhancing technology to commit crimes,
the police can (and should) be able to use such technology to conduct investigations and
hold them to account.

(C) No, because the police violated Tony's Fourth Amendment rights by focusing their attention on his home without probable cause or even reasonable suspicion that he was involved in criminal activity.

(D) Yes, because the police did not violate Tony's Fourth Amendment rights because he failed
to take sufficient steps to protect his privacy.

After work, Billy Mott stopped at Sal's Bar and drank several cocktails. When the bartender
asked if he wished for a cab to be called, Mott, with slurred speech, declined the invitation. Mott
then entered his car and drove away. Tragically, about three-quarters of a mile away, Mott
slammed into another car that was waiting at a red traffic light. V, the driver of the latter car,
was killed immediately upon impact. A pedestrian near the accident phoned the police, and two
officers quickly arrived at the scene. Upon their arrival, Officers Riley and Hill immediately
smelled alcohol on Mott, and Riley subjected Mott to a series of field sobriety tests, which he
failed. Officer Riley then arrested Mott and took him to the hospital for medical care. Meanwhile,
Officer Hill arranged for Mott's vehicle to be towed to the police impoundment lot. After the
vehicle arrived at the lot, the police realized that it had an "event data recorder," a box-shaped

[Handwritten margin note, top right: Exceptions to search warrant × Exig Circs × Plain View × SIA × Auto?]

[Handwritten margin note, top left: Container?]

device located under the floor carpet of the driver's seat. The device was installed by the vehicle's manufacturer and measures information on the vehicle's speed, braking, acceleration, and other similar data. Without securing a search warrant, police accessed the data. The data showed that Mott was travelling well over the speed limit at the time of the accident and failed to brake before hitting V's car.

[Handwritten margin note, right: —destroy ev —safety —mobile]

8. Can the prosecution use the information secured from the event data recorder when Mott is tried for vehicular manslaughter? What if any additional information might be useful in answering the question? (For this question, presume that any exceptions to the federal exclusionary rule do not apply.) *[Handwritten: No, needed warrant & no exception applies]*

Bob is a 1L student who is trying to finance his legal education by selling drugs at the law school. One evening, while studying at home, Samantha knocked on Bob's door. Samantha is in Bob's class at law school, but the two are not particularly friendly. Bob knew that Samantha lived in another building in the same apartment complex. Samantha said she dropped by to ask for help with a Criminal Law question. Samantha is a former police officer, a fact Bob did not know. Also unbeknownst to Bob was the fact that Samantha had been asked by a police officer acquaintance to befriend Bob and find out whether he was, in fact, dealing illegal drugs. Bob answered Samantha's Criminal Law question while standing at the door, but when Samantha feigned ignorance and prolonged the discussion, Bob invited Samantha into his apartment. *[Handwritten: Consent]*

During their discussion about mistake of fact and law, Bob offered Samantha a beer. Bob went into the kitchen to retrieve two beers, and Samantha followed as the two continued to discuss the nuances of mistake of fact. There, on the kitchen counter, Samantha observed a large supply of glassine envelopes, a scale, and, sticking out from under aluminum foil, a white powdery substance. Thereafter, while Bob remained in the kitchen, Samantha walked over to a laptop computer sitting on the dining room table, opened it, touched the "space" bar on the keyboard, and saw what appeared to be a child pornography image on the screen. She then quickly closed the top of the laptop. After drinking the beer, Samantha left the apartment and told her police officer acquaintance what she had seen. Based on Samantha's statements, search warrants were obtained and, armed with the warrants, police searched Bob's apartment and found the white powdery substance which turned out to be cocaine, and a trove child pornography on Bob's computer. Bob was charged with possession for sale of an illegal substance and possession of child pornography.

[Handwritten margin note, right: Not plain view]

9. Is the evidence seized with the search warrants admissible at trial for the drug and child pornography offenses? (For this question, presume that any exceptions to the federal exclusionary rule do not apply.)

    ANSWER: *[Handwritten: Plain view exception for warrant for drugs but no exception applies including PV× Exig Circs× SIA× Auto×]*

Police Officer Stano was on patrol one sunny afternoon and observed Wiley Durant, a man of Polynesian ancestry, standing against a stop sign on a public street. Having nothing else to do, and having a disdain for people of Polynesian ancestry, Stano decided to hassle Durant, who Stano

[Handwritten margin note, bottom: sucks but doesn't matter his subjective intent]

knew was involved in the distribution of methamphetamine. The following discussion occurred between the two: *vexed on what?*

> Stano: "What are you doing out here—don't you have anything better to do than hang out?"

> Durant: "It's none of your business, officer. I'm not doing anything unlawful."

> Stano: "What's in that gym bag by your feet? Is it your bag?"

Durant said nothing in reply and Stano reached down toward the bag, prompting Durant to reach toward the bag, which Stano deflected. Upon feeling the bag, Stano immediately discerned an aluminum foil-wrapped, brick-like package, which he knew based on his training and experience usually contained methamphetamine. Stano then placed Durant under arrest for drug possession.

10. Can defense counsel raise a Fourth Amendment challenge against the admissibility of the methamphetamine?

(A) No, because Stano knew that Durant was involved in the illegal drug business and the search and arrest were therefore valid.

(B) No, because Durant abandoned any privacy interest in the gym bag and its contents.

(C) Yes, because Stano engaged in racial/ethnic profiling.

(D) Yes, because Stano engaged in an unlawful search.

X Exig Circs
X SiA
X PV
X Auto

Bond (2000)

Private Searches

Walter Whitney is the town snoop and he prided himself on both knowing everyone's business and on providing what he thought invaluable information about his neighbors to the police. On one occasion, his information led directly to an arrest and conviction. The Chief of Police told the media after that trial that without good citizens like Walter, his officers would be at a distinct disadvantage in the war on drugs and they relied on people like Walter to keep them informed about what was happening on the streets.

Larry Fitzsimmons was widely known to be a drug dealer. Frustrated that the local police were unable to gather enough evidence to arrest Larry, Walter decided to take things into his own hands. After Larry left for work one morning, Walter went over to Larry's house. Walter first looked through the windows but saw nothing incriminating. Undeterred, Walter went to the back of the house where he knew Larry kept a ladder. Using the ladder, Walter climbed up to a second story window and entered Larry's house.

Once inside the house, Walter searched every room and discovered no evidence of any drug activity. He did, however, find Larry's laptop computer in a drawer of a desk and took the laptop with him.

Walter returned home and powered up the laptop. He searched the files hoping to find any evidence proving his belief that Larry was a drug dealer. He found none. But he did find pictures of what appeared to be young women in various stages of undress and engaging in what appeared to Walter to be sexual activity. Thinking these images might be child pornography, Walter raced to the police station to turn over what he discovered.

Based solely on the images found on Larry's computer, multiple charges of possession of child pornography were brought against Larry.

11. Should the evidence obtained by Walter be suppressed?

(A) The evidence should not be suppressed because it was found by a private citizen who was not constrained by the Fourth Amendment.

(B) The evidence should be suppressed because Walter was an agent of the police and the entry into Larry's home was done without a warrant.

(C) The evidence should not be suppressed because Walter was only an unofficial agent of the police and so his entry into the home was not constrained by the Fourth Amendment.

(D) The evidence should be suppressed because Walter's entry violated state trespass laws and therefore violated the Fourth Amendment.

Topic 5

Questions

Motion to Dismiss

Change the facts in Question 11. Assume that Walter was always on the alert for illegal activity by others, though he had never reported anyone to the police and no one in the police department had ever heard of Walter. His entry into Larry's house was the first time he had broken into someone else's property and the first time he told the police about the results of his snooping. The judge, after the suppression hearing on the Larry's Motion to Suppress, was extremely upset at police use of information by someone who, though a private citizen, illegally obtained the information by breaking into a home. Instead of suppressing the child pornography evidence alone, she dismissed the entire pornography case with prejudice. The state appealed.

12. How should the court of appeals rule?

ANSWER:

Search Warrants

A search warrant was issued for the home of suspected drug dealer Abigail Hunter. In the brief affidavit accompanying the warrant, the officer generally described the varied suspected illegal activities of Abigail, including drug dealing witnessed by the officer. The affidavit claimed that Abigail was engaged in drug distribution and other crimes and was the head of a notorious gang plaguing the city.

The judge issued the warrant authorizing the officer to search Abigail's home for "evidence of any felonies." Police executing the warrant found evidence of drug dealing and loan sharking. A multi-count indictment was brought charging Abigail with violation of multiple statutes involving illegal drug trafficking and loan sharking.

13. Is the search warrant itself valid? (For this question, presume that any exceptions to the federal exclusionary rule do not apply.)

    (A) The search warrant was invalid because it was vague and did not instruct the police to search for evidence of specific offenses.

    (B) The search warrant was valid because the affiant presented sufficient evidence to search for multiple offenses.

    (C) The search warrant was invalid because there clearly was no probable cause.

    (D) The search warrant was valid because the police had established the general criminal notoriety of the target.

Police secured a warrant to search the hotel room of Emile Savoca who police believed was a serial robber who used a black ski mask. This conclusion was based on an anonymous informant, eyewitness interviews, and security camera footage at seven robberies Savoca allegedly committed. The seven robberies described in the affidavit occurred over an unspecified period of time. The warrant authorized a search of Savoca's hotel room for evidence of the robberies, listing the victims and locations of each, but not the dates. During the search of the hotel room, police found objects taken from five of the seven robbery victims. Prior to trial, the defense claimed that the warrant was invalid and sought to exclude the evidence.

14. How should the court rule? (For this question, presume that any exceptions to the federal exclusionary rule do not apply.)

    ANSWER:

Los Angeles police intercepted a Federal Express package containing cocaine, which was addressed to the defendant in Dayton, Ohio. The LAPD sent the package to Dayton police, who sought a warrant in anticipation of a controlled delivery of the cocaine. Based on this information, a search warrant was issued authorizing the Dayton police to search the defendant's home following the controlled delivery of the package by an undercover police officer in a Fed Ex uniform. Police then searched the home seizing the package. A motion to suppress was filed in the case.

15. How should the court rule?

   (A) The court should suppress the evidence. When the warrant was issued the magistrate did not have probable cause to believe that the evidence was presently at the house to be searched.

   (B) The court should not suppress the evidence. When the warrant was issued the magistrate had probable cause to believe that the evidence would be at the house when police executed the warrant.

   (C) The court should suppress the evidence because the police caused the package to be delivered to the defendant's house.

   (D) The court should not suppress the evidence because police knew what was in the package and had possession of the package when the warrant was issued.

A confidential, reliable informant phoned Detective Roberts to tip him off that Angel Smith, a major drug dealer in Metropolis, had just received a large shipment of marijuana and cocaine at his home. The informant, an employee of Smith, was present when the drugs arrived. Detective Roberts prepared the following affidavit:

> The affiant, Detective Roberts, has good cause to believe that a large quantity of marijuana and cocaine is presently at the home address of Angel Smith, whom the affiant and other police know is operating a major drug distribution out of his home. Whereupon, affiant requests a warrant issue for the search of Angel Smith's home for marijuana and cocaine.

The magistrate issued the warrant and Detective Roberts executed the warrant and found marijuana and cocaine in Angel Smith's home. Smith was later prosecuted and the defense filed a motion to suppress the evidence found during the search.

16. Should the court grant the motion to suppress the evidence?

   (A) The court should deny the motion to suppress because Detective Roberts conducted the search in objective good faith reliance on the warrant.

   (B) The court should grant the motion to suppress because Detective Roberts failed to inform the issuing magistrate about the informant's identity.

   (C) The court should deny the motion to suppress because there was probable cause to support the warrant.

(D) The court should grant the motion to suppress because the affidavit was so lacking in probable cause as to make police reliance on the judicial finding of probable cause unreasonable.

One summer afternoon, David Daniel was taken into custody by an officer who had a warrant for his arrest, supported by probable cause, based on his alleged littering in a public space, a low-level, local municipal offense. At the time of his arrest, Daniel vigorously protested and proclaimed his innocence. The arresting officer related "I don't know anything about it. I'm just executing the warrant; doing my job." Daniel was arrested and released on his personal recognizance. Soon thereafter, he retained a lawyer. After some investigation, the lawyer learned that the magistrate issuing the arrest warrant, Mike Tammy, was a local lawyer who lacked a valid license to practice law (due to failure to satisfy his continuing legal education requirements).

17. Presuming the arrest warrant was supported by probable cause, can Daniel file a Fourth Amendment claim because Tammy issued the warrant?

(A) Yes, because the officer did not personally observe the alleged littering, which is a non-breach of the peace offense.

(B) Yes, because Tammy was constitutionally unqualified to decide whether probable cause existed to support an arrest warrant.

(C) No, because the Fourth Amendment does not permit a custodial arrest for such a minor offense.

(D) No, because the arrest warrant was supported by probable cause.

Searches without Warrants

On a June evening, as the defendant exited a private residence and entered the parking lot of a YMCA, an area known to the police as a high-crime area, he was approached by two plainclothes officers. The officers were driving in an unmarked police vehicle. The defendant was gingerly carrying a brown paper grocery bag with the words "Kash 'n Karry" and "Loaded with Low Prices" printed on the outside. One of the officers, Thomas, immediately recognized the defendant as the person who sold him marijuana two weeks before.

When Officer Thomas identified himself as a police officer, the defendant stopped and placed the bag at his feet. Officer Thomas thereafter opened the bag and found inside a loaded revolver. Thomas, knowing that the defendant was not lawfully entitled to possess a firearm (because he was a convicted felon), told the defendant that he was under arrest.

Defendant was charged with drug trafficking and unlawful possession of a weapon. Prior to trial, defendant sought to suppress the gun found in his bag.

18. How should the court rule on the defense motion to suppress the gun?

   (A) The evidence should not be suppressed because the police had reasonable suspicion to stop the defendant and make sure he was not armed.

   (B) The evidence should not be suppressed because the officer had probable cause to search the bag based on his prior purchase of drugs from defendant.

   (C) The evidence should be suppressed because the evidence was not discovered incident to a lawful *Terry* stop.

   (D) The evidence should not be suppressed because it was discovered incident to a lawful arrest.

Officer Matterly was walking her assigned beat. Her patrol area included a notorious open air drug market. As she was walking by the market, she saw a man she later learned was Reggie Holt talking with two women. Matterly knew the two women talking to Holt were prostitutes with multiple arrests. When Holt saw Officer Matterly he put his hands in his pockets and walked away from the women. Officer Matterly approached the two women and asked them who Holt was. One of the women stated that he was SnugglyBear, their pimp, who was giving them their daily work assignments. Officer Matterly followed and stopped Holt. She told him he was under arrest for promoting prostitution. She ordered him to take his hands out of his pockets and when Holt complied a baggie of cocaine fell out of his pocket. Holt was subsequently charged only with drug possession. The defense moved to suppress the drugs based on a lack of probable cause for the arrest.

19. How should the court rule on the defense motion to suppress the evidence?

ANSWER:

A police officer patrolling a downtown neighborhood late on a Sunday night observed Wilson and a male companion venture onto a sidewalk located in front of a post office. The officer saw a few other people in the vicinity, but they were some distance away from the post office. A minute later, dispatch informed the police officer that a silent alarm within the post office had sounded. Dispatch related that the post office had been illegally entered via a window. The officer turned on his patrol car roof lights and detained Wilson and his companion. After both men provided evasive answers to the officer's questions concerning why they were out at that time of night, and whether they had been to the post office, the officer arrested both men.

Prior to placing the two men in the police car, the officer searched them, finding paint chips in Wilson's pocket. The paint chips were later traced to the window of the post office that had been jimmied open causing the alarm to sound. Wilson was charged with unlawful entry of a federal facility. Wilson's attorney moved to suppress the evidence because the officer did not have probable cause to make an arrest.

20. Should the evidence be suppressed?

    (A) Wilson's presence in the immediate vicinity of the post office where a silent alarm had sounded and evasive answers provided probable cause for the arrest, and the evidence was seized incident to the lawful arrest.

    (B) Wilson's presence in the vicinity of the post office was not incriminating and the evidence was seized incident to an unlawful arrest.

    (C) Wilson's presence in the vicinity of the post office was sufficient to justify a *Terry* stop, and an officer may conduct a search prior to placing a suspect in a police car.

    (D) Wilson's presence in the vicinity of the post office was sufficient to justify a *Terry* stop, but the officer had no authority to search Edwards.

Police officer Justin Huey was driving in a Metropolis patrol car when he received a radio call that fellow officers had witnessed Ike Newton rob a convenience store and that Newton was driving a purple Ford Mustang eastward on W. 44th Street. Officer Huey intercepted the Mustang going east on W. 44th Street and arrested Newton. Huey searched Newton but found nothing incriminating on him. Huey then activated a key fob he found in Newton's pocket, which popped upon the trunk of the Mustang. Inside the trunk, in plain view, Huey saw several bags of marijuana. The car was impounded. Newton was charged with marijuana possession, and the defense has moved to suppress the drugs.

21. Is the marijuana admissible?

ANSWER:

Darius Dalton, after having many beers at Sal's Bar early one evening, was pulled over by Officers Shelton and Harris on suspicion of drunk driving. When Dalton asked why he was detained, Shelton replied that the officers had observed Dalton exceed the posted speed limit and repeatedly cross the centerline. Shelton observed that Dalton's eyes were bloodshot and he smelled of alcohol. After Dalton performed poorly on several field sobriety tests, Shelton asked Dalton to use a portable breath test device to measure his blood alcohol concentration (BAC), which Dalton refused. Shelton thereafter placed Dalton under arrest for drunk driving and began transporting him to a local hospital for a blood test, to better confirm his blood alcohol concentration. Shelton drove the patrol car and Harris sat alongside him, with each officer out loud bemoaning the recent increase in drunk driving arrests. Dalton sat in the backseat. When the three men arrived at the hospital, Dalton refused to comply with the blood test, and Shelton told him that state law allowed a test to be taken when an individual is lawfully arrested for drunk driving. Dalton still refused. Shelton directed a hospital staff member to take the blood sample. The sample revealed that Dalton's BAC was well above the legal limit of .08 percent.

22. Should the evidence of BAC be suppressed? (For this question, presume that any exceptions to the federal exclusionary rule do not apply.)

   (A) Yes, because the officer was required to get written consent of the party providing the blood sample.

   (B) Yes, because the officer needed to secure a warrant under the circumstances.

   (C) No, because state law allowed the taking of a blood sample under the circumstances.

   (D) No, because a blood draw was needed after Dalton refused to comply with the less intrusive breath test.

One July day in the late afternoon, police received a 911 call. The caller, who refused to identify herself, said she heard a scream at 123 Park Ave. and that someone yelled "No, no, please let me go." When police arrived at 123 Park Avenue, they saw a young adult female stabbed to death on the threshold of the front door, which was open. Detectives learned that the victim was Katy Sellers, who owned a realty company with her husband Huey Sellers. About an hour after the police arrived, and shortly after Katy Sellers was taken away, Huey Sellers drove up to the house wearing sweat clothes. When told about the stabbing Huey cried out "I never should have left her for that run. I would have been home, and I could have protected her." Police, who were aware that the Sellers couple had significant marital difficulties, decided not to ask Huey about his possible involvement. However, after leaving the scene, they accessed film footage from a police camera mounted on a public utility pole located across the street. The camera, which had within its scope of vision the Sellers's front door, clearly showed Huey stabbing his wife at the threshold of the door.

23. The prosecution wishes to use the camera footage in the Huey Sellers homicide trial. Which of the following decisions would be most useful to the defense in its motion to suppress the camera footage?

(A) *Illinois v. Gates*, 462 U.S. 213 (1983).

(B) *Brigham City v. Stuart*, 547 U.S. 398 (2006).

(C) *Carpenter v. United States*, 138 S. Ct. 2206 (2018).

(D) *Collins v. Virginia*, 138 S. Ct. 1663 (2018).

Probable Cause: Police Truthfulness

Detective Roberts submitted the following affidavit with an application for a search warrant:

> The affiant, Detective Roberts, has good cause to believe that a large quantity of marijuana and cocaine is presently at the home address of Angel Smith, whom the affiant and other police know is operating a major drug distribution out of his home. This information comes to us from a reliable, confidential informant who was present at Smith's home three days ago when the drugs were delivered. The informant has provided reliable information three times in the past which led to three successful convictions. Whereupon, affiant believes that a large quantity of marijuana and cocaine will be found now at Angel Smith's residence and requests that a warrant issue for the search of Angel Smith's home for marijuana and cocaine.

Prior to submitting the affidavit and the warrant application to the magistrate, Detective Roberts contacted another informant who had purchased on several occasions both marijuana and cocaine from Smith with police buy-money. Roberts directed the informant to attempt another purchase from Smith. Several hours later, the informant called Roberts and told him he had visited Smith at his apartment and tried to purchase marijuana and cocaine, and that Smith told him that he was out and did not expect a shipment for two weeks. The day after receiving this information Detective Roberts submitted the above-noted affidavit and warrant application to the magistrate without informing the magistrate of the information received from the second informant.

The warrant was issued and executed that day. During the subsequent search, Roberts found no marijuana or cocaine or other evidence relating to drug charges. However, pornographic pictures of children were discovered while searching for the drugs. Prior to trial, Angel Smith learned of the second informant who told Smith what he had told Detective Roberts. On the basis of that information, a motion to suppress the pornographic materials was filed.

24. Should the motion to suppress be granted? (For this question, presume that any exceptions to the federal exclusionary rule do not apply.)

ANSWER:

At the conclusion of the suppression hearing in the previous Question, the prosecutor argued that, even if the court found that the omission was material and the affidavit as submitted lacked probable cause, the evidence should not be excluded because the police reasonably relied upon the warrant.

25. How should the court rule?

    (A) The court should deny the suppression motion because the evidence is admissible under the good faith exception to the exclusionary rule.

    (B) The court should deny the suppression motion because, even without the omitted information, there was adequate probable cause to support the warrant.

    (C) The court should grant the suppression motion because the "good faith" exception to the exclusionary rule is not applicable in the face of substantiated claim of material falsehood in the affidavit.

    (D) The court should grant the suppression motion because the judiciary should not be viewed as facilitating the wrongful securing of evidence by police.

Search Warrants: Particularization

A magistrate issued a search warrant based on probable cause that evidence of a major stolen jewelry operation would be found at Carl Smith's residence. The probable cause established that Smith was the city's major fence for stolen jewelry and was running the business out of his home. The warrant authorized police to search Smith's "residence and Carl Smith's person." Police went to execute the warrant at Smith's residence and at Smith's place of employment, a major insurance underwriter. The officers found evidence of the fencing operation at Smith's residence. At the same time, officers went to Smith's place of employment and searched him, finding in his pocket a large diamond ring that turned out to be stolen. A motion to suppress the ring was filed.

26. Should the ring be excluded from evidence at Smith's trial?

(A) No. The warrant ordered that Smith's person be searched, and police were complying with the terms of the warrant.

(B) No. A search warrant's order is global. The validity of the execution should not turn on where Smith happened to be at the time of the search.

(C) Yes. The search warrant did not specify that Smith could be searched at his place of employment.

(D) Yes. Probable cause did not exist to believe that Smith would have the evidence sought anywhere but at his residence.

Probable cause was established that the defendant, John Peters, transmitted two images containing child pornography from a laptop computer in his home. A warrant issued ordering police to search Peters' home and to seize his "laptop computer" and "any physical photos depicting minors engaging in sexually explicit conduct." During the search of the home, the police located the laptop computer as well as a tablet computer. The police searched the laptop computer and found the two specific images; they did not find any physical photos. The police then searched the files on the tablet computer and found multiple images containing child pornography. The defense argued that the warrant authorized only a search of the laptop computer and not the tablet.

27. Should the files found on the tablet be suppressed?

(A) No. Probable cause existed to believe that Peters possessed child pornography images and given the seriousness of the crime a search of the entire house was permitted.

(B) No. Where a warrant authorizes a search of a specific computer, police may search all computers during the execution of the search warrant.

(C) Yes. The warrant did not specify that the tablet computer could be searched.

(D) Yes. Once the police found the two files, they were required to terminate the search.

Execution of a Search Warrant

At 3 p.m. one afternoon, federal agents executed a lawful search warrant authorizing the search of a house. Probable cause existed that narcotics and proceeds of drug sales were in the house. The search warrant did not authorize a no-knock entry. When they arrived on the scene, officers knocked on the door and entered immediately. They ordered the people in the house out of bed, and conducted the search described in the warrant. The police found narcotics and a large quantity of money, mostly in $20 denomination. The defendant filed a motion in federal court to suppress the evidence.

28. Should the evidence be suppressed?

   (A) Yes. The Fourth Amendment requires that a search warrant be executed only after police knock and announce their presence.

   (B) Yes. The failure of police to adhere to the Fourth Amendment requirement that police knock and announce their presence prior to entering to execute the warrant should shock the conscience of the court and lead to suppression of the evidence.

   (C) No. The warrant was supported by probable cause and the failure to knock and announce does not trigger the federal exclusionary rule.

   (D) No. Evidence of narcotics may be easily destroyed by flushing down the toilet and the need to prevent the destruction of evidence created an exigency allowing police to disregard Fourth Amendment requirements for the execution of searches.

Police conducted several controlled buys of heroin from 136 Park Street, a single family residence. Over the course of several weeks, they conducted surveillance of the address, observing multiple visitors briefly visiting the address and behavior consistent with an illegal drug business being operated there. Examination of property records revealed that Albert Hill, who was well known to the police, was the owner and occupier of the residence. Based on the foregoing, police obtained a valid, probable cause-based warrant to search the property for "heroin, material and items used to manufacture and sell heroin, and the search of the person of Albert Hill." About a half hour before the warrant was to be executed, police observed a young man they did not recognize leave the Park Street address and walk to a convenience store several blocks away. One of the officers, suspicious of wrongdoing, pursued the young man, who turned out to be Barry Dillard. The officer detained Dillard in the store and demanded that he empty his coat pockets. This revealed a small revolver, which Dillard was not lawfully entitled to possess (as a convicted felon). Shortly after Dillard's arrest, police executed the search warrant on 136 Park Street, which disclosed a large amount of heroin.

29. Dillard has moved to suppress the revolver. Should the revolver be suppressed?

    (A) No, because police are permitted to secure persons associated with the property targeted for search to ensure their personal safety and the orderly completion of the search.

    (B) Yes, because the convenience store was not specified in the search warrant.

    (C) No, because police always have the right to conduct a weapons frisk in a public place.

    (D) Yes, because Dillard was detained before the search occurred and was located in an area beyond the immediate vicinity of the premises to be searched.

The police had probable cause to believe that Jonathan Snicker was operating a fraudulent stock investment company. The evidence demonstrated that Snicker was using email to target senior citizens, seeking to entice them to invest in non-existent companies. Based on this, a magistrate issued a warrant for Snicker's Internet service provider (ISP) for all his emails with the phrases "hot deal," "investment opportunity," or "stock tip." The warrant was executed, and the ISP provided several thousand emails. Based on these emails and resulting investigation, charges were filed against Snicker. Snicker filed a motion to suppress the content of the emails.

30. Should the motion to suppress be granted?

    (A) No. Snicker has no expectation of privacy in the content of his email communications and therefore the conduct of the police does not constitute a search under the Fourth Amendment.

    (B) No. Snicker does have an expectation of privacy in the content of his email communications, but the warrant was predicated on probable cause validating the search.

    (C) Yes. Snicker has an expectation of privacy in the content of his email communications and executing the warrant at the third party ISP violated Snicker's reasonable expectation of privacy.

    (D) Yes. The terms of service between Snicker and the ISP provide a shield against search warrants because the terms specifically state that the ISP will provide secure and private email service.

Plain View

Police operating with a valid search warrant searched John Broadley's dormitory room and its adjoining shared bathroom as authorized by the warrant. The bathroom door to the room of John's neighbor, Tom Kimberling, was open. The police officer could see into Kimberling's dorm room. From the threshold to Kimberling's room, the officer saw on the top of a dresser against the far wall a stack of loose marijuana and rolling papers. Recognizing both items, the officer walked into Kimberling's room and seized the contraband and arrested Kimberling. Kimberling's lawyer moved to suppress the marijuana. The prosecuting attorney claimed that the marijuana was in plain view.

31. Should Kimberling's motion to suppress be granted?

(A) No. The contents of the room were in plain view.

(B) Yes. The contents of the room were in plain view, but the officer did not have authority to enter the room and seize the contraband.

(C) No. A dorm room is not the same as a home or apartment and is subject to unannounced inspections for contraband.

(D) Yes. The contraband was not in plain view because the officer did not have the authority to look into the adjacent room.

Walter Franklin was driving home from work late on a Friday evening. As he drove past the town's speed trap, Officer Martin O'Shea's radar indicated that Franklin was traveling at 58 miles per hour in a 55 miles per hour zone. Officer O'Shea decided to pull Franklin over. Franklin immediately stopped when Officer O'Shea activated his blue lights. O'Shea later testified at the suppression hearing that, as he approached Franklin's car, he noticed Franklin's bumper sticker that read "They can have my Smith & Wesson when they pry it from my cold, dead fingers."

O'Shea also testified that he looked through the windows "to see what I could see." On the rear seat, O'Shea saw what he believed was a women's wallet. O'Shea decided that he was going to give Franklin a verbal warning to slow down and, as was his practice, he ordered Franklin out of the car and to the rear of the car so that O'Shea's dashboard camera would capture the warning.

As Franklin was standing behind the car, O'Shea opened the rear door to "do a protective sweep for weapons." Seeing none, O'Shea grabbed the women's wallet, opened it, and discovered that it belonged to his Captain who reported it stolen two days earlier. Prior to his trial, Franklin filed a motion to suppress the wallet.

32. The motion will be:

   (A) granted because O'Shea was possibly entitled to do a protective sweep for weapons but the seizure and search of the woman's wallet was improper.

   (B) granted because Officer O'Shea had no legal authority to enter the car.

   (C) denied because the officer had reasonable suspicion to believe that the woman's wallet was stolen.

   (D) denied because O'Shea was entitled to do a protective sweep and the woman's wallet was in plain view of this sweep.

Police officers driving through a high crime area of the city at 1 a.m. noticed the defendant leaning into a car. When the officers drove around the block and returned, the defendant remained on the street corner but the car was gone. Thinking that some criminal activity might be happening, the officers stopped their car. At the same time, the defendant walked away from the corner. The officers approached the defendant and detained him. Immediately upon stopping the defendant, one of the officers patted the defendant down. In the defendant's outer jacket pocket, the officer felt two thimble-sized objects. The officer reached into the pocket and retrieved the two objects, which contained crack cocaine. The defendant was charged with possession and moved to suppress the crack cocaine. At the suppression hearing, the officer testified that he did not believe the object was a weapon but thought that they might be objects used to carry crack cocaine.

33. How should the court rule on the motion to suppress?

   ANSWER:

Custodial Arrest for Petty Offenses

Joe Descarte jaywalked while crossing a busy intersection in the financial district on his way to his bar admission character and fitness interview. He was stopped by a police officer who intended to write Joe a ticket for jaywalking. Joe explained to the officer that he was a law student and needed to be at his interview if he was going to be admitted to the Bar. Joe told the officer he was too busy to stop but offered to leave his driver's license with the officer.

Joe's attitude annoyed the officer, and the officer arrested Joe, who missed his interview. Jaywalking is a minor misdemeanor in the state, carrying a penalty of a $100 maximum fine and no jail sentence. State law authorizes a police officer to arrest or issue a summons for any misdemeanor offense. Following the arrest, the officer searched Joe and found the remnant of a marijuana cigarette in the pocket of Joe's suit. Joe is charged only with possession of a controlled substance, also a misdemeanor. Joe's attorney filed a motion to suppress the marijuana.

34. How should the court rule on the motion to suppress?

   (A) The court should grant the motion because a custodial arrest for an offense that carries no jail penalty violates the Fourth Amendment; the search therefore was not incident to a lawful arrest.

   (B) The court should grant the motion because, even though the arrest was lawful, the search of Joe's person on the street for jaywalking violated the Fourth Amendment.

   (C) The court should deny the motion because the arrest did not violate the Fourth Amendment, and the evidence was found incident to a lawful arrest.

   (D) The court should deny the motion because the marijuana was unrelated to the basis for the arrest, which was jaywalking.

Arrest

On December 18, Officer Petome was investigating a call reporting increased traffic in an undeveloped area in the Lionshead neighborhood. The neighborhood teens refer to this undeveloped area as "the spot." Officer Petome arrived at the scene and saw a dirty red pickup truck that he believed to have been recently off-road leaving "the spot." Officer Petome unsuccessfully tried to follow the truck but later saw the truck parked in the driveway of 13 Shintonshire Road. He knocked on the door of the residence in order to investigate why the red pickup had been off-road at "the spot."

Ms. Hanson, remaining inside the house, answered the door, and Officer Petome inquired as to who had been driving the red truck. She denied any knowledge regarding who was driving the truck or who owned it. While Ms. Hanson was speaking with Officer Petome, Tyrice Hanson, her son, was standing behind her inside the residence. Officer Petome told Ms. Hanson that he had seen Tyrice driving the red truck away from "the spot" and asked if he could speak with Tyrice outside regarding what he was doing at "the spot." Ms. Hanson refused to allow Officer Petome to speak with Tyrice outside and demanded to know why Tyrice had to go outside. Officer Petome advised Ms. Hanson that if she continued to impede his investigation she would "regret it." After Ms. Hanson again interrupted Officer Petome, Officer Petome departed, but remained in his vehicle outside the Hanson residence. About fifteen minutes later, Ms. Hanson emerged, and Petome arrested her for carrying an unlawful switchblade knife (protruding from her shirt pocket). In a search of Hanson conducted incident to the arrest, Petome found cocaine in her pants pocket. Hanson was charged with possession of the illegal knife and cocaine.

35. Ms. Hanson filed a motion to suppress the cocaine based on an illegal arrest. The motion will be:

    (A) granted because the warrantless arrest was illegal because Officer Petome arrested Ms. Hanson due to personal animosity.

    (B) granted because a full custodial arrest, such as occurred, was an unreasonable seizure under the Fourth Amendment.

    (C) denied because the warrantless arrest was lawful and so was the search incident to arrest.

    (D) denied because of the seriousness of the offense of possessing an unlawful switchblade.

At 2:33 a.m., Officers Richard Hough and William Lynch, Jr., received a dispatch advising them that there was a group of men outside on the 3400 block of Old York Road, and that one of them was armed with a gun. The allegedly armed man was a white male wearing a brown leather jacket over a black hooded sweatshirt. The officers arrived at 3434 Old York Road about five minutes after receiving the dispatch.

Cindy Delaine was standing outside on the porch of her home at said address and approached the driver's side door of the cruiser to speak with the officers. While they were speaking, Officer Hough noticed a man standing nearby who matched the description of the suspect. The officers knew the man to be one Clifford Mallory, a convicted felon not entitled to carry a firearm (a felonious offense in the jurisdiction). It is undisputed that Mallory was outside and in view of the officers. At one point, Mallory spoke with Officers Hough and Lynch who were still in the cruiser. As Mallory did so, his jacket lifted to reveal a revolver stuck in his waistband. When Officer Hough observed this, he exclaimed "gun!" in order to alert his partner to the presence of a weapon. Officer Hough exited the vehicle, told Mallory that he was under arrest and ordered Mallory to stop, but Mallory instead ran into the house he shared with Jack Delaine, shutting the door behind him.

The officers gave chase. Jack Delaine briefly blocked the officers' entry, shouting that they had no right to enter without a warrant. They pushed him aside and Officer Hough kicked the door, breaking the latch. Mallory was inside blocking the door from opening, and Officer Hough kicked the door several more times, breaking loose a lower panel on the door. Mallory relented and Officer Hough opened the door. Officer Lynch placed Mallory under arrest, searched him, and discovered the revolver earlier observed. In his prosecution for unlawful possession of a firearm, a felony, Mallory has challenged the validity of a search of his person that found the revolver.

36. Should the motion to suppress be granted?

    (A)   Yes, because Mallory's arrest was invalid because he was inside the house and the police did not have a warrant to enter.

    (B)   Yes, because Mallory's arrest was invalid because the police lacked probable cause to arrest him because it was possible that Mallory was legally carrying a fake gun.

    (C)   No, because the police had probable cause to arrest Mallory for a felony and were in hot pursuit when he entered the home.

    (D)   No, because Mallory's arrest was valid because the police had probable cause to arrest him.

Jim Dudd was a wanted man: police had probable cause to arrest him for a series of armed robberies of elderly men and women. On July 23, in the morning, the Police Commissioner ordered all officers on duty to be on the lookout for Dudd and to take him into custody. Officers Talent and Sims took this command seriously, indeed so seriously that they arrested Dudd later that same morning in his home, without first securing an arrest warrant. The Commissioner was relieved to hear the news of the arrest and that Dudd later confessed to the robberies at the police station (after being provided *Miranda* warnings and waiving his rights). But the Commissioner was disappointed that Talent and Sims did not get an arrest warrant and worried about the effect this might have on the prosecution of Dudd for the robberies.

37. Did the actions of Officers Talent and Sims jeopardize the prosecution of Dudd?

ANSWER:

The police obtained a valid warrant for the arrest of James Falco. The warrant listed Falco's home address. On the way to Falco's home, the officers stopped at the home of Falco's elderly grandmother. The officers knocked on the door and Grandma Falco answered the door. The officer standing in front of the door looked through the open door and saw James Falco sitting at the kitchen table enjoying a piece of apple pie and coffee. The officer yelled "Police, we have a warrant!" and entered the home to arrest James. A search of James revealed two OxyContin tablets, which Falco unlawfully possessed. James's attorney filed a motion to suppress the tablets based on the illegal entry.

38. How should the court rule on the motion to suppress?

ANSWER:

Judicial Review of an Arrest

Tom Quill was arrested at 4:00 p.m. on Friday afternoon on a street corner after Officer Kumerline saw him buy heroin from a known drug dealer. Quill was transported to the local jail and locked up. Because his shift was nearly over, Kumerline filled out the paperwork to establish probable cause for Quill's arrest and left it on the desk of the weekend officer for presentation to the magistrate on Saturday morning. The weekend officer failed to see Quill's paperwork and his arrest was not presented to the magistrate for a probable cause determination.

When Kumerline returned to his desk on Wednesday (after taking several vacation days), he found the probable cause memorandum that he wrote and noticed that no marking had been made to show that a probable cause hearing had been held. Upon investigation, Kumerline discovered the oversight and immediately took Quill's case to the magistrate. At 11:00 a.m. on Wednesday, the magistrate determined that probable cause existed for the arrest and detention of Quill. After returning to the police station, Officer Kumerline met with Quill and advised him of his rights under *Miranda v. Arizona*. Quill agreed to speak with him. During the interrogation, Quill made incriminating statements. After getting Quill's confession, Kumerline left the room. At trial in state court, Quill's attorney filed a motion to suppress Quill's statement.

39. Is the confession admissible?

ANSWER:

Pretextual Stops and Arrests

On April 11, at approximately 4:00 p.m., State Highway Patrol ("SHP") Trooper R.J. Jacks ("Jacks") stopped Defendant for alleged traffic violations committed while traveling westbound on U.S. 35. Jacks testified at the suppression hearing that he was in a marked police cruiser parked on a strip between east and west U.S. 35 and observed "a vehicle probably half a mile to three quarters of a mile away, in the left-hand westbound lane, passing a semi-truck." The speed limit in the area was 55 miles per hour and the vehicle had suspiciously slowed its speed, eventually pulling back in behind the semi. Using a radar gun, Trooper Jacks checked the vehicle's speed three times as it approached, and it registered at about 53 miles per hour. Jacks continued to monitor the vehicle, and as the vehicle drove by, Jacks assessed the behavior of the vehicle's driver, Alicia Dukes. Jacks asserted that "As she drove by, I noticed that she didn't look over at me. She seemed extremely tight. She was—her hands were locked at the 'ten and two' position on the steering wheel, leaned up on the steering wheel, staring straight ahead as she went by." Jacks found this behavior "suspicious," and he decided to follow her to "see if [he] could observe any more unusual driving behaviors and also any kind of offenses that I might stop her for."

Jacks left the median strip and caught up with Dukes. He noticed that Dukes was "weaving in her lane," and he felt that "maybe she [was] watching [him] in her mirror." Dukes, however, never drove outside of her lane, and, at all times, she continued to drive "unusually slowly." Jacks then "decided to pull up beside of her, just to look, take a look at her to see, you know, if I could see anything, if she would look over at me, what her behavior was when I pulled up beside of her." Upon doing so, however, Defendant kept her eyes on the road, and, according to Trooper Jacks, she "looked exactly the same as when she drove by me [before].... She's still locked on the steering wheel, staring straight ahead. I pulled up beside her. I'm looking at her through my side glass. She never glances over at me, just kept driving."

Ultimately, Jacks testified that Dukes had committed two traffic violations. First, Dukes "followed too closely" to a very large truck. Second, Jacks testified that although Dukes used her turn signal to change lanes, she did not turn on her signal until she had already started to change lanes. As a result of these violations, Jacks decided to pull Dukes over for an "education stop." At the suppression hearing, it was established that the SHP does not formally authorize anything termed an "education stop."

At the hearing, Jacks further testified that when he approached the car, he asked Dukes for her license and registration. When Dukes opened her purse, he could see a baggie inside the purse with what he believed to be marijuana. Additionally, he claimed that he smelled a faint odor of marijuana inside the car. At this point, Jacks arrested Dukes for possession of marijuana.

Dukes moved to suppress the marijuana on the basis of an illegal traffic stop. The trial court suppressed the marijuana. How should the court of appeals rule on the Government's appeal?

40. The evidence found during the search of the vehicle is:

(A) inadmissible because Officer Jacks did not pull her over for any traffic violation but for a non-existent "education stop."

(B) inadmissible because a reasonable police officer would not have made the stop for such minor traffic violations.

(C) admissible because police had probable cause to search the car.

(D) admissible because the stop was lawful.

Protective Sweep of a Home

An undercover police officer learned that members of the "Heartless OG" gang had committed a series of burglaries and armed robberies involving automatic weapons. Jonathon Break was the leader of the gang and was known to be hiding in his home located in woods at the outskirts of the city. The house was known to be the gang's hangout. The police obtained a "no-knock warrant" to arrest Break, eliminating the need to knock and announce before entering the home, and then entered it without knocking or announcing. The police entry caught Break unawares. Break was sleeping on a couch in the front room close to the door when the police entered.

Police handcuffed Break and then walked into an adjacent room and opened the door of a closet located inside the room. No one was hiding in the room or in the closet. However, in the closet they saw a number of automatic weapons and ammunition, which they seized. A test of one of the weapons matched a bullet found in the body of a person who had been murdered six months earlier, unrelated to the recent series of burglaries or robberies. Break was charged with that murder. Break's attorneys filed a motion to suppress the automatic weapon and the subsequent ballistic test on the ground that police illegally searched the closet without a warrant.

41. Was the search of the closet, resulting in discovery of the weapon, lawful?

    (A) The warrantless search of the closet was illegal because Break was in custody and could not have reached the weapons in the closet.

    (B) The warrantless search of the closet was illegal because police could have secured the premises and obtained a search warrant.

    (C) The warrantless search of the closet was legal because police may check areas adjacent to the room where the arrest took place to protect their safety.

    (D) The warrantless search of the closet was legal because police had probable cause to believe that weapons and the proceeds of the burglaries and robberies were on the premises.

After seizing the weapons, the police officers swept the entire house for Break's confederates. During the sweep, a police officer opened a small cabinet hanging on the wall in the basement. Police found inside the cabinet a large quantity of stolen jewelry. Break has filed a motion to suppress the items found in the cabinet.

42. Are the stolen jewelry items found in the cabinet admissible?

ANSWER:

Search of a Person or Item Incident to Arrest

On November 15, a police officer saw Elliot Freeman travelling over the speed limit while driving through an intersection. As the officer pursued the automobile, she observed Freeman make an illegal right turn on a red light. After stopping Freeman's automobile, the officer spoke to Freeman and determined that Freeman was intoxicated. The officer arrested Freeman for driving while intoxicated. At the scene, and prior to taking Freeman to the police station, the officer patted down Freeman to determine if he had a weapon or contraband on his person. The officer felt an object in Freeman's coat pocket that she knew was not a weapon. Nonetheless, she reached into the pocket and retrieved a glassine bag of cocaine; she thereafter removed from Freeman's shirt pocket a vial of cocaine. A number of pills of various kinds and some drug paraphernalia were also recovered from Freeman's other coat pockets. Freeman was charged with illegal possession of cocaine. Prior to trial, the defense filed a motion to suppress the contraband.

43. Is the contraband found in Freeman's pockets admissible?

    (A) The evidence is inadmissible because the officer knew when he reached into Freeman's pockets that he was not carrying a weapon.

    (B) The evidence is inadmissible because the search should have been conducted as an inventory search at the police station.

    (C) The evidence is admissible because the officer had probable cause to conduct a search of Freeman's person once he felt the objects in the pocket.

    (D) The evidence is admissible because it was a lawful search incident to arrest.

Officer Smythe stopped Jennifer Henry after he saw her drive through a stop sign. After issuing Henry a traffic citation, Officer Smythe ordered Henry out of the car and to the rear of her car so that his dashboard camera could record the interaction. Once at the rear of the car, Officer Smythe ordered Henry to empty her pockets and place the contents on the trunk of the car. Henry complied and Officer Smythe saw a small bag of what appeared to be cocaine. Officer Smythe then arrested Henry for drug possession.

44. Is the cocaine admissible at Henry's trial?

   (A) The evidence is admissible because it was seized incident to a lawful custodial arrest.

   (B) The evidence is admissible because it was seized incident to a lawful traffic stop.

   (C) The evidence is inadmissible because a search incident to arrest may not precede the lawful arrest.

   (D) The evidence is inadmissible because a police officer may not conduct a search incident to arrest unless the person is actually arrested.

While sitting in his patrol car, Officer Jenson watched Ben Apten talk with an unknown female. Apten was well known to Officer Jenson as a drug dealer because Officer Jenson had arrested Apten multiple times in the past. While watching the two, Officer Jenson saw the unknown female hand Apten some crumpled money. Apten took the money, looked around, and then handed the female something that Officer Jenson could not identify. The female then hurried away.

Officer Jenson got out of his car and approached Apten. As he approached, Apten saw him, reached into his pocket, placed something in his mouth, and started to swallow. Officer Jenson jumped on Apten and grabbed him by the face in an attempt to force open Apten's mouth. Officer Jenson ordered Apten to open his mouth. When he refused Officer Jenson slapped Apten in the ear causing Apten to yell out in pain. When Apten yelled, a small baggie of white "rocks" fell out of Apten's mouth.

At his trial for possession of crack cocaine with intent to distribute, Apten's lawyer challenged the admissibility of the crack cocaine.

45. How should the court rule?

   ANSWER:

Search of a Home Incident to Arrest

On April 16, at approximately 7:10 a.m., three officers assigned to the Parma Fugitive Task Force arrived at 555 Pearl Road looking for the defendant with the intent to arrest him on outstanding felony warrants. They knew that defendant lived at that address and had reason to believe that he was home at the time.

When they arrived, the officers approached the rear, first-floor apartment door of the two-family home and entered an enclosed porch. The door to the apartment was open and they began shouting "police" to announce their presence. No one responded. Police then entered the house and heard a noise upstairs where there was only one bedroom and a bathroom. The officers went into the bedroom with their weapons drawn, shouting for the defendant to come out of the closet with his hands up. When the defendant did not comply, two officers entered the closet to extricate him. After a brief struggle, the officers pulled the defendant out of the closet into the main area of the bedroom, at which time the other officer held him face down on the floor, about six feet from the closet. The officer then handcuffed him, with his hands behind his back. This process, from the time the officers entered the bedroom to the time they subdued the defendant on the floor, took one minute or less.

After the defendant was removed from the closet, one officer searched him and found a small, clear plastic bag containing 30 ecstasy pills in his pocket. With the defendant still prone on the floor, one officer watched over the defendant while the two other officers searched the closet to look for a weapon. The closet was dark and messy, and the officers needed flashlights to conduct the search. After looking for five to 10 minutes, they recovered no weapon but discovered a bag near where the defendant had been hiding containing three plastic bags of ecstasy pills. One bag contained seven pills, one bag contained 20 pills, and the third bag contained 132 pills. The pills retrieved from the closet, like the pills found in the defendant's pocket, all had the letter "G" imprinted on one side and the silhouette of a woman imprinted on the other side.

Prior to trial, the defendant filed a motion to suppress the drugs found both in the closet and on his person.

46. How should the court rule on the motion to suppress?

    (A) The court should deny the motion because all of the evidence was secured incident to a lawful arrest with a warrant.

    (B) The court should deny the motion because the police had probable cause to believe that evidence of guns would be found wherever the defendant was found.

(C) The court should grant the motion because police should have sought a search warrant in addition to an arrest warrant.

(D) The court should grant the motion because the search did not fall under the search incident to arrest exception to the warrant requirement.

The police set up a sting operation to catch men cruising in the Old Town neighborhood looking for prostitutes. As part of the sting operation, an undercover policewoman is stationed at the corner of Elm Road and an alley. From an unmarked car, the police witness Joshua Zimmer drive up to this corner and stop his car. Zimmer calls to the undercover policewoman who approaches Zimmer's car. Zimmer and the undercover policewoman talk. The undercover policewoman gives the signal that a solicitation for prostitution has been made. Complying with the undercover officer's suggestion, Zimmer pulls his car into the parking lot around the corner where the police are waiting in unmarked cars. Zimmer is arrested and removed from his car. The arresting officer takes Zimmer to the rear of Zimmer's car and begins the booking process by asking identification questions. Zimmer is not handcuffed. While this process is happening, a second officer searches Zimmer's car. Under the front seat, the officer finds a single ecstasy pill (an illegal substance).

Zimmer is charged with possession of an illegal substance. His lawyer sought to exclude the ecstasy pill by challenging the validity of the search of Zimmer's car.

47. How should the trial court rule?

ANSWER:

The police obtained a warrant to arrest Lilly Joinder for failure to pay child support. Two male police officers went to Joinder's home and properly executed the warrant. Joinder was arrested in her living room but had just stepped out of the shower and was wearing only a towel. Joinder asked permission to put on clothes before being taken to the police station. The police agreed and escorted her into the bedroom. As Joinder approached her dresser drawer in the bedroom, the officer observed on the top of the dresser a gun, which he seized. Later inspection of the gun indicated that it lacked a serial number (it had been filed off). Joinder now faces felony weapons charges.

Joinder filed a motion to suppress the gun asserting that the search exceeded the scope of a search incident to arrest.

48. Should the court grant the motion to suppress?

(A) No. Entry of the room and seizure of the gun were proper.

(B) No. Entry of the room and seizure of the gun were justified by exigent circumstances.

(C) Yes. Police had no authority to enter the bedroom. Because the officers were men they should have stood at the door and observed Joinder getting the clothing.

(D) Yes. The entry into and search of the dresser constituted an invasion of Joinder's privacy and police should have secured a search warrant.

Exigent Circumstances

Police answered a 911 call with no one on the other end and received a busy signal when they repeatedly tried to call back. Officers were then dispatched to the 911 call address. Upon their arrival, they saw a bed sheet with blood on it draped across the front door, obscuring their view into the house. The officers banged on the outside of the house next to the door. After a couple of moments, the defendant poked his head around the sheet. The defendant appeared surprised by the presence of the officers and very nervous. The defendant denied calling 911 and said that all was okay inside the residence. When police asked if they could come in and look around, the defendant said no. The officers entered without his permission. They walked through the entire house and found marijuana located in a dresser drawer. The defendant was charged with drug possession.

The defense moved to suppress the marijuana.

49. Should the court suppress the marijuana?

    (A) Yes. Even if the entry of the home without the defendant's consent was legal the taking of the marijuana exceeded the scope of the entry.

    (B) No. The entry was legal when the defendant refused to provide consent, creating probable cause that someone inside the home was in danger.

    (C) No. The marijuana was located in a place where a weapon could be stored, which might pose risk of injury to the police.

    (D) Yes. The police, instead of entering the home, should have opted for a less intrusive technique to allay their concerns, such as peering in the windows of the home from outside.

The police were sitting in their squad car outside of the home of a suspect's girlfriend waiting for a warrant to search the house to be obtained. The police already had a felony arrest warrant for the suspect. The suspect, unaware that the police were outside, walked out of the house and down to the street to get his morning newspaper. The police saw him outside the home and rushed towards the suspect. The police identified themselves as police and ordered the suspect to "freeze." The suspect turned and ran back into the house. The police ran after the suspect, entered the home, searched for, and found, the suspect under a bed. The police arrested the suspect and discovered on him a firearm that he, as a convicted felon, was not entitled to possess.

50. Should the handgun be suppressed?

    (A) Yes. The gun was found only after the police entered the home without a search warrant.

    (B) No. The police legally entered the home and therefore had authority to arrest and then conduct an incidental search of his person.

    (C) Yes. The police believed a search warrant was going to be issued shortly so they should have waited for the warrant to arrive.

    (D) No. The police had authority to enter the home because a warrant was going to be issued soon allowing the entry.

Using the facts in Question 50, add the following. As the officers were taking the suspect out of the home, he told the police "You'll never find my stash!" At that moment, the girlfriend arrived at her home and was denied permission to enter. One of the officers stayed at the home and remained at the doorway, stopping anyone from entering while the second officer took the suspect to the police station and went to get a warrant to search the girlfriend's home for drugs. At one point, the girlfriend, required to stay on the porch outside the front door, asked to use the restroom and was told that she could not because the officer was male and would have to watch her at all times to prevent the destruction of evidence. The second officer returned to the home two hours later without a warrant, which had been denied because of a lack of probable cause. The girlfriend then filed a § 1983 action asserting that the continued presence of the first officer at the home without a warrant violated her Fourth Amendment rights.

51. How should the court rule?

    ANSWER:

As of 3 p.m. on July 3, police had probable cause to believe that Delbert possessed three ounces of cocaine and that he was staying in room 280 of the Hearts at Home Hotel. Around 6 p.m. on July 3, three uniformed officers visited the hotel and secured a key card to room 280 from the hotel clerk. One of the officers tried to use the key card to gain entry to the room but the card did not work. At that point, the same officer blocked the door peephole, knocked on the door, and announced "housekeeping." Delbert soon thereafter partially opened the door but when the officer flashed his police badge Delbert quickly attempted to push the door shut. The officers then used a battering ram to force the door open. After entering, the officers saw three bags of what appeared to be cocaine on a bedside table near the front door. Delbert was immediately arrested; a subsequent search of the hotel room revealed no other contraband. Delbert's lawyer has filed a motion to suppress the cocaine.

52. How should the court rule?

ANSWER:

Community Caretaking Function

Around 6:00 p.m., John Maluck was at the wheel of the first vehicle stopped at a traffic signal light in Chicago, Illinois. Two Chicago police officers, Armondo Santiago and Anthony Swimmer, were in their squad car, which was located a few cars behind Maluck's car. The light at the intersection changed, but Maluck's car did not respond, and motorists started honking their horns. Someone coming from the opposite direction on Michigan Avenue told the officers that there was a car blocking traffic, and that the driver was either asleep at the wheel or passed out.

The officers activated their squad car roof lights and pulled up next to Maluck's car. Officer Swimmer went over to Maluck's car and observed that Maluck was asleep behind the wheel with his head down. The gear of Maluck's car was in "drive," and his foot was on the brake. Maluck's window was open, and Swimmer attempted to wake him by calling to him, but Maluck did not respond. Swimmer reached in through the open window of Maluck's car, shifted the gear into "park," and while doing so noticed a bag of what he knew to be marijuana on the front seat next to Maluck.

53. Under the Fourth Amendment, did the officer have the right to reach into the car and see the marijuana?

    (A) Yes. The search was a limited search for anything dangerous to the officers or Maluck.

    (B) No. There was no probable cause to search the car for anything.

    (C) Yes. The marijuana was in plain view as a result of the officer exercising a caretaking function.

    (D) No. The search exceeded the officer's authority under the caretaking function.

Search of an Automobile Incident to an Arrest

Peter Laval was a middleman for a major drug dealer. Laval sold and delivered substantial quantities of drugs to mid-level sellers. Late one night Laval was driving along Interstate 95, weaving all over the road. Suddenly, he saw a police car behind him signaling him to pull over. The officer observed Laval weaving and wanted to check him for drunk driving. He ordered Laval out of the car and subjected him to field sobriety tests. Laval was sober and had no trouble passing the tests.

The officer prepared to write Laval a ticket and entered Laval's information into the police computer records system. Laval had forgotten to renew his driver's license that had expired four months earlier. The officer arrested Laval for driving without a license, pursuant to a state law that authorized arrests in such cases. He handcuffed Laval and put him in the back of the police car. The officer then searched Laval's automobile and found a large quantity of marijuana in the trunk of the vehicle. The police officer seized the marijuana and Laval was charged marijuana possession. Laval's lawyer moved to suppress the marijuana found in the trunk of the vehicle.

54. Is the marijuana admissible at Laval's trial, solely on the basis of the search of his car trunk incident to arrest?

 (A) The marijuana is admissible because it was found in a search incident to a lawful custodial arrest.

 (B) The marijuana is admissible because it was found during a search under the automobile exception to the warrant requirement.

 (C) The marijuana is inadmissible because the arrest of an unimpaired driver for a traffic offense is unlawful under the Fourth Amendment, and the subsequent search is tainted by the illegal arrest.

 (D) The marijuana is inadmissible because the search of the trunk was unlawful.

Rufus Daily was driving his 1968 Lincoln Continental on a rural back road. He drove past a state trooper on drug interdiction patrol. The trooper used his radar gun to check Rufus's speed and confirmed that Rufus was traveling five miles per hour over the speed limit. The trooper pulled Rufus over and approached his car. Rufus gave the trooper his license and registration. The trooper checked the license and found that Rufus had outstanding arrest warrants for burglary. The trooper ordered Rufus out of the car, told him that he was under arrest, placed him in handcuffs, and situated him in the backseat of his trooper patrol car. The trooper then returned to Daily's car and rummaged around inside to see if he could discover any contraband. Under the car's front driver's seat, he found what appeared to be a plastic baggie containing cocaine and a cell phone, which he readily activated (by entering "1,2,3,4,5,6") and discerned on its screen a picture of Daily holding a large rifle.

55. Daily, a convicted felon, has been charged with the burglaries, as well as unlawful possession of cocaine and possession of a firearm by a convicted felon. He has filed a motion to suppress the cocaine and the photo connecting him to the firearm. Regarding the lawfulness of the searches incident to arrest alone, the court likely will:

(A) Deny both motions to suppress because the trooper acted lawfully.

(B) Grant the motion to suppress the cocaine and deny the motion to suppress the photo.

(C) Deny the motion to suppress the cocaine and grant the motion to suppress the photo.

(D) Grant both motions to suppress.

Automobile Exception

Officer Trapper saw the defendant run a red light. After stopping defendant's car, the officer walked up to the driver's window and instructed the defendant to lower the window. As soon as the window was lowered, Officer Trapper observed on the passenger seat floor what she knew was a machine gun, which it was unlawful for defendant to possess. Trapper told defendant that he was under arrest for unlawful possession of a firearm and searched him, finding nothing but his car keys. Trapper placed defendant in handcuffs and situated him in the backseat of his police squad car. Trapper then searched the car's interior and found nothing of an incriminating nature. Frustrated, Trapper then turned her attention to the trunk of the car. When she opened the trunk, she discovered several large glassine bags containing what she knew to be marijuana. The defense has filed a motion to suppress the marijuana found in the trunk.

56. Based on authority afforded by the automobile exception alone, the marijuana found in the trunk by Officer Trapper at the scene of the stop is:

    (A) admissible under the automobile exception to the warrant requirement.

    (B) not admissible under the automobile exception to the warrant requirement.

    (C) admissible because the defendant possessed an unlawful machine gun.

    (D) not admissible because police lack authority to search a car trunk incident to the lawful arrest of a suspect.

Let's change the facts in the previous Question. Assume that just after the stop, a fellow officer arrived at the scene with a drug detection dog named Tango. Tango approached the trunk of the car and promptly alerted to the presence of drugs in the trunk. Based on Tango's response, Officer Trapper opened the trunk and discovered a sealed shipping box. Officer Trapper opened the shipping box and discovered several bricks of marijuana. Upon finding the drugs, Trapper arrested the driver. The defense filed a motion to suppress the marijuana found in the trunk. How should the trial court rule?

57. The evidence found during the warrantless search of the trunk by Officer Trapper is:

(A) admissible because it was found incident to a lawful custodial arrest.

(B) admissible because it was found during a search under the automobile exception to the warrant requirement.

(C) inadmissible because there was no exigent circumstance to justify a search of the trunk under the automobile exception.

(D) inadmissible because search of a trunk of the car is more invasive than a search of the passenger compartment and therefore does not come within the automobile exception, even when probable cause exists that the trunk contains contraband.

Officer Oscar Williams spent a year cultivating an informant inside a local crime syndicate. This informant provided useful and reliable information about the inner workings of the syndicate, including detailed information about the movement of large quantities of cash and narcotics. One day, the informant called Officer Williams and reported that the boss of the syndicate, Harden James, was suspicious that a snitch was working inside the syndicate. James was planning to flee the country taking the proceeds of the latest narcotics sale, some $250,000 with him. The informant reported that James would leave his house at 4730 Campbell Street at 5:30 p.m. with a suitcase full of cash in the back of a black SUV.

At the appointed hour, Officer Williams arrived at James's home and observed James load a large suitcase into the back of his black SUV. James then got in the car and drove out of the driveway and started down the street.

Officer Williams activated his lights and pulled James over. Officer Williams then observed that Judge Russo was riding in the car with James. Judge Russo explained that he was riding with James because they were going away for a romantic weekend together.

Officer Williams opened the rear of the SUV and observed two identical suitcases. One was labeled H. James and the other labeled F. Russo. Officer Williams removed both suitcases and opened them. Inside the suitcase labeled H. James, Officer Williams discovered nothing more than clothing and personal items. However, inside the suitcase labeled F. Russo, Officer Williams discovered a loaded handgun. Unfortunately, Judge Russo did not have a valid permit for the gun and Officer Williams arrested him. No money was found in either suitcase.

Judge Russo filed a motion to suppress the gun as the result of an unconstitutional search of his luggage.

58. The gun found in Judge Russo's suitcase is:

(A) inadmissible because Officer Williams did not have probable cause to believe that Russo was involved in James's illegal activities.

(B) admissible because Officer Williams had probable cause to search the suitcases in James's car.

(C) inadmissible because Judge Russo was illegally seized, and the search was fruit of the illegal seizure.

(D) admissible because Officer Williams had probable cause to arrest everyone in the car, and the search was incident to the lawful arrest.

Search of Containers

Janice Albion was sitting in the Greyhound Bus Station waiting for the 10:15 bus to El Paso, Texas, located on the border near Mexico. She was arrested when a police officer recognized her from the wanted poster on display in the Greyhound station. The wanted poster identified her as a bail jumper and major heroin dealer. She was arrested without incident. The police officer searched Albion and found a luggage claim ticket in her pocket. Albion was removed to a private office inside the Greyhound terminal. The police officer had the Greyhound security officer retrieve the luggage that matched the claim ticket. The luggage was delivered to the police officer in the private office. Albion identified the luggage as hers and told the officer that he could not open it. The police officer then opened the unlocked luggage and found inside a black zippered bag that he then opened. Inside the bag was a large glassine bag containing marijuana.

59. The search of the luggage was:

   (A) lawful incident to Albion's arrest.

   (B) lawful because the officer had probable cause to believe that evidence would be found inside, and exigent circumstances prevented her from getting a warrant.

   (C) not a lawful search incident to arrest because the luggage was not within Albion's grab area at the time of the arrest.

   (D) not a lawful search incident to arrest because the officer did not have probable cause to conduct a search.

Jason Andrews was well known to the local police as a drug courier who stashed his illegal drugs in his home. Based on reliable information from a police informant, who had supplied reliable information for several years, and a legal wiretap of Andrews's phone, the police learned that Jason was going to send his next delivery via a local delivery service and that the delivery service would pick up the drugs at 1:00 p.m. on May 5. The police set up a stakeout near Jason's home to watch the transfer to the delivery vehicle. At the appointed hour, the police saw the delivery van arrive at Jason's home. Jason came out of the house and walked to the delivery van. Before the police could get there, however, Jason gave the package to the delivery driver and went back into his house. The delivery van then pulled out of the driveway. At that moment the police stopped the delivery van. One of the officers entered the van, took the package that Jason gave the driver and opened the package. Inside the officer found cocaine.

60. Are the drugs admissible against Jason in a trial for drug trafficking?

   ANSWER:

Impoundment and
Inventory Search of a Vehicle

While on routine patrol, an officer noticed an unoccupied vehicle parked in a no parking zone on a public street. Consistent with policy, the officer called for a tow truck to remove the vehicle. The truck arrived and towed the vehicle to the police impound lot. When the car arrived at the lot, the officer in charge used a special tool to unlock the driver door. Also pursuant to policy, the officer conducted an inventory search of the car. The search produced nothing of consequence until the officer removed a door panel. Inside the officer found cocaine.

61. The cocaine is:

   (A) inadmissible because the impoundment and inventory were illegal.

   (B) inadmissible because the search inside the door panel was invalid.

   (C) admissible because the impoundment and inventory were legal.

   (D) admissible because the inventory was legal.

Tina Mesa's car was totaled following an accident in Metropolis, and she was taken to the hospital by ambulance from the accident scene. Tina was cited for failing to yield during a turn. Metropolis policy required that the vehicle be towed and impounded because it was blocking traffic. Metropolis inventory policy directed officers in the field, who have ordered a car to be towed after a serious collision, to search the passenger compartment and the trunk. The policy authorized the opening of passenger compartments and closed containers when police are unable to discern their contents by virtue of exterior visual inspection alone. Before towing Mesa's car, the officer decided to conduct an inventory of the car because, in his words, "Mesa seemed nervous about something." In the glove compartment, the officer found a diamond watch that turned out to be stolen; in the trunk of the vehicle behind the spare tire, the officer discovered an opaque-wrapped brick-size package that the officer opened and saw that it contained marijuana. Mesa was charged with receiving stolen property and possession of marijuana. The defense filed a motion to suppress the objects found in the vehicle.

62. How should the court rule on the motion to suppress?

   (A) The watch and marijuana are admissible because they were found during a lawful inventory of the disabled car's contents.

   (B) The watch is admissible, but the marijuana is not because the inventory of the trunk was illegal.

(C)   The watch and the marijuana are both inadmissible because an inventory is limited to objects that are visible from outside the car.

(D)   The watch and the marijuana are both inadmissible because the inventory policy was discretionary and was equivalent to an impermissible generalized warrantless search.

Comparing Different Justifications for the Search of an Automobile

Around 5:00 p.m. on a Friday evening in July, a man was slumped in the driver's seat of a vehicle located in the middle of the public street in front of 125 Oak Street, a single family home. Officer Hold, when driving by the address on routine patrol, observed the vehicle, which had its engine running and its break lights activated, indicating that the driver had his foot on the break. Concerned for the driver's safety, the officer knocked on the roof of the car, but was unable to rouse the driver. The officer then reached into the vehicle, and shook the driver's shoulder, which had the effect of partially awakening the driver. The officer said, "This is a public space, you'll need to do your sleeping somewhere private, please provide me with your driver's license," to which the driver replied, "Huh?" Frustrated, and believing that the driver was drunk or under the influence of an unlawful substance, the officer reached into the driver's pocket and retrieved his driver's license, which provided the name and address "John M. Maluck, 125 Oak Street."

The officer thereafter peered into the passenger compartment of Maluck's car and saw on the front seat a white substance in a clear, unlabeled plastic bag sticking out more than halfway from inside an open, unzipped backpack. Based on his extensive experience as a police officer, the appearance and packaging of the white substance, and Maluck's impaired condition, the officer believed that the powder was likely heroin. The officer reached into the car and removed the plastic bag from the backpack. He then removed the backpack from Maluck's car and after rummaging through it found burrowed deep inside a brown bottle. The outside of the bottle had inscribed on it the word "Cynomel," yet lacked formal prescription drug information on it. The officer did not know what was in the bottle, but he believed that it was a prescription drug that Maluck had obtained illegally. Maluck's car, which was impounded and inventoried, contained no contraband or evidence.

The officer arrested Maluck for being intoxicated in public and drug possession and, after handcuffing Maluck, situated him in the backseat of his police squad car. After doing so, it occurred to the officer that he had heard Maluck's name before—the police had probable cause to believe he had stolen a red Camaro automobile. The officer then saw what appeared to be a vehicle covered by a dark green tarp in the driveway adjacent to the 125 Oak Street residence. With Maluck asleep in the squad car, the officer walked up the driveway, which was situated alongside the front lawn and up a few yards past the front perimeter of the residence. The top part of the driveway had a wall, in front of which the tarped vehicle was situated. One of the other two sides the driveway was enclosed by a brick wall about the height of the car, and the third side of the driveway abutted the side door to the house, providing access to the driveway. Upon reaching the car, the officer lifted the tarp and saw underneath a bright red Camaro. After taking a picture of the car, the officer radioed for assistance, and when backup arrived, the officer transported Maluck to the station.

Subsequent testing revealed that the white powder was indeed heroin. The officer also discovered upon further investigation that Maluck lacked a prescription for Cynomel. Out of an abundance of caution, the officer secured a search warrant for the brown bottle, opened it, and later learned from lab tests that the substance inside was indeed Cynomel, a drug that required a prescription to obtain legally.

Ultimately, Maluck was charged with public intoxication, heroin possession, unlawful possession of a prescription drug, and auto theft, and he filed a motion to suppress the heroin and the Cynomel, as well as evidence relating to the allegedly stolen auto.

63. How should the judge rule on the motion to suppress?

ANSWER:

Stop and Frisk

Police were investigating drug activity complaints in a Metropolis public housing unit. When they entered the hallway, they saw Aldo Glick leaning against the wall in the hallway. Three officers walked over to Glick and began asking him questions. Glick testified during the suppression hearing that the officers did not raise their voices, did not use profanity, and did not draw their weapons. Glick also testified that, at first, he ignored the officers and did not respond to their questions but that they persisted. He started to walk away from the officers, but they walked with him. Finally, he engaged them in conversation when he realized that they would not let him ignore them and leave. One of the officers told Glick that tenants had complained that drugs were being dealt in the hallway. The officer asked Glick where he lived. He responded, untruthfully, that he did not live in the building and was just waiting for a friend.

They asked to see his I.D., and Glick fished out his driver's license from his wallet and handed it to the officer. The officer checked the license and told Glick he had lied to them about not living in the building. Glick asked for his license back so that he could go up to his apartment. One of the other officers told Glick that he could have his license back and leave if he allowed them to search his backpack for a weapon. Glick testified that he believed that the officers would not let him leave until he let them search. He handed over his backpack which one of the officers opened and then removed several glassine envelopes containing rocks of cocaine. Glick was arrested and charged with illegal possession of crack cocaine. The defense filed a motion to suppress the evidence seized from Glick's backpack.

64. Are the packets of crack cocaine admissible at Glick's trial?

    (A) The evidence is admissible because Glick consented to the search of his backpack.

    (B) The evidence is inadmissible because Glick was lawfully on the premises at the time of the search.

    (C) The evidence is admissible because it was found during a legitimate search for weapons.

    (D) The evidence is inadmissible because it was found during an illegal search.

Reginald Starkie was seen standing near a 1992 Ford Taurus in what Officer Sammie testified was in a high-crime area at 11:00 p.m. on a hot, humid midsummer night. Starkie was wearing a fully zipped winter coat and a winter hat. Officer Sammie watched Starkie approach and then unsuccessfully attempt to open the door to a business that had closed at 9 p.m. Starkie then returned to the Taurus and spoke with a man who turned out to be Starkie's cousin, Timothy Drone. Drone was also standing outside the idling Taurus.

When Officer Sammie hailed Starkie, Starkie moved to the other side of the car, hunched over, and appeared to fiddle with something in his waistband. Sammie told Starkie to show his hands, but Starkie did not comply. Sammie heard the somewhat muffled sound of metal hitting the ground and saw Starkie pick up an object of some kind and place it in his coat pocket. Officer Sammie then told Starkie to put his hands on the car, and Starkie complied.

Officer Sammie looked on the ground near and under the car and did not see anything suspicious. Sammie then patted Starkie down and felt a bag with hard, metal items. Though he did not think the items were weapons, his training and experience immediately caused him to believe that they were burglary tools. Sammie removed the bag from the outer pocket of Starkie's coat and observed that the bag in fact contained burglary tools. Starkie was arrested and charged with possession of burglary tools and attempted breaking and entering. Starkie filed a motion to suppress the bag and its contents.

65. How should the court rule on the motion to suppress?

   (A) The officer had reasonable suspicion to make a *Terry* stop and reasonable suspicion to search for a weapon and the search of the bag was within the scope of a valid *Terry* frisk.

   (B) The officer did not have reasonable suspicion to make a *Terry* stop.

   (C) Although the officer had reasonable suspicion to make a *Terry* stop, the search exceeded the frisk allowed under *Terry*.

   (D) The officer had probable cause to believe that a break-in was about to occur and, therefore, probable cause to arrest Starkie and to secure the bag in his coat as a result of a search incident to arrest.

Officer Carbonari was investigating reports of drug sales on a street corner, in a neighborhood known to have a high crime rate. Carbonari watched Willie Warble for several minutes, as motorists and pedestrians engaged Warble in very short conversations. Carbonari did not see money or objects change hands. Carbonari drove right up to the corner where Warble was standing. When Warble saw the police car, he walked away from the corner. Carbonari started after Warble and told him to stop, but Warble started running away. Carbonari saw Warble reach into his pocket, while he was running, and throw away several objects. Warble was tackled at the end of the block by Carbonari's partner. Carbonari found the objects thrown away by Warble. Those objects were small glassine envelopes containing small quantities of cocaine.

66. Is the cocaine admissible at Warble's trial?

   ANSWER:

Officer Jessie was stationed roadside on Highway 98 one afternoon when the radio dispatch operator relayed to him a 911 report by an anonymous cell phone tipster that a late model red Ford Bronco had almost run her off the road and was being driven very erratically in the westbound lane of Highway 98. The caller, before hanging up, indicated that the Bronco was located at mile marker 47 of Highway 98, and provided a license plate number for the Bronco. Officer Jessie, who was situated at mile marker 60 soon saw a late model Bronco with the license plate number conveyed by the dispatcher. Jessie thereafter followed the Bronco for approximately five minutes; during such time the Bronco abided by all traffic laws.

Concerned that the driver was drunk or high, however, Officer Jessie activated his patrol car roof lights and the Bronco slowly pulled over. Jessie approached the Bronco and immediately smelled what he knew to be burnt marijuana emanating from the Bronco. He ordered the driver, one Ted Harris, to get out of the Bronco, and when Harris did so, Jessie saw lying on the driver seat of the vehicle a large glassine bag containing what Jessie knew to be marijuana. Harris is facing a charge of marijuana possession and filed a motion to suppress the marijuana found by Officer Jessie.

67. Will the motion to suppress succeed?

    (A) No, because the anonymous tip justified the traffic stop, resulting in plain view discovery of the marijuana.

    (B) Yes, because Officer Jessie, while entitled to follow the Bronco, failed to confirm the tipster's allegation of erratic driving.

    (C) Yes, because anonymous tipsters cannot qualify as a basis for reasonable suspicion to justify a stop.

    (D) No, because the marijuana was viewable only after Officer Jessie acted unlawfully in ordering Harris from the Bronco.

A police officer stopped Sumner Wells for running a red light. The officer approached Wells's car, advised him of the reason for the stop, and got Wells's driver's license and proof of insurance. The officer returned to his vehicle and ran a records check on Wells. The record check revealed no warrants for Wells, so the officer returned to Wells's car and issued a warning for running the red light. Wells asked if he was free to leave and the officer stated that he had one more piece of paperwork to complete and then Wells could leave.

The officer returned to his vehicle and issued a radio call for a K-9 unit. The officer sat behind Wells's car for about 15 minutes until the K-9 arrived at the scene. The K-9 officer approached Wells's car with his dog and walked slowly around Wells's car. The dog reacted to the presence of drugs in the trunk of the car. The officer took Wells's keys from the car and opened the trunk. Inside the trunk was a large quantity of drugs. Wells was charged with possession of the large quantity of drugs. His lawyer has filed a motion to suppress the drugs.

68. The drugs are:

    (A) admissible because the use of the drug dog provided probable cause for a warrantless search of the automobile.

    (B) admissible because the search of the vehicle was incident to the lawful traffic stop.

(C) inadmissible because the drug dog sniff occurred after the traffic stop was improperly extended.

(D) inadmissible because there was no reasonable suspicion to justify use of the drug dog to ascertain whether there were drugs in the automobile.

Checkpoint Stops

Metropolis police set up a roadblock at the corner of East 55th Street and Central Avenue where a shooting had occurred at the same time two days earlier. Police hoped that someone traveling through the intersection would have information about the shooting. The police stopped every car and handed the driver a handbill asking for information about the shooting. David Evans's car was in line. When his car reached the front of the line, a police officer asked Evans to roll down his window. As the officer gave Evans the handbill, he noticed that Evans was nervous, and his speech slurred. Instead of being waved on, Evans was ordered to the side of the road where another officer ordered him out of the vehicle and told Evans to perform field sobriety tests. Evans failed. Evans was arrested, taken to the police station, and given a Breathalyzer exam which reported that his blood alcohol level was over the legal limit. Evans was charged with driving under the influence. Evans's attorney moved to exclude officers at the scene of the checkpoint stop from testifying about Evans's condition as well as the results of the Breathalyzer exam.

69. How should the court rule on the motion to suppress?

ANSWER:

Traffic Stops:
Duration and Scope of Inquiry

One day while on patrol, Officer Anderson noticed Robie Morgan leaving a Frisbee golf course and lawfully pulled him over for speeding. Before exiting his patrol car, Anderson requested that a colleague bring a drug-sniffing dog to the scene of the traffic stop, based on his past experience that "Frisbee golfers use weed." Anderson thereafter checked Morgan's driver's license, proof of insurance, and registration and, finding nothing amiss, issued Morgan a written warning for his speed and returned his paperwork. At that point, Officer Anderson asked Morgan if he enjoyed playing Frisbee golf. Morgan answered yes and told Officer Anderson that he had just left the golf course.

Officer Anderson told Morgan that, in his experience, Frisbee golf players liked to smoke marijuana. Officer Anderson asked Morgan if that was his experience as well. Morgan said nothing in response but at that point became visibly nervous. Anderson then related that he perceived Morgan's nervousness, and that nervous people "usually had something to hide."

Officer Anderson then said that he would like to check Morgan's car for contraband. Morgan gave a heavy sigh and said "go ahead." Just as this occurred, a drug-sniffing dog arrived at the scene and indicated that marijuana was in Morgan's car trunk. Anderson then opened the trunk and found several ounces of marijuana (which was unlawful in the jurisdiction).

70. Presuming no exception to the exclusionary rule applies, the marijuana found in Morgan's trunk is:

    (A) admissible because it was found incident to a lawful search.

    (B) inadmissible because once Officer Anderson wrote the warning and returned Morgan's papers, he was no longer allowed to ask Morgan any questions.

    (C) inadmissible because use of the drug-sniffing dog was unlawful.

    (D) admissible because Officer Anderson had probable cause to search the car.

Administrative Searches

Billy Baldus owns several apartment buildings near a law school. He rents his units primarily to law students who are grateful for relatively cheap housing close to campus. Because Baldus charges below market rates for his apartments he has taken to cutting costs wherever possible. These cost-cutting methods include postponing needed repairs, neglecting or ignoring safety regulations, and generally running a slum landlord operation.

Karen O'Malley, a law student, rents one of Baldus's apartments. As she is preparing for final examinations, the local housing inspector arrives at her apartment. He demands entry into the apartment to make sure the apartment is up to housing code. He explains that the apartment is due for inspection as a matter of routine based on a two-year cycle of inspections. That is, every apartment in the city is inspected every two years. O'Malley refuses to allow the inspector to enter. After making repeated requests for permission to enter and being denied, the housing inspector calls the local police department, and an officer is dispatched to obtain an administrative search warrant authorizing a routine search of O'Malley's apartment. When the officer arrives with the warrant, a final request to enter to conduct a housing inspection is made and again refused. At this point, O'Malley is arrested, and the housing inspector makes his inspection, finding numerous housing code violations.

Prior to her trial for obstruction of justice, O'Malley files a motion to dismiss asserting her Fourth Amendment right to refuse entry to the housing inspector.

71. The trial court should:

   (A) dismiss the charges because O'Malley's refusal to allow the search was justified given the need to prepare for her exams.

   (B) dismiss the charges because the housing inspector did not have probable cause to believe that there were any housing code violations to support a search of O'Malley's apartment.

   (C) deny the motion to dismiss because Baldus's history of safety violations supported a finding of probable cause and therefore the housing inspector had a right to enter and search.

   (D) deny the motion to dismiss because the authority to enter and search was based on an administrative search warrant predicated on the need to conduct routine safety inspections.

Special Needs Searches

On January 18, 2015, United States Border Patrol Agent Zane Chokan was on duty at the immigration stationary checkpoint on State Route 467, 42 miles north of the U.S.-Mexican border and the Lukeville Port of Entry (POE). State Route 467 is the primary route north from the Lukeville POE. At approximately 10:10 a.m., Agent Chokan received a radio call from Lukeville POE agents advising that a suspicious vehicle had entered the United States from Mexico. The Lukeville POE agents described the vehicle as a red Ford Explorer with an Arizona license plate of BEN 9729. Agent Chokan testified that the POE agents indicated that the Explorer had two occupants and no luggage. The Explorer was driving north on Route 467 toward the checkpoint.

Agent Chokan testified as follows:

> The 42 miles between the checkpoint and Lukeville POE was known as a significant center of drug smuggling activity.

> Individuals have been known to pull over along State Route 467, have their vehicles loaded with recently smuggled narcotics, and proceed north, and then try to sneak the illicit cargo through the Border Patrol checkpoint on SR 467.

> At approximately 11:15 a.m. on January 18 he saw a red Ford Explorer pull into the primary inspection lane at his checkpoint. The Ford Explorer had two occupants, identified as the Defendants, and the license plate matched the POE report. He walked around the Ford Explorer, looked through its tinted windows, and saw some clutter in the backseat and two large duffel bags in the cargo area.

> The area between the Lukeville POE and the SR 467 checkpoint is a national park, with the checkpoint located just beyond where the national park land ends. One could see the national park's border clearly from the checkpoint and that there is no place in the park that someone could buy luggage like the duffel bags found in Defendants' vehicle.

> Based on elapsed time from the 10:10 a.m. radio report from the border to the 11:15 a.m. arrival of the Explorer at the checkpoint, any stop by the Explorer could not have lasted more than several minutes.

> He was familiar with several illegal narcotics seizures at the checkpoint involving luggage found in cars coming through the Lukeville POE. Two recent narcotics seizures involved duffel bags that were similar in size, shape, and color to those seen in Defendants' vehicle.

After observing the duffle bags in the back of Defendants' vehicle, he directed the Explorer to the secondary inspection area because he believed that the vehicle contained narcotics. At the secondary area, he went to the rear of the vehicle, raised the lift gate, and opened the duffle bags, in which he found approximately 92 kilograms (approximately 204 pounds) of marijuana.

A motion to suppress was filed, limited to the issue of the checkpoint stop and search.

72. How should the court rule on the motion to suppress the marijuana?

ANSWER:

In a cost-saving move, the State Department of Corrections terminated the state employees responsible for preparing the food for prisons and contracted the food service out to a private company. Almost immediately, the prisons saw a dramatic increase in inmate substance abuse, which Department investigators determined was in significant part the result of drugs being smuggled into the prisons by private food service company personnel. The Department instituted a drug testing procedure that mandated urinalysis drug testing of every employee of the private food service company that worked in any State prison. Failure to comply with the testing would result in the worker being banned from working in the prisons.

73. Is the Department of Correction's policy valid under the Fourth Amendment?

(A) The suspicionless drug testing of all food service workers is an unreasonable search.

(B) Suspicionless drug testing of food service workers working in a state prison facility does not violate the Fourth Amendment requirement that searches be reasonable.

(C) The testing of food service workers violates the Fourth Amendment because it is not applied to all state employees who also have the opportunity to import drugs into the prisons.

(D) The testing of some prison workers and not others violates the Equal Protection Clause of the Fourteenth Amendment.

Consent Searches

Kimberly Hutton is a third-year law student who traveled to the big city for her character and fitness interview as part of her bar application process. She was running a little late and was worried that she would not arrive on time at the interview. As she quickly crossed the parking lot near the interview location, a police officer approached her and asked if he could be of assistance. Hutton told the officer of her predicament and he offered to help her find her way. As they walked to the building where the interview was to occur, the officer asked Hutton if she understood the difference between *Terry v. Ohio* and consent. Hutton said she did. The officer then asked if Hutton would allow the officer to look inside her purse. Because she did not want to be late and was frazzled over possibly being late, she said "sure." The officer looked inside the purse and saw a baggie of green leafy substance that he recognized to be marijuana. He then arrested Hutton for drug possession.

74. The marijuana is:

   (A) inadmissible because Hutton's consent was involuntary because of the stress of the interview.

   (B) admissible because Hutton consented to the search of her purse.

   (C) admissible because there was reasonable suspicion to search Hutton since law students are known to use marijuana during stressful times and she was moving quickly.

   (D) inadmissible because the officer did not advise Hutton that she could say no to the request to search.

Frances Dixon was lawfully arrested for drunk driving and taken to the local police station. Dixon was well known to the police as she was suspected of dealing in stolen historical artifacts that she obtained during her work as a Red Cross relief worker around the world. The police believed that she would travel to distressed areas of the world, steal artifacts, and smuggle them into the United States. Repeated investigations, however, failed to turn up any actionable evidence.

While Dixon was in custody, Officer Smaltz went to Dixon's house and spoke with a gentleman he knew to be her husband. Officer Smaltz told Mr. Dixon that his wife was in jail. Mr. Dixon asked if he had to bail her out or if he could just leave her there. Smaltz told Mr. Dixon that he could leave her there if that is what he wanted. Mr. Dixon simply smiled. Sensing an opening, Smaltz told Mr. Dixon of his suspicions about Mrs. Dixon's smuggling operation and asked if he could enter the house and look around. Mr. Dixon was shocked to hear this information, thought for a moment, and invited Smaltz in, saying "I hope you find the stuff and put her away forever.

She is a witch and I hate her." Smaltz searched the house and soon discovered significant evidence of Mrs. Dixon's smuggling operation.

The defense attorney moved to suppress everything found in the house.

75. The evidence found in the house is:

    (A) admissible because Mr. Dixon's consent to search the house was voluntary.

    (B) admissible because exigent circumstances justified not getting a warrant.

    (C) inadmissible because Mr. Dixon's consent to the search of the home was motivated by his hatred of his wife.

    (D) inadmissible because the officers should have sought a warrant before they went to the Dixon family home.

Alter the facts in Question 75. Presume that as Smaltz began a search of the home he found a room in the basement that was locked. Smaltz asked Mr. Dixon for the key to the room but Mr. Dixon said he did not have a key because the room was his wife's work room and only she had a key. Officer Smaltz asked if he could force open the door to which Mr. Dixon replied "Sure. I don't care." Officer Smaltz forced open the door causing minor damage to the door jamb. Inside the room, Smaltz located a vast quantity of stolen antiquities.

Mrs. Dixon's attorney filed a motion to suppress all evidence found at the house. The state claimed that the evidence in the basement was lawfully found with the consent of Mr. Dixon.

76. How should the court rule on the motion to suppress?

    ANSWER:

Police received a report from a neighborhood watch leader that a large number of people were visiting the home of Johanna Coleman. The report stated that the visitors would go up to the front door, speak briefly with Ms. Coleman, and then leave.

Two police officers went to Ms. Coleman's home without a warrant. They asked her if they could come into her house and talk to her in her living room. She opened the door and invited the officers into her home. While Ms. Coleman sat in the living room talking to one of the officers and denied any illegal conduct, the other officer wandered into the bedroom and found a large quantity of drugs under the bed. Ms. Coleman was arrested and charged with possession of illegal drugs with the intent to sell.

Her lawyer filed a motion to suppress. The officers testified that they did not tell Ms. Coleman that she could refuse to allow them to enter the house and search.

77. What should be the result?

    (A) The evidence should be suppressed because the police did not inform the defendant of her right to refuse to allow the police officers to enter her home and conduct a search.

    (B) The evidence should be suppressed because the defendant did not consent to the search that uncovered the drugs.

    (C) The evidence should be admitted at trial because the defendant was simply unwise to let the police into her home.

    (D) The evidence should be admitted because the officers had probable cause to conduct a search and could have entered without the defendant's permission.

Police were investigating reports that Dennis, a graduate student, had become a principal supplier of illegal narcotics at the university. Police watched Dennis' movements and visited his rented duplex apartment when Dennis was out. The police went to the property manager and explained their suspicions about Dennis' activities. The manager stated that he was shocked because Dennis seemed like such a nice boy and that he had been in the apartment just the day before to fix a leaky faucet and did not see anything unusual. The manager agreed to let the officers into the apartment. The police entered the apartment and searched for evidence of drug use or transactions. In the closet in Dennis' bedroom, the officers found an army duffle bag loaded with drugs. Dennis was charged with trafficking.

His attorneys moved to suppress the evidence. The state countered with the claim that the search was legal pursuant to the property manager's consent.

78. The evidence should be:

    (A) suppressed because the property manager did not have authority to consent to a search of Dennis' apartment.

    (B) suppressed because the police lacked probable cause to enter the apartment.

    (C) admitted because the property manager had actual and implied authority to enter the apartment and could consent to a search of the apartment.

    (D) admitted because Dennis had no expectation of privacy in a rented apartment.

Police had probable cause to arrest Mr. Masten on charges related to the sexual assault of his step-daughter. They secured an arrest warrant and went to the Masten home. When they arrived at the house, Mrs. Masten let them into the house where they arrested Mr. Masten. The arrest involved a brief scuffle in which Mr. Masten was knocked to the ground, hitting his head and sustaining a small cut.

Police asked for permission to search the remainder of the house, but Mr. Masten refused. The officers handcuffed Masten, took him outside, and placed him in an ambulance that transported him to the hospital. Mr. Masten objected to being taken to the hospital and yelled to his wife on the way out of the house not to let the officers search the home. The officers returned to the house approximately 15 minutes later and asked Mrs. Masten for permission to search the residence. She granted permission. In the Masten's bedroom closet, police found a small rectangular box on the shelf that contained sexually explicit photos of Masten and his step-daughter. Masten's attorney moved to suppress the photographs.

79. How should the court rule on the motion to suppress?

ANSWER:

Electronic Eavesdropping

Blackbeard, a name used on the internet by an unknown person, was the target of an intensive investigation into an international child pornography ring. Blackbeard was believed to be the man behind an Internet website known as the "kidconnexion." This site permitted anonymous file sharing of child pornography. Unfortunately for the FBI, Blackbeard was a sophisticated programmer who managed to conceal his true identity despite multiple efforts by the FBI to flush him out. During the course of the investigation, the FBI made contact with one user who agreed to cooperate with the police. Based on the statements of the informant, the FBI obtained a warrant to create a "mirror" computer for the kidconnexion server in order to collect all of the communications of the site. The warrant did not direct how the FBI was to create the mirror computer. According to the agent in charge, the creation of the mirror involved hacking into the computer server and installing a program that directed all communications to the government computer while also allowing the communications to proceed to the target.

After 15 days of tracking, the FBI had sufficient information to identify Blackbeard as James Andrews. The FBI found that Andrews was running kidconnexion from a Wi-Fi connection at the local public library. The FBI staked out the library and watched Andrews enter the library and establish an Internet connection. At that moment the FBI arrested Andrews and secured his laptop.

Over the course of the 15 days of tracking Andrews' computer use, the FBI collected 20,000 images believed to be child pornography, receipts for 500,000 bitcoins, and Internet addresses and other items.

80. Is the evidence admissible?

ANSWER:

Exclusionary Rule

A Metropolis municipal police officer observed the defendant driving a car just before the driver crossed the city boundary line of Metropolis and into a neighboring suburb. State law does not allow a municipal police officer to arrest a suspect outside the territorial jurisdiction of her municipality, unless in hot pursuit. The Metropolis police officer nonetheless followed the defendant into the neighboring jurisdiction. Five minutes later, the officer observed the defendant driving erratically. The officer stopped the defendant's car to determine if the defendant was drunk. The officer administered field sobriety tests, which the defendant failed, and then arrested the defendant.

Prior to trial, the defendant's lawyer claimed that the arrest was illegal and sought to dismiss the charges. The trial court concluded that the officer violated the defendant's federal Fourth Amendment rights and excluded the testimony of the officer and dismissed the charges. The state court of appeals reversed the ruling and held the evidence admissible. The defendant appealed to the U.S. Supreme Court.

81. How should the U.S. Supreme Court rule?

ANSWER:

Good Faith Exception

Officer Ahmed Alzahabi was on routine patrol in his squad car at 11 p.m. one evening when he noted a tall, slender woman waiting alone at a bus stop. Naturally inquisitive, he exited his car, walked up to her, and asked her name and why she was out so late. The woman replied that her name was Helen Bixbee and that she was waiting for the 11:20 p.m. bus. After saying thanks, the officer returned to his squad car and ran the name Helen Bixbee in the records database contained in his laptop computer. A search of the database revealed an arrest warrant for one Helen Bixbee, issued by a neighboring county. Based on this warrant, Officer Alzahabi returned to the car and arrested Bixbee. During a search of Bixbee the officer discovered a bag of heroin.

When Officer Alzahabi returned to the police station, it was learned that the arrest warrant for Bixbee had actually been revoked, which the clerk in charge of updating the database negligently failed to note in the database. Nonetheless, Bixbee was charged with drug possession.

82. The evidence is:

   (A) admissible because Officer Alzahabi's had probable cause to arrest Bixbee and found the heroin during a valid search incident to arrest.

   (B) inadmissible because the warrant was invalid.

   (C) admissible because, even if the warrant was invalid, Officer Alzahabi was entitled to rely on the warrant.

   (D) inadmissible because the warrant was invalid, and Officer Alzahabi could not reasonably rely on the warrant.

Officer Conrad submitted this affidavit for a search warrant:

> The affiant is a commissioned officer with the Metropolis Police Department. The affiant has been a member of the Department's Narcotics Squad for 11 years. Affiant received a tip from a confidential informant who has proved reliable in the past that Morgan Washington, residing at 2204 Main Street, within the city, possibly was in possession of a large quantity of uncut powder cocaine at his residence and was dealing said cocaine out of his house.

> Washington, who drives a 2007 Honda Accord, uses the car to transport cocaine. The affiant's investigation has verified the informant's information. A search of Washington's residence two years ago netted an ounce of cocaine, but the case against Washington was dismissed on a legal technicality.

The affiant, possessing probable cause, asks this court to issue a search warrant for Washington's residence and automobile.

The magistrate issued the warrant, which was executed by Officer Conrad. Police found no cocaine in Washington's home but did find 60 imitation Gucci purses. Washington was charged with 60 counts of trafficking in fraudulent goods. Conviction of each offense carries a 10-year mandatory prison sentence. The defense moved to suppress the purses found at Washington's home. The state argued that the search warrant was valid, but if not, the purses are admissible under the good faith exception to the warrant requirement.

83. How should the court rule on the motion to suppress?

ANSWER:

In summer 2016, federal agents suspected that Ronald Rungun headed a criminal syndicate unlawfully transporting and selling firearms. After trying without success to follow his car, they obtained a court order under the federal Stored Communications Act directing Rungun's cell phone company to provide "cell site location information" (CSLI) covering the prior two weeks. Analyzing the information, agents deduced that Rungun repeatedly visited several locations where large shipments of unlawful guns had been discovered. Agents used this information to secure a search warrant of Rungun's home, where they discovered multiple unlawful firearms, ledgers of unlawful firearm sales, and a large amount of cash. Rungun was later indicted in federal court for unlawful trafficking in firearms. While the case was still being adjudicated, prosecutors learned that the U.S. Supreme Court in *Carpenter v. United States*, 138 S. Ct. 2206 (2018) held that obtaining historical CSLI constituted a search under the Fourth Amendment, requiring a warrant based on probable cause, not a court order based on the lower quantum of evidence required by the Stored Communications Act ("specific and articulable facts showing that there are reasonable grounds to believe" that the records sought "are relevant and material to an ongoing criminal investigation").

The federal trial court now has before it a defense motion to suppress the evidence found in the search of Rungun's home.

84. How should the court rule on the motion to suppress?

ANSWER:

Interrogation and Confession: Custody

The Department of Human Services ("DHS") began an investigation regarding allegations of sexual contact between Donald Daffo and his 15-year-old stepdaughter, Sandra. A social worker from DHS telephoned Carol, Sandra's mother, to tell her that she and Donald had to appear at the social worker's office for an interview about the allegation. Mrs. Daffo testified that when she asked what would happen if they failed to go to the interview the social worker stated that the child would be removed from their home. The social worker testified she did not say this.

Mrs. Daffo testified that she had not wanted to go to the DHS office and asked that the social worker come to the family's residence to talk with the family. The social worker insisted that the interview must take place in the DHS office. Mrs. Daffo testified that she believed, if they did not go to the interview and cooperate, that her daughter would be removed from their home.

The next day Donald, Mrs. Daffo, and Sandra went to DHS for the interview. Over the objection of Donald and Mrs. Daffo, the child was interviewed for half an hour on an individual basis by the social worker and Police Sergeant Conner. Donald and his wife requested they go with the child, but they were told that the child would be questioned separately. After the child was questioned, Donald and his wife were questioned, outside the child's presence. Donald, Mrs. Daffo, the Social Worker, and Sergeant Conner were present during this interview.

Prior to their arrival at DHS, Donald and his wife did not know that a police officer would be present for the interview which took place in a small private office with the door closed. Sergeant Conner sat very close to Donald and his wife. Conner himself testified that he sat facing Donald while questioning him, moving from a position "2–3 feet away to possibly inches from the defendant." Conner also testified that, at one point, Donald backed up his chair, and expressed discomfort at Conner's proximity to his body. Sergeant Conner, who is 6 feet 5 inches tall and weighs 330 pounds, controlled the interview and asked the vast majority of questions. Donald was told he was free to leave and that he was not under arrest. However, he was not given any of the *Miranda* warnings. The interview lasted over an hour.

During the interview, Donald made several incriminating admissions concerning the suspected sexual contact. At the conclusion of the interview, the family was permitted to leave and return home. A week later, Donald was indicted for criminal sexual contact with his stepdaughter.

85. Are the statements Donald made during the interview admissible at his trial?

ANSWER:

Carrie Clepto and her two infant children were observed via closed circuit television in a Target store. Carrie was stuffing women's and children's clothing in pockets sewn into the lining of her coat. A store detective, Donald Dick, who worked for a private security company hired by Target and had been observing Carrie in the store for weeks, grabbed her at the checkout counter and took Carrie and her children to a windowless back room. Dick closed the room's door, locked it from the inside, and showed Carrie the store's video tape. He then triumphantly told her that she was going to prison unless she helped the store identify, apprehend, and convict the ring leader of the gang that had been, for a number of months, stealing almost daily from this particular Target store. When Carrie hesitated, Dick threatened that Child Services would take her two children from her custody, and she would never regain custody. By now, the two infants were screaming and crying, and Carrie agreed to tell all. She told Dick that, in fact, she was part of a shoplifting ring that had stolen thousands of dollars' worth of merchandise from this Target store over a period of 10 weeks. She identified the ring leader and promised to testify against him. Her statement was video recorded. After she made the statement, local police were summoned to the store where the officers arrested Carrie and read her *Miranda* rights.

Carrie was charged with felony theft after she was released on bail and refused to cooperate with prosecutors. Her defense attorney moved to suppress the video tape made at the time she gave her incriminating statement to the store detective.

86. What result?

(A) The statement is inadmissible because Carrie was not given *Miranda* warnings prior to being questioned.

(B) The statement is inadmissible because it was not voluntary, being the result of the threat to take away her children.

(C) The statement is admissible because she was not in custody when she was questioned.

(D) The statement is admissible because the store detective who questioned Carrie was not a government agent.

Interrogation and Confession: Public Safety Exception

Officer Charles was a rogue cop. Since he was a child, he wanted to be a police officer, but Charles also had a fondness for easy money. Charles stole drugs and money from drug dealers, and then sold the stolen drugs to other street dealers. His commanding officers were suspicious of Charles, but they never were able to get proof of his illegal activities.

One night, Charles was stopped for driving under the influence. Charles was quite evidently drunk, and the officer who stopped the car arrested Charles, although at the time he did not know that Charles was a fellow officer. Charles had pulled into a lawful parking space seconds before his encounter with the police officer. Since the car was lawfully parked, the car was not towed or impounded.

Charles was transported to the police station where he was identified as a police officer. The arresting officer, without administering the *Miranda* warnings, asked Charles about his service revolver. Charles related that it was in the trunk of his vehicle. When officers went to the vehicle to search the trunk for the service revolver, they found a large quantity of drugs and cash. Officer Charles has been charged with D.U.I., possession of the drugs, and possession of stolen property (the cash).

87. Defense counsel sought to suppress the drugs and money because the trunk search, based on Charles' statements in violation of *Miranda*, provided the only reason for the trunk search. The evidence should be deemed:

   (A) admissible because the car was searched incident to the arrest.

   (B) admissible because the public safety exception to *Miranda* allowed the officer to ask Charles about the location of the gun prior to issuance of the warnings and the money and the drugs were in plain view.

   (C) inadmissible because Officer Charles should have been given the *Miranda* warnings because he was in custody and subject to police interrogation.

   (D) inadmissible because Officer Charles was legally entitled to possess the gun and the search of the car was illegal.

Interrogation

Barry Brewster, age 43, was arrested for drunk driving. He refused to take a Breathalyzer test and was booked for drunk driving. During the booking process, Brewster was told to stand in a boxed-out area on the floor so that his answers and responses could be captured on videotape.

The videotape captured a stumbling Brewster who spoke with hesitating and slurred speech. The videotape was strong evidence that Brewster was inebriated when he was brought to the police station. Asked to spell his name, Brewster first misspelled it and then corrected himself. He had similar difficulty with his address. Brewster was then asked for his date of birth and on what date he would turn age 52. He was able to recite his date of birth but not when he would turn 52. The booking and fingerprinting took about 30 minutes, during which time Brewster never received *Miranda* warnings. Prior to his trial for drunk driving, Brewster's lawyer moved to suppress evidence about Brewster's responses to the questions asked during the booking.

88. The motion should be:

(A) denied because drunk driving poses a serious public threat and police needed to acquire the information sought to ascertain whether he was intoxicated.

(B) denied because the booking questions, concerning routine issues needed to administratively process an arrestee such as Brewster, are pedigree questions which need not be preceded by *Miranda* warnings.

(C) granted as to the inability to recite his name and address because Brewster should have been advised of his *Miranda* rights as soon as he was arrested.

(D) granted as to evidence pertaining to his inability to project ahead in time when he would become a 52-year-old.

Danny was a small-time Chicago criminal hood who had been in and out of trouble numerous times. He gained notoriety after killing his brother-in-law and, after being convicted, filing a successful appeal that invalidated his conviction. The Supreme Court threw out his conviction because incriminating statements he made to police were in violation of his right to counsel. Not too long after that conviction was reversed and Danny went free, he was arrested again.

A police dispatcher sent a patrol car to a retail establishment after midnight where a silent alarm indicated that a break-in was in progress. When the police car pulled up to the store, the officers saw a smashed plate glass window. The officers got out of the car, drew their weapons and shined their flashlights into the store through the broken window. Immediately, Danny came out of the store through the broken window with his hands in the air. He said to the officers, "You've got me this time." They handcuffed Danny and placed him in the back of the police car.

During the ride downtown, Danny, without being spoken to by the officers, talked freely about the break-in and about how arresting him red-handed should assure the two officers' promotions. Just before they got to the jail, Danny also told the officers that nothing he told them could be used against him since they had forgotten to give him *Miranda* warnings. Danny's attorney moved to suppress the statements made to the police officers.

89. The statements are:

(A) admissible because they were volunteered.

(B) admissible because Danny knew his rights and spoke anyway.

(C) inadmissible because the officers should have administered the *Miranda* warnings when Danny was arrested.

(D) inadmissible because the officers should have *Mirandized* Danny on the ride to the police station.

The defendant, known as "Hothead" Grant, was arrested for the brutal murder of his girlfriend, Lola. Hothead and the victim had lived together for two years. Everyone who knew the couple was aware of their stormy relationship. The two quarreled in front of family and friends, and period-ically each would turn up with bruises and bandages. When Lola's lifeless body was found in an alley behind their apartment, Hothead was arrested immediately and taken to the police station.

Following his booking, Hothead was told to sit in the seat next to the investigating detective's desk in a public entry area in the police station. That seat was four or five feet away from the public area of the police station. While Hothead sat, the detective ignored him and focused on paper work, presumably about the homicide. However, several members of Lola's family soon entered the area, sat about five feet away from Hothead, and began threatening him. After about 20 min-utes of constant abuse, Hothead turned to the detective and said, "If you take me out of this room, I will tell you how and why I murdered my girlfriend." The detective moved Hothead immediately, and Hothead gave a full confession. After Hothead confessed, he was read *Miranda* warnings, and he without prompting signed a waiver and a written verbatim copy of his confession.

The defendant's attorney, prior to trial, moved to suppress the confession.

90. Is the confession admissible?

ANSWER:

Instead of the facts above, consider the following alternative facts. Following Hothead's arrest and booking, he was placed in a jail cell to await a court appearance. Shortly after Hothead's arrival in the cell, another inmate was locked in the cell with Hothead. The two began to trade information about why they were there. While they talked about their criminal exploits, Hothead confessed to the murder of his girlfriend and provided details in response to questions from his cellmate. In fact, the cellmate was an undercover police officer pretending to be another detainee in order to pump Hothead about the murder. That police officer will testify at trial about Hothead's admissions obtained in the jail cell.

91. The officer's testimony about Hothead's statements is:

   (A) admissible because Hothead's statements were not the product of custodial interrogation.

   (B) admissible because the statements were spontaneously made.

   (C) inadmissible because the questioning should have been preceded by *Miranda* warnings.

   (D) inadmissible because Hothead's statements where the product of deceit and trickery.

Miranda Warnings

Police arrested the defendant and took him to the police station where he was placed in an interrogation room. Detective Kurt Wallender told the defendant that he wanted to talk to him about a burglary that had occurred the night before on the defendant's street. First, Detective Wallender told the defendant, "I have to read you your *Miranda* rights." Wallender told the defendant that he had the right to remain silent, and that anything he said could be used against him in a court of law. Wallender also told the defendant that he had the right to talk to a lawyer for advice before being asked any questions, and that a lawyer "would be appointed if and when he went you go to court." After Detective Wallender asked the defendant if he understood those rights and wished to waive them, the defendant answered affirmatively.

During the interrogation, the defendant admitted committing the burglary. Wallender also asked the defendant about a number of recent robberies, and after some hesitation, the defendant also admitted to committing them.

At trial for the burglary, the defense moved to suppress the defendant's confession as to the burglary.

92. Is the confession admissible?

ANSWER:

Based on the same facts as Question 92, assume that the defense attorney also moved to suppress the defendant's statements pertaining to the robberies. The defense motion was based upon the fact that Detective Wallender only informed the defendant that he wished to question him about the burglary.

93. The motion to suppress should be:

  (A) granted because the defendant waived his *Miranda* rights only to questions related to the burglary.

  (B) granted because the detective's failure to inform the defendant about the other crimes he wanted to question him about constituted trickery and deceit.

  (C) denied because the defendant knowingly, intelligently, and voluntarily waived his *Miranda* rights.

  (D) denied because trickery and deceit do not affect the quality of a defendant's waiver.

Waiver of *Miranda* Rights

Harlan Stone, a member of a notorious biker gang involved in major drug dealing in Los Angeles County, was arrested in connection with the brutal murder of a police snitch. Even before police were done booking Stone, at 10 a.m. a lawyer retained by the gang to represent Stone was at the police station demanding to see him. Police told the lawyer to wait until after jail inmates were given their lunch. Following the booking, Detective Svedborg took Stone into an interrogation room. Stone had not seen the lawyer and did not know that a lawyer had been retained, was in the building, and had asked to see him.

Detective Svedborg read Stone his *Miranda* rights and then asked Stone if he understood the rights and was prepared to waive them. Stone said, "I guess so." In the two hours that followed, Stone admitted to killing the snitch. At the end of the two hours, Stone was informed about the lawyer waiting to see him. Stone made it clear that, if he had known that the lawyer was at the jail, he would not have answered any questions before talking to the police. A pretrial motion to suppress Stone's confession was filed.

94. The motion should be:

(A) granted because Stone should have been permitted to see the lawyer retained to represent him.

(B) denied because Stone did not exercise his *Miranda* right to counsel.

(C) granted because Stone made clear his desire to exercise his *Miranda* right to counsel and in fact did so, albeit belatedly.

(D) denied because Stone knowingly, intelligently, and voluntarily waived his right to counsel.

Johnny Dealer was caught on videotape selling crack cocaine to an undercover police officer during a buy and bust operation. Dealer was arrested the next day. Police hoped to turn Dealer into a state's witness against his supplier, who, they hoped, would lead to the next person up the chain. Dealer was interrogated by Officer Krupke who read him the *Miranda* warnings. Krupke told Dealer that he thought they could help each other out, but Dealer said he wanted a lawyer. Krupke asked him, "What for? I can do more for you right now than a lawyer can." Dealer asked the officer to explain, and Krupke told Dealer that he was prepared to go to bat for Dealer and make sure he did little or no time in return for supplier-related information. Dealer thought about it for a few minutes, agreed to talk with Krupke, and signed a written waiver of *Miranda* rights. While they talked, Dealer implicated himself in several crimes but got cold feet and was unwilling to talk about his supplier. He told Krupke that if he talked, he'd be a dead man. Dealer's statement resulted in additional criminal charges being filed against him. At trial, Dealer's attorney moved to suppress his statement.

95. What will be the result of the motion to suppress?

ANSWER:

First Confession without Warnings

When Officer Harris arrested and handcuffed Freddy Felon in Felon's home for a string of home burglaries, one of which resulted in the death of the home owner, Officer Harris falsely told Freddy that his fingerprints were found all over the home where the death occurred. The officer did not read Freddy his *Miranda* rights prior to telling him this. Freddy responded, angrily, that he committed the burglary, "but I'm not going to take the fall for the murder." No further comments were made by the officer or Freddy.

Freddy was taken from the home and transported to jail. Once at the jail, Freddy was booked and then taken to an interrogation room. Two hours later, a detective assigned to the case was informed of the statement made to Officer Harris at Freddy's home. The detective met with Freddy and advised him of his *Miranda* rights. Freddy agreed to waive his rights and wrote a confession admitting to the burglaries and the accidental death of the home owner. Prior to trial, the defendant's attorney moved to suppress both the confession at Felon's home and the one at jail.

96. Should the confessions be suppressed?

(A) Both confessions should be suppressed because the first was given without *Miranda* warnings and is inadmissible, and the second confession is inadmissible because the "cat was already out of the bag" and the defendant's second confession was the result of the first.

(B) Both confessions are admissible because the first confession was not the product of custodial interrogation, and the second confession was given in full compliance with *Miranda*.

(C) The first confession is inadmissible because it was not secured in compliance with *Miranda*, but the second confession was secured by a different officer in different surroundings following the reading of *Miranda* warnings and is therefore admissible.

(D) The second confession is admissible because it was secured in full compliance with *Miranda* rules, and the first confession is admissible because, at worst, its admission would be harmless error.

Nate Ramirez was at home one afternoon when he received a phone call from Grimshaw, whom police knew to be his accomplice in the burglary of Jane's home that resulted in her murder. Grimshaw was in police custody at the time of the call. Shortly after the call, a sheriff's deputy wearing a badge and carrying a firearm, saw Ramirez walking down the sidewalk near his home. With her hand on her holstered gun, the deputy told Ramirez that he was to accompany her to the police station.

Ramirez was then transported to the police station, placed in a small room, and questioned by two detectives. The entire interrogation at the station was videotaped. The lead detective began the interrogation stating: "What I want you to do is I want you to be honest with me. The indication we have is that both you and Grimshaw are involved. . . . I want you to tell me what happened that night. I know you were there. I wouldn't be here if I didn't know that. You know what I'm saying?" After these statements by the detective, Ramirez admitted breaking into the victim's house the night of the murder.

The two detectives then left the room for about an hour, only to be replaced by another detective, Larry Smith, who entered the room alone. Smith offered Ramirez a drink of water, casually said "Let's begin where you left off, with you discussing the break into Jane's home," and provided *Miranda* warnings to Ramirez. Ramirez waived his rights to counsel and silence, and then provided a full confession of his involvement in the burglary and murder of Jane.

97. Are Ramirez's statements admissible?

ANSWER:

Exercising *Miranda* Rights

Prior to a planned interrogation, a police detective read the *Miranda* rights to a suspect who had been arrested the previous night. When the detective asked the suspect if she understood her rights and was willing to waive them and answer the detective's questions, the suspect answered: "Maybe I should talk with a lawyer. What do you think?" The detective did not respond to the question, but asked the suspect if she was ready to get down to business and answer questions. The suspect nodded, and the detective began the interrogation which produced answers implicating the suspect in a series of armed robberies.

98. Are the answers admissible at trial?

   (A) The defendant's answers are inadmissible because they were secured without a valid waiver of the defendant's *Miranda* rights.

   (B) The defendant's answers are inadmissible because she invoked her right to counsel.

   (C) The defendant's answers are admissible because she did not invoke her right to counsel and then waived her rights.

   (D) The defendant's answers are admissible because the defendant's willingness to answer the detective's questions revoked her earlier invocation of the right to counsel.

Invoking the Right to Remain Silent

Allison Aide, a nursing assistant in a retirement home, was arrested for battering residents in her care. Allison was transported to the police station, booked on the charges, and given *Miranda* warnings. Allison signed a written waiver of rights and agreed to questioning. After about half an hour, the questions became much more difficult and incriminating. At first, Allison did not respond to the tougher questions, sitting in absolute silence. She then answered a few questions.

When the officer asked her specifically about her actions with one of the alleged battered victims, Allison replied: "I'd rather not make any other comments at this time." The officer did not press Allison to answer the question, instead he asked her about other incidents. Allison answered these questions. The interrogation continued for another hour by which time Allison had confessed to battering four of the residents of the nursing home. Allison's attorney filed a motion to suppress all of her answers to questions after she had informed the officer that she did not want to "make any other comments at this time."

99. The motion should be:

(A) denied because Allison waived her rights in writing.

(B) granted because Allison rescinded her waiver and invoked her right to stop questioning.

(C) denied because Allison continued to answer questions.

(D) granted because she had the right to see an attorney prior to the resumption of questioning.

Resumption of Interrogation

Thad Lewing, age 18, was arrested for the purse snatching-robbery and murder of a woman on the street. Lewing matched the description given by a person who witnessed the robbery-murder. Police arrested Lewing at his mother's home. Once at the police station, Lewing was taken to an interrogation room where he was read his *Miranda* rights and signed a written waiver. During the interrogation, when confronted by a detective with information that he had been identified by a witness, Lewing said, "I didn't do it and that's all I'm going to say." The interrogation stopped immediately. Lewing was told to remain in the room.

About 15 minutes later, the detective walked back in the room and asked Lewing if he was ready to help himself and admit to the robbery-murder. Lewing agreed to talk. Over the next hour, Lewing answered all of the detective's questions and admitted to the robbery and killing.

100. Is Lewing's confession admissible?

ANSWER:

Deputies arrived at the residence of defendant Francis Scott in response to a complaint concerning gunshots in the neighborhood. When Mr. Scott was eventually apprehended, he was lying at the bottom of a small ravine behind his residence. He was handcuffed immediately with his hands behind his back and read his *Miranda* rights. The first officer asked if he wanted a lawyer. Mr. Scott answered, "You bet." While being led to a police cruiser, Scott made a belligerent remark to a second officer and made further statements, innocuous and non-inculpatory, such as "I don't believe this is happening." Mr. Scott was placed in a cruiser for a period of about 10 to 15 minutes.

After 15 minutes, a third officer took Scott out of the police cruiser. Scott said to him that "This is bull—." After this statement, the third officer asked whether Mr. Scott had been advised of his rights. Mr. Scott answered, "Yeah." That officer further asked whether he was aware that he had the right to an attorney. Mr. Scott again answered, "Yeah." Then the officer asked him what had happened. Mr. Scott replied that there had been a "hassle." The officer asked with whom. Mr. Scott answered, "Glenda." When asked whether he had shot a gun, Mr. Scott replied that he had shot into the air.

101. Are Scott's statements to the officer admissible?

ANSWER:

The defendant was arrested when his girlfriend called police and reported that he assaulted her. Read the *Miranda* warnings, he told the investigating officer that he wanted to see an attorney. Later that day, the defendant met with the public defender. At the end of their meeting, the public defender told the defendant that he would be back the following evening and instructed the defendant not to talk to the police or even his cellmate. On his way out of the police station, the defender also instructed the police not to interrogate his client.

The following morning, the investigating officer took the defendant from his cell and told him that now that he had seen and talked with a lawyer, it was time for the defendant to talk to the officer. The defendant agreed to talk to the officer and began answering the officer's questions about the alleged assault. His answers incriminated him.

102. Will the defendant's incriminating statements be admissible at trial?

(A) The defendant's incriminating statements are admissible because the defendant consulted with counsel prior to the interrogation.

(B) The defendant's incriminating statements are admissible because the defendant knowingly, intelligently, and voluntarily waived his *Miranda* rights.

(C) The defendant's incriminating statements are inadmissible because they were secured in violation of his *Miranda* right to counsel.

(D) The defendant's incriminating statements are inadmissible because the officer failed to read him his *Miranda* warnings at the outset of the second interrogation session.

Sixth Amendment Rights

Arthur was charged with drunk driving. During a first court appearance, he pleaded not guilty, and an attorney was appointed to represent him. He was held in jail pending trial. During this time, police received a tip from a reliable informer that just prior to the drunk driving arrest, Arthur had robbed a local branch of the American Savings and Loan Bank and shot and killed the bank's security guard.

Following the tip, police placed an undercover agent in the cell with Arthur to question him about the bank robbery. Eventually, the agent, without giving Arthur *Miranda* warnings, engaged Arthur in conversation, including asking him if he had ever "done" anybody. Arthur ended up discussing the bank robbery and the murder of the guard. He also told the cellmate/agent that after the bank robbery he got blind drunk to forget about the killing and that's when he got arrested for drunk driving.

Arthur was charged with the robbery and murder of the guard. Before trial on the robbery and murder charges, Arthur's attorney moved to suppress the statements made to the undercover agent.

103. Is Arthur's robbery and murder confession to the undercover agent admissible under the Fifth Amendment (*Miranda*) and the Sixth Amendment right to counsel?

   (A) The confession is inadmissible because it was secured in violation of defendant's *Miranda* rights.

   (B) The confession is inadmissible because it was secured in violation of defendant's Sixth Amendment right to counsel.

   (C) The confession is admissible because even though defendant's Sixth Amendment right to counsel had attached, he volunteered the statement to the undercover agent.

   (D) The confession is admissible because it did not violate defendant's rights when he did not know he was talking to a police undercover agent.

104. Will the undercover agent be permitted to testify about Arthur's confession about drunk driving at the trial on that charge?

   ANSWER:

Interrogation and Confessions: Due Process (Voluntariness)

The defendant was arrested and charged with robbery of a pedestrian who was walking towards a subway station at night. The defendant was picked up just a couple of blocks from the subway station. He had never been in trouble with the police. Immediately after his arrest, he was transported to the subway stop. There the victim said that he was not sure but he thought the defendant was the person who had robbed him.

The defendant was taken to the police station where he was given *Miranda* warnings. The defendant agreed to talk to the police and signed a written form waiving his rights. The interrogating officer told the defendant that he had been unequivocally identified by the victim so that he might as well confess. The defendant insisted that it was a mistake and that he had not committed any crime. This exchange went on for 11 hours. The officer's partner filled in for him for an hour.

During the 11 hours, the conversation changed very little. The officer or his partner insisted that they knew the defendant was the robber, and the defendant insisted, sometimes crying hysterically, that he was innocent. In the morning, at the end of the 11th hour of questioning, the defendant finally agreed with the officer that he had committed the robbery. The officer read the *Miranda* warnings again and then asked the defendant to sign a written statement of his oral confession. The defendant did so while sobbing.

The defendant has now recanted the confession and insists that he is innocent. Without the confession, the victim's shaky identification will not be enough to assure the defendant's conviction.

105. Is the defendant's confession admissible?

(A) The confession is admissible because the defendant waived his *Miranda* rights.

(B) The confession is admissible because it was voluntarily given.

(C) The confession is inadmissible because it was secured in violation of *Miranda*.

(D) The confession is inadmissible because it was involuntary.

Suzie, a 22-year-old finishing up her education degree as a student-teacher at a suburban high school, developed a crush on Ben, a 17-year-old junior at the school. The teacher and student had a sexual relationship that lasted for three months. Their relationship ended when the Ben became involved with a classmate. He told his new girlfriend about his prior relationship with Suzie, the teacher, and word about their relationship spread throughout the high school. When the principal heard about the affair, he notified the superintendent's office and the police. The 17-year-old refused to cooperate with the police on the advice of his parents. The police then obtained a sexual assault arrest warrant for Suzie and arrested her on a Friday afternoon as she left the school.

Suzie was given *Miranda* warnings, and she waived her rights. The investigating officer then told her that if she cooperated and told the truth, he would get the case moved to juvenile court because the victim was still a juvenile and that she would definitely receive a probation sentence in juvenile court. Suzie, who was not sophisticated about legal matters and had no prior arrests, thought that this was a very promising development. She did not know that because she was an adult her case could not be handled in juvenile court. Looking for any break she could get, she told the officer that she didn't force herself on Ben but admitted having sex with him over a period of three months.

Without Ben's cooperation, Suzie's admission was the only evidence the state had.

106. Suzie's statement is:

(A) admissible because she waived her *Miranda* rights.

(B) admissible because she waived her *Miranda* rights and confessed immediately thereafter.

(C) inadmissible because her statement was involuntary.

(D) inadmissible because she should have been allowed to consult with an attorney and have an attorney present during questioning.

Eyewitness Identification

The defendant was arrested and charged with crimes arising out of a home repair fraud scheme to defraud elderly pensioners. She was indicted by a grand jury and then arraigned on the indictment. Just prior to trial, the prosecutor had arranged a lineup. The defendant appeared in a lineup along with five other women of similar height, weight, and hair color. The four victims who viewed the lineup that morning all identified the defendant as the person who had promised extensive home repairs, got them to give her thousands of dollars in deposits, and failed to do any of the work.

Later in the afternoon, three other elderly victims, who had not made it to the morning lineup, were shown a photo of the defendant along with photos of five other women who closely resembled the defendant. These three victims also picked the defendant from the photo array. The prosecutor did not notify the defendant's lawyer in advance of the lineup or the photo identification.

107. Is evidence about the lineup identification admissible at trial?

ANSWER:

108. May the witnesses who identified the defendant at the lineup testify at trial and identify the defendant as the perpetrator of the fraud?

ANSWER:

109. Is the pretrial identification testimony of the three victims who picked the defendant out of the photo array admissible at trial?

(A) The witnesses' testimony about the pretrial photo identification is admissible because the Sixth Amendment right to counsel does not attach to a photo array identification.

(B) The witnesses may identify the defendant at trial as the person in the photo array but may not also identify the defendant in court as the person who committed construction fraud on them.

(C) The witnesses' pretrial photo identification is inadmissible because the defendant's attorney should have been notified and given an opportunity to attend the presentations of the photo array to the witnesses.

(D) The witnesses' pretrial photo identification is inadmissible because it was likely suggestive.

Tina, looking out her apartment kitchen window while washing dishes at dusk, saw a man walk into the parking lot of her building, open the driver's door of her neighbor's vehicle, look around, get in, and drive out of the parking lot. Tina explained that while the individual was opening the door, he "did look up and glance like a three-quarter turn." Her view of the car thief lasted less than a minute. She contacted the police who came to interview her. She described the individual to the officers as: "Early 20's, a white male, about 145 pounds, five eight. He had dark brown curly hair, a dark blue jacket, a white shirt underneath, and blue jeans."

Two weeks later, following a raid on a used car parts chop shop where her neighbor's car was found and nine men were arrested, the officers interviewed Tina again and showed her a photo array of nine color mug shots of white males. The purpose of the array was to determine whether Tina could identify the thief who stole the automobile. Before presenting the photos to Tina, the officers permitted her to review the actual theft report containing her description of the thief.

At the photo array, the officer handed the nine photographs face up in a stack to Tina. Looking at just the fronts of the photographs, she selected the defendant's picture without hesitation. Four of the nine photographs were of four of the people arrested at the auto parts "chop shop." A fifth picture was of a suspect who was also "wanted in connection" with the shop. The other four photos were of individuals without any suspected connection to auto theft. Following Tina's photo identification of the defendant, he was charged with grand theft auto.

At trial, Tina easily identified defendant as the person she had seen outside her window. Defendant's attorney moved to exclude Tina's trial identification of the defendant. At the suppression hearing, Tina agreed that seven of the nine photos depicted men having straight hair. Of the two remaining pictures, one was of a man who has curly brown hair but who barely had any hair on the top of his head. The ninth photo was of the defendant who had curly brown hair. The other eight photos were of men who were considerably older than the defendant, and five of the photos were of men who were considerably heavier than the defendant. On cross-examination at the trial, Tina agreed that she had told the officers that the thief's hair was "fluffy" and worn in an "Afro" style.

110. Defendant was charged with auto theft for stealing the neighbor's car. Tina's trial identification testimony is:

(A) admissible because the photo identification was made prior to the time the defendant was charged and his Sixth Amendment right to counsel had not attached.

(B) admissible because Tina's trial identification testimony was reliable; she had no reason to lie.

(C) inadmissible because the defendant had been arrested in connection with the used car parts store chop shop raid, and his attorney should have been contacted about the presentation of the photo array.

(D) inadmissible because the photo identification was impermissibly suggestive, a fact which tainted Tina's in-court identification.

One stormy night in March, Elle was depositing her garbage in the receptacle outside her apartment building when she heard glass breaking. She looked in the direction of the sound of the breaking glass and saw the face of a white male, approximately 6'5" tall with a red hat on his head, enter the first-floor apartment of her friend Pam. Fearful for her safety, Elle quickly ran home and phoned the police. Elle, who was very fond of Pam, was very angry about the incident, which resulted in the loss of Pam's treasured jewelry, and she readily agreed to help police identify the burglar. She agreed to review several volumes of police "mug shots" but was unable to identify the burglary suspect. One afternoon after review mug shots, Elle was seated in a corridor of the police station, frustrated that she could not help, and awaiting a ride home from her boyfriend Bill. Bill eventually phoned and arranged to meet Elle outside. As she was getting up to approach the police station door, Elle saw an officer chaperoning a tall man with a red hat on his head, and immediately exclaimed "that's him — that's the burglar." Police then took the man into custody, who turned out to be Bret Hall, who police had coincidentally arrested for a robbery of a gas station.

111. Elle's eyewitness identification of Hall is:

(A) admissible because the identification occurred in the hallway of a busy police station, where Elle was more likely to be at ease and capable of making an accurate identification.

(B) admissible because police did not arrange the identification procedure.

(C) inadmissible because, as a matter of policy, witnesses who are frustrated and motivated by personal bias are not the proper subject of consideration.

(D) inadmissible because the defendant was in custody and his *Miranda* rights had attached.

Standing

Twenty-six-year-old defendant Jeremy Harris was a passenger in a car being driven by his girlfriend, Laura (who was also twenty-six years old). The car was a brand new Cadillac, owned by Laura's father. A police officer, stopped at a red light next to the Cadillac, decided to follow the car because it seemed unusual for two young people to be associated with such a fancy car. After following for about a mile, the officer observed the Cadillac fail to come to a full stop at a stop sign. The officer turned on his roof top light and pulled the Cadillac over.

The officer ordered the occupants out of the car and demanded that the car's trunk be opened. Inside the trunk, the officer found a backpack with the name "Jeremy Harris" written on its exterior. In the back pack, the officer found clothing, toiletries, and a significant quantity of cocaine. The defendant was charged with possession with intent to distribute. Defendant's attorney moved to suppress the evidence.

112. The motion to suppress will be:

   (A) granted because the officer conducted an illegal search.

   (B) granted because the officer lacked authority to order the occupants of the vehicle out of the vehicle.

   (C) denied because the officer, based on her reasonable belief that the drivers were up to no good, had probable cause for the vehicle stop.

   (D) denied because the search was lawful incident to a valid stop of the vehicle.

Let's change the facts in the previous Question. What if Jeremy Harris is now driving the Cadillac, which is actually a rental vehicle, and that girlfriend Laura, the passenger, lawfully rented the vehicle, allowing Jeremy to drive it (even though he was not expressly listed as an authorized driver on the rental agreement). Assume further that after following the vehicle for a mile, the officer did not observe any traffic violations. At the end of the mile, the officer decided to pull the car over because he did not like rich people. After ordering the occupants out of the vehicle, the officer immediately searched Jeremy and found cocaine on his person. Jeremy's attorney moved to suppress the evidence.

113. The motion to suppress will be:

   (A) granted because the officer acted with discriminatory intent.

   (B) granted because the search was incident to an illegal stop.

   (C) denied because Jeremy lacked standing to challenge the search.

(D) denied because Jeremy operated the vehicle in violation of the rental contract.

Police, armed with a search warrant, arrived at a party to search for illegal drugs. They informed all the guests that they were free to leave as soon as they were searched. The defendant, who was with a date at the party, stashed his drugs in his date's purse, which she had slung over her shoulder. The police searched the purse and found the drugs; the defendant admitted that the drugs were his. The defendant was charged with illegal possession of narcotics. The defendant's attorney moved to suppress the drugs, but the state countered that the defendant did not have standing to challenge the search.

114. Will the motion to suppress the drugs be granted?

ANSWER:

The defendant, Carter, had spent an evening at a house party in the home of a casual friend, Sara Thompson. After the party, when all of the other guests had left, Carter, a drug dealer, sat at Thompson's kitchen table and cut a kilo of cocaine and divided it into packets for sale. He gave Thompson a small quantity of the cocaine in return for letting him use her apartment.

Just after this occurred, police, who suspected Carter of being a drug dealer, broke into the house, seized the cocaine on the table, and arrested Carter who admitted that the cocaine was his. Carter was charged with possession of cocaine for sale. Prior to trial, Carter's attorney moved to suppress the cocaine. The state claimed that Carter did not have standing to challenge the search of Thompson's apartment.

115. The motion to suppress should be:

(A) granted because any individual in a home has standing to contest an illegal search.

(B) denied because the police entry was lawful to prevent the destruction of the evidence.

(C) denied because the defendant lacked standing to challenge an illegal search.

(D) granted because the defendant was a lawful social guest, and the police could not enter without a warrant.

Appellate Review of a Motion to Suppress

At the conclusion of a suppression hearing to determine whether evidence secured during the stop and search of an automobile should be admitted at trial, the judge ruled that the police officer's testimony was credible, and the driver and her passenger's testimony were not. The court ruled that the evidence could be used by the prosecution at trial because the defendant had failed to prove that she did not consent to a search of her car. On appeal, the defendant claimed that the police officer's testimony was not believable and that the trial court erroneously applied the law of consent searches.

116. The trial court's finding that the police officer's testimony was credible and the defendant's and her witness's testimony not credible:

   (A) was erroneous because the one officer's testimony was contradicted by two witnesses.

   (B) will be overturned by the court of appeals if the court finds the defendant and her witness's testimony to be more credible.

   (C) will likely stand because appellate courts are very deferential to the court of appeals virtually never substitutes its judgment for that of the trial court credibility determinations and assessments of on a question of fact.

   (D) will stand because the trial court's finding on a question of fact is not subject to review on appeal.

117. Using the facts in Question 116, the trial court's conclusion that the defendant failed to prove that the search was illegal:

   (A) will be reversed on appeal because the conclusion is based upon an erroneous finding of fact.

   (B) will be reversed on appeal because it is based upon an erroneous conclusion of law.

   (C) will be affirmed because the trial court's findings are entitled to deference.

   (D) will be affirmed because the moving party seeks to upset the status quo and bears the burden of proof.

A police officer observed a young man wearing gym shorts and a T-shirt hanging around a street corner late at night, a street corner known to police as a high drug-trafficking location. As the officer approached the corner, the young man turned his back on the officer, crossed the street and walked in the opposite direction. The officer followed. Two blocks from where the officer first observed the young man, the officer ordered him to stop. The young man stopped in his tracks and turned towards the officer. The officer pushed the young man up against the store front, told him to put his hands over his head against the glass and to spread his legs. The officer then reached into the front of the young man's gym shorts and found a clear plastic baggy containing several rocks of crack cocaine.

The defendant was charged with possession of crack cocaine for sale. The defense moved to suppress the evidence seized from the defendant's shorts. At the suppression hearing, the officer and the defendant testified identically about what happened the night of the arrest. At the conclusion of the evidence, the trial court denied the motion to suppress, holding that the officer had probable cause to arrest the defendant, and the evidence was found during a lawful search incident to arrest. The defendant entered a conditional plea to the charge and was found guilty. The defendant appealed the conviction, claiming that the trial court erred in its ruling on the legality of the arrest and search.

118. How should the court rule on the appeal?

ANSWER:

What if the judge in the previous Question had granted the defendant's motion to suppress and the state elected to appeal immediately from that ruling? The state asked the appellate court to hear its interlocutory appeal so that the evidence would be available to the prosecution at trial.

119. Will the appellate court consider the interlocutory appeal?

ANSWER:

Derivative Evidence

Defendant Larry Carter, charged with aggravated trafficking in cocaine, moved to suppress evidence gained from a search of his residence and garage. Officer Lowe testified he was in an unmarked cruiser when he noticed a white Bronco truck parked behind a garage in an alley. Lowe said he observed Larry Carter seated in the driver's seat and he noticed Chris Ross standing by the corner of a garage carrying some type of bundle in his arms. Lowe said Ross switched the bundle from his left arm to his right arm. Lowe said the bundle seemed heavy and was wrapped in something gray. Lowe said he watched Ross, holding the bundle, get in the passenger seat of the Bronco, and Carter then drove the Bronco down the alley onto Everett.

With back up assistance, Officer Lowe made a "felony stop" on the car; the subjects were ordered out of the vehicle at gunpoint and told that they were under arrest. Officer Lowe looked in the car and saw a gray bundle lying on the front floorboard and it appeared to be the bundle he saw Ross carrying into the Bronco. Lowe said he unwrapped the gray bundle and found a small package wrapped in brown opaque paper. He unwrapped the package and found two pounds of cocaine.

A search warrant was obtained to search Carter's home and garage where Officer Lowe first observed the defendants. The search uncovered a large quantity of cocaine in the garage. Carter was charged based upon the evidence found in the garage. Officer Lowe admitted upon cross-examination that he did not observe Carter or Ross violate any traffic law prior to the stop.

The defendants moved to suppress the evidence found in the car and the garage.

120. How should the court rule?

ANSWER:

Derivative Evidence:
Miranda Violation

The defendant, arrested a block away from a jewelry store that had just been robbed, met the description given by the proprietor. Immediately following the arrest, the arresting officers searched the defendant and found a gun sticking out of his pants. They asked him what he had done with the stolen jewelry. The defendant told the police that he discarded the jewelry in the trash container at the corner when he saw the patrol car with flashing lights approaching. One of the officers retrieved the jewelry from the container.

Prior to trial, the defendant moved to suppress his response to the officer's question and the jewelry.

121. How should the court rule?

   (A) Both the defendant's statement and the jewelry should be suppressed because the officer failed to give the defendant *Miranda* warnings and the jewelry is derivative of the *Miranda* violation.

   (B) Both the statement and the jewelry are admissible because *Miranda* warnings need not be given during a public safety emergency.

   (C) The defendant's statement is inadmissible because of the *Miranda* violation, but the jewelry is admissible.

   (D) The statement and the jewelry are inadmissible because the defendant's statement was involuntary and taints the derivative evidence.

Derivative Evidence: Causal Connection

A wealthy art collector called the local police to report that an art expert had just informed her that she had purchased a fake Degas painting from the Memex Art Gallery. A month before, two reliable informants in the local art community told police that Fenton Gaston, a virtually unknown artist, had been making excellent reproductions of work by famous artists and was selling them as originals through the Memex Gallery.

That evening, the police went to Gaston's home studio and knocked on the front door. No one responded. Police then entered the unlocked back door and found Gaston in a back room working on a painting. He was immediately arrested, and the home studio searched. Five reproduction paintings were found, including one allegedly painted by Degas.

Gaston was taken to the police station, given *Miranda* warnings, and questioned for a few minutes. He waived his *Miranda* rights and confessed to making the reproductions. Defense counsel for Gaston has moved the court to suppress the confession.

122. How should the court rule?

(A) The warrantless entry of the defendant's home studio and the subsequent arrest were justified by exigent circumstances to prevent the destruction of evidence because the police had no way of knowing whether someone was inside destroying the reproductions; therefore, the confession secured with *Miranda* warnings is admissible.

(B) The warrantless entry of the defendant's home studio and the subsequent warrantless in-home arrest were Fourth Amendment violations, and the confession is inadmissible because it is the fruit of the poisonous tree.

(C) The warrantless search of the studio and arrest of Gaston were without probable cause, and the confession is inadmissible because it is derivative of the Fourth Amendment violation.

(D) The warrantless entry of the defendant's studio to search was a Fourth Amendment violation, but the confession is not derivative of that violation.

Derivative Evidence:
What May Be Suppressed

Police received a call that an average-size Asian man was seen leaving a house near the corner of South and Elm Streets, carrying a computer. The caller identified herself as a neighbor who lived at 4719 Elm Street. Police went to the corner of South and Elm and discovered a house on Elm Street near that corner had been burglarized. They interviewed the neighbor who had made the call and who repeated the information about the average-sized Asian man.

The police then looked in the area within a mile from the burglary and found an average-size Asian man who was walking 10 blocks from the burglarized house. The defendant was arrested. He was carrying a bag filled with groceries but not a computer. The stolen computer was found the next day in a trash can, a block from where the defendant was arrested.

At a lineup held the day after the arrest, the neighbor identified the defendant as the Asian man she had seen. The neighbor also testified in court and identified the defendant. She testified that she had ample opportunity to view the defendant as he left the burglarized home and she watched him pass in front of her house and continue down Elm Street. The defendant was convicted of burglary and appeals on the ground that the in-court identification was inadmissible.

123. How should the court rule on appeal?

(A) The in-court identification of the defendant was legal even though his presence in court was derivative of an illegal arrest.

(B) The in-court identification of the defendant was legal because he was lawfully arrested following the lineup identification.

(C) The in-court identification of the defendant was illegal because it was derivative of an illegal arrest.

(D) The in-court identification of the defendant was illegal because it was derivative of an illegal lineup.

After an extensive undercover investigation involving a "sting" operation, police obtained a warrant to search the home (including any computers) of Petra Santos for evidence of her involvement in international money laundering. They arrived at her house and entered immediately through an unlocked back door. When Santos came downstairs in response to the noise, she was served with the warrant. The search of her home computer found extensive records of deposits and withdrawals in foreign bank accounts.

Defense counsel has filed a motion to suppress everything found in the search, arguing that the police failed to follow the knock-and-announce rule mandated by the Fourth Amendment.

124. How should the court rule on the motion to suppress?

   (A) The motion to suppress should be granted because the judge issuing the search warrant did not authorize a no-knock entry, and therefore the police violated the defendant's Fourth Amendment rights.

   (B) The motion to suppress should be denied because, even though the police violated the defendant's Fourth Amendment rights by failing to knock and announce their presence, the evidence was seized pursuant to a valid search warrant and the exclusionary rule does not apply to a violation of the knock and announce rule.

   (C) The motion to suppress should be granted because there was no exigency to justify the no-knock entry.

   (D) The motion to suppress should be denied because the Fourth Amendment does not require police to knock and announce themselves and wait before entering to execute a valid search warrant.

Derivative Evidence: Exceptions

An undercover officer who had infiltrated a violent gang reported that gang members were buying guns and bullets from a house at 8517 Washington Street. Police staked out the location and saw young "gangers" enter the house, and then leave the house a few minutes later carrying a paper bag and a long box. Some of the boxes appeared to be heavy. A young man from another gang was arrested for selling drugs and, during interrogation, confirmed that his gang, too, bought weapons from the Washington Street house.

A police officer broke into the Washington house to check it out. This officer reported a large cache of weapons in the basement. Police then obtained a search warrant based on the information they had received from the infiltrating officer, the police stake out, and the other gang member. The subsequent search found weapons and ammunition in the basement as well as a closet in the master bedroom. Defense counsel has filed a motion to suppress the weapons found during the search. (When answering, do not consider the so-called "good faith" exception to the exclusionary rule.)

125. How should the court rule on the motion?

ANSWER:

Police suspected that Donnell Watson was selling marijuana from a room at the Seaside Motel. Police officers concealed in an unmarked police van in the parking lot near the motel room's door saw people arrive and park in the parking lot, knock on the room's door, enter for a short time, then leave and drive away. When police saw Watson leave the room and drive away, they knocked on the door, announced their presence, entered, and thoroughly searched the motel room when no one answered the door. They were shocked to find 100 pounds of marijuana stacked in bales in the corner. Watson has been charged with possession of 100 pounds of marijuana.

Defense counsel has filed a motion to suppress the marijuana because the police had no warrant or exigent circumstances to conduct the search. The prosecution responds that the inevitable discovery rule would apply because a maid was scheduled routinely to clean the room within a few minutes after Watson left the area and would have informed the police of the marijuana cache, in accordance with motel policy about immediately reporting all illegal drug activity directly to the police.

126. How should the court rule on the motion to suppress?

(A) The motion should be granted because the search was incident to a search without probable cause or a warrant.

(B) The motion should be denied because of the exigent circumstances that someone may have been in the room destroying important evidence.

(C) The motion should be denied because the drugs would have inevitably been discovered by police when the maid cleaned the room according to the motel rules that dictated the room be cleaned a few minutes after a guest (such as Watson) left at that time of day and the police be notified immediately of all illegal drug activity at the motel.

(D) The motion should be granted because Watson was not available to consent and the police did knock and announce their presence.

Officers Harris and Jones observed an individual that they thought was the subject of a lawful outstanding arrest warrant. Harris, who was driving, turned the patrol car around to get a better look at the individual. However, by this time, the individual had entered a convenience store. The officers entered the store and made contact with the individual, who turned out to be Lanny Loser. Jones asked for Loser's identification card and determined that he was not the individual who was the subject of the arrest warrant, one Byron Bobo. The officers then left the store. Before leaving, however, Harris said, "I want to double check that I.D., he could have slipped us a fake one," and reentered the store. As Harris got closer to Loser, he realized that there was no way that he was Bobo, who he recalled was much taller, but nonetheless again requested Loser's I.D. and asked, "you have any warrants out on you?" Loser stated that he did not, and Harris replied that he would keep the I.D. for a few moments to run a warrants check. Loser then continued shopping in the store, and a few moments later, Harris approached him saying that there in fact was a valid warrant for his arrest (for trespassing). Harris told Loser to walk to the front of the store where Loser was arrested. During a search incident to arrest, officers found a bag of heroin in Loser's front pocket.

127. Defense counsel for Loser has filed a motion to suppress the heroin. How should the court rule on the motion?

(A) Deny the motion because an officer is free to run a database check and the warrant was valid.

(B) Deny the motion because the heroin would have been inevitably discovered when Loser was arrested at some point.

(C) Grant the motion because the attenuation doctrine does not apply.

(D) Grant the motion because police cannot ask anyone for identification without a legal basis.

Impeachment

Police routinely follow Patricia Haskell, a known gang member, as she drives her Hummer around the neighborhood. Just to "let her know we are watching her," one night Officer Zanzig pulled over Haskell, approached the Hummer and looked inside. Haskell was alone in the vehicle. Officer Zanzig spotted the butt end of a pistol sticking out from the bottom of the passenger seat, searched the Hummer, found the pistol, and immediately arrested Haskell.

Haskell is charged with unlawful possession of a firearm by a convicted felon. At Haskell's trial, a police informant testified that two weeks before the arrest, he told police he had just seen a pistol under the seat in Haskell's Hummer. Police did not act on this information because they wanted to wait until they had finished gathering evidence of Haskell's involvement in more serious offenses.

During pretrial motions, the judge suppressed evidence about the pistol found in the Hummer because the stop of the Hummer was an illegal seizure in violation of the Fourth Amendment.

Haskell testified at trial. In response to questions on cross-examination, she said, "I have never had a weapon of any kind in my car and never will. Weapons are dangerous."

The prosecutor then asked Haskell about the pistol found in the Hummer during the illegal search. Defense counsel objected because the pistol was suppressed as the product of an illegal search and should not have been asked about by the prosecutor.

128. How should the trial judge rule?

(A) The judge should deny the motion and allow the defendant to be questioned about the weapon seized in violation of the Fourth Amendment.

(B) The judge should deny the motion because the stop was reasonable because of Haskell's known gang affiliation and the community's strong interest in controlling gang members.

(C) The judge should grant the motion because to allow the prosecution on cross examination to elicit Haskell's statement denying having the weapon, then allowing the prosecution to interrogate her about the weapon found in the illegal search, is to allow the government to create an issue (the denial) then benefit from its own illegality by asking about the suppressed evidence.

(D) The judge should grant the motion because the evidence was suppressed.

A police officer on foot patrol was fatally shot in a drive-by shooting. A month before, this officer had shot and seriously wounded a mob enforcer who was caught beating a store owner for refusing to make extortion payments to mob boss Anthony "Big Man" Carini. After a massive effort to find the cop killer produced many leads and some significant evidence, police arrested Bradley Fulton, a reputed assassin who worked for Carini, the same mob boss as the mob enforcer wounded by the deceased police officer. Police speculated that the drive-by shooting of the officer was retaliation for the earlier incident.

Fulton was taken to the police station where he was interrogated. No *Miranda* warnings were given. When presented with the overwhelming proof the government had accumulated, Fulton confessed and said he had been paid by mob boss Carini to "get even."

At Fulton's murder trial, Fulton testified and denied knowing anyone named Anthony Carini or having anything to do with retaliation for the earlier shooting. The prosecution impeached Fulton with his confession. Fulton was convicted and appeals.

129. Should the conviction be reversed?

   (A) Yes. A confession secured without *Miranda* warnings is inadmissible for any purpose.

   (B) Yes. The confession may not be used to impeach the defendant's credibility but may be used to impeach a defense witness's credibility.

   (C) No. A confession secured without *Miranda* warnings may be used to impeach a defendant's testimony.

   (D) No. The confession may only be used in a case for perjury, not during the criminal trial itself because of the *Miranda* violation.

Let's change the facts in the foregoing question. Again, the detective did not read Fulton the *Miranda* rights, but he also interrogated Fulton for 13 straight hours, taking a break only to allow Fulton to go to the bathroom. Fulton was not offered food or water during this period. The detective repeatedly yelled at Fulton, telling him that Fulton was a cop killer and would "get the needle" unless he confessed then and there. The detective slapped Fulton in the face whenever Fulton dozed off. The detective also lied and said an eyewitness to the drive-by shooting had looked through a mirrored window in the interrogation room and picked out Fulton as the killer. Hearing this, Fulton said, "I guess you got me" and made a full confession.

At Fulton's murder trial, Fulton again testified that he had never heard of Anthony Carini and knew nothing about the cop killing or any retaliation. The prosecutor sought to impeach Fulton with the earlier confession. Defense counsel objected.

130. Should the court sustain the objection?

   (A) Yes. The statement may not be used because of the *Miranda* violation.

   (B) Yes. The statement may not be used because it was involuntary and violated Fulton's due process rights.

   (C) No. The statement may be used for all purposes because Fulton elected to testify and then lied.

(D) No. The statement may be used to impeach Fulton's credibility because a *Miranda* violation permits the confession to be used to impeach but not during the government's case in chief to prove guilt.

The defendant stabbed a man to death during an altercation at a bus stop. An arrest warrant for murder was issued for the defendant. Several months later, the defendant was arrested and was silent when told of the murder charges. He was taken to the police station, and informed, during booking, why he was arrested. He did not respond. Later after the booking, the defendant was advised of his *Miranda* rights and he asked for a lawyer.

At trial, the defendant took the witness stand and testified that he had stabbed the victim in self-defense. During cross-examination the prosecutor sought to use the defendant's failure to tell the arresting officer or the booking officer that he had killed in self-defense. The defense attorney objected.

131. How should the court rule?

(A) The court should allow the prosecutor to use, on cross-examination, the defendant's failure to come forward and his subsequent failure to tell the police at any time, before or after *Miranda* warnings are given, that he killed in self-defense. It is reasonable to expect someone who killed in self-defense to say this when questioned by police about the death.

(B) The court should allow the prosecutor to use the defendant's failure to come forward and his failure to tell the police that he killed in self-defense at the time of his arrest; the prosecutor may not use the defendant's post-arrest silence to impeach him.

(C) The court should allow the prosecutor to use the defendant's failure to come forward and his failure to tell the police at the time of the arrest that he killed in self-defense; the prosecutor may not use for impeachment the defendant's silence after he was taken to the police station.

(D) The court should allow the prosecutor to use the defendant's failure to come forward and his silence at the time of and following his arrest until the defendant was given the *Miranda* warnings.

Questions

Practice Final Exam

Part I

A police officer and his drug-detection dog walked through the hallways of a multi-unit apartment building. The departmental policy authorizes officers to walk through the common hallways of such buildings to detect the presence of illegal drugs. The dog signaled a positive alert in front of Apartment 14D. Using the dog alert as probable cause, police secured a search warrant for Apartment 14D and found, during the execution of the warrant, a small quantity of marijuana.

132. Is the evidence seized during execution of the search warrant admissible? (When answering, do not consider the objective good faith exception to the exclusionary rule. *United States v. Leon*, 468 U.S. 897 (1984).)

ANSWER:

Detective Roberts submitted an application for a search warrant based on information received from a confidential unnamed informant. After considering the affidavit, the magistrate informed Roberts that the probable cause section was insufficient. The magistrate then administered the oath to Roberts and asked him questions that might serve to supplement the probable cause finding. The magistrate digitally recorded Roberts' supplemental testimony. After hearing Roberts' additional information, the magistrate told Roberts and the assistant prosecutor that she was not convinced that the informant really existed. The magistrate ordered Roberts and the assistant prosecutor to produce the informant in chambers the next morning.

133. Must the prosecutor produce the informant?

(A) Yes. The prosecutor must comply or forgo the warrant.

(B) Yes. The prosecutor must comply with the order. It does not really matter because the informant will have to be produced at trial.

(C) No. The prosecutor need not comply because the informant's privilege protects the prosecutor from ever having to disclose the informant's identity.

(D) No. The prosecutor need not comply because the judge has no right to that information.

A search warrant authorized police to conduct a search at "210 Centre Street, a four apartment complex, front apartment number 3 on the second floor, belonging to Angel Smith." When police arrived at the 210 Centre Street, they discovered that Apartment 3 was at the rear of the second floor; the name on the door plate read Angel Smith. They executed the warrant, entered Apartment 3 and found large quantities of illegal drugs. Prior to trial, the defense moved to suppress the evidence on the ground of a faulty warrant.

134. Should the court grant the motion to suppress?

   (A) Yes. The search warrant misdirected the police.

   (B) Yes. A search warrant must particularly describe the place to be searched; here the description was inaccurate.

   (C) No. The search warrant described the place to be searched with adequate specificity.

   (D) No. The police acted in objective good faith reliance on the search warrant.

Police investigating a street shooting recognized the victim, Charles Todd, who was a major drug trafficker in the upper west side of the city. Missing from the victim's body was a heavy gold necklace with a crucifix which the victim always wore. The officers speculated that the necklace had been ripped away from Todd's body. Later the same night, police received a tip from an informant, who was a regular police source of reliable information about drug trafficking, that Todd had been murdered by John Sanford, a competitor whose territory had been encroached upon by Todd's people. Sanford was also known as a major drug dealer in the same part of the city, and the informant said that Sanford was sitting on an enormous cache of drugs.

Armed with the information from the informant, police presented a magistrate with probable cause to believe that Sanford was involved in Todd's murder and requested a warrant to search Sanford's home for the necklace. The officers did not present the magistrate with information about drugs. The warrant only specified the necklace as the target of the search and authorized police to search Sanford's home for the necklace. The warrant did not mention drugs.

Prior to entering Sanford's home, the commanding officer instructed the search team to look for the necklace and drugs. Once in the house, police scoured the premises for drugs and the necklace. In two walk-in closets on the first floor, police found large quantities of drugs. Police then searched the rest of the house. On the second floor of the home, in a child's dresser drawer, police found the necklace. They thereafter found a gun that was located under the couch, which seemed to match the kind of gun used in Todd's murder. Sanford's lawyer filed a motion to suppress the necklace, drugs, and gun.

135. How should the court rule on the motion to suppress?

   ANSWER:

Police officers had a lawful warrant to arrest Tom Feola for embezzlement. When they went to Tom's house, his mother informed them that he was not at home. She told the officers that Tom was at his girlfriend's house. She provided the police with the name and address of Tom's girlfriend. Police went directly to the girlfriend's house, entered and arrested Tom. Tom claims the arrest was illegal.

136. Was the arrest illegal?

    (A) The arrest is legal because the officers had a lawful arrest warrant.

    (B) The arrest is legal because of exigent circumstances since the defendant may have learned from his mother that the police were looking for him.

    (C) The arrest is illegal because police entered a home to search for a non-resident without a search warrant.

    (D) The arrest is illegal because police entered without permission or exigent circumstances.

Evelyn Piersall was arrested for drunk driving, a misdemeanor. For a first-time offender such as Piersall, the normal procedure in Metropolis is to book drunk driving suspects, strip search them, and then place them in a jail cell with other inebriates until sober. Once sober, they are released from jail on bail and issued a summons to appear in court.

Piersall was booked and then strip searched by a female police officer. The officer found a small bag of marijuana hidden in Piersall's underwear. She was charged with D.U.I. and possession of marijuana, a misdemeanor. In a motion to suppress the marijuana, Piersall's lawyer has challenged the strip search.

137. Is Metropolis' strip search policy constitutional?

    (A) The policy is consistent with Fourth Amendment standards because the standardized policy at jail intake controls police discretion and protects the prisoner's privacy interest as well as the jail's security and evidence needs.

    (B) The policy is consistent with Fourth Amendment standards that allow a full search of the person based on exigency, incident to a lawful custodial arrest.

    (C) The policy violates the Fourth Amendment because evidence of drunk driving is not likely to be found on the person of the arrestee.

    (D) The policy violates the Fourth Amendment because a search of such intrusiveness must be based on individualized probable cause.

A Metropolis ordinance authorized warrantless inspections by police of vehicles in auto sales lots, junkyards, and other vehicle salvage facilities. The regulatory scheme required proprietors of such establishments to present, on demand by a law enforcement officer during regular business hours, titles, or other documentary evidence of ownership in vehicles located on the premises.

The owner of the "Cheap Used Cars" lot was previously convicted in connection with a chop shop operation, which stripped away viable parts from stolen cars and sold them. Officer Krupke entered the "Cheap Used Cars" sales facility located at the rear of the lot and demanded to see the title for a 1997 Cadillac Eldorado for sale on the lot. When the owner refused Officer Krupke's demand for the title, the owner was charged with violating the inspection statute, a misdemeanor.

138. Is the statute valid?

ANSWER:

Craig is a Mr. Fix-it. He makes his living doing minor repairs for busy people. Generally, a home owner leaves a key under a doormat so that Craig can get in the house when no one is home and attend to repairs. One day, as Craig was fixing a leaky sink in a kitchen, police drove up to the house and rang the doorbell. Police told Craig, who answered the door, that they wanted to search the bedroom of the family's 16-year-old daughter suspected of involvement with two male students who were threatening classmates.

Craig identified himself to the police as a handyman making some minor repairs at the house and volunteered to help. He showed them to the girl's locked bedroom. He also showed the police a key to the room which was sitting on the ledge above the bedroom door. He unlocked the room for the police and let them in. Inside the room, the police found pictures of the girl with the two principal suspects in the school threats case. The girl and the two boys were holding automatic weapons and hand grenades. Subsequent lawful searches found the weapons and grenades.

The girl and the two boys were arrested and charged with illegal possession of automatic weapons and hand grenades. The girl moved to suppress the pictures found in her bedroom.

139. Are the pictures admissible?

(A) The pictures are admissible because Craig was the home owner's surrogate and waived the owner's Fourth Amendment rights.

(B) The pictures are admissible because police could have entered the house to search based on exigent circumstances.

(C) The pictures are inadmissible because police could not reasonably rely on Craig's consent to search.

(D) The pictures are inadmissible because police must seek the permission of the target of an investigation in order to search the bedroom of that target.

Police received an anonymous tip that William Grass was operating a marijuana grow operation on his three acre farm on the outskirts of Metropolis. Two police officers were dispatched to investigate the tip. Officer 1 walked up Grass' driveway and around to the back patio connected to the family room of the home. Walking onto the patio, Officer 1 observed six marijuana plants growing in pots on the patio. Meanwhile, Officer 2 climbed over a locked fence, posted with No Trespassing signs, about 150 yards from Grass' home. Officer 2 walked through a cultivated field which contained tomato plants and corn. At the back of the cultivated area, Officer 2 discovered 100 marijuana plants.

In preparing a probable cause affidavit to secure a search warrant of the Grass residence and its associated property, the Officers detailed what they saw in the field but made no mention of the discovery of the marijuana plants on the patio. The warrant was issued by a magistrate and authorized a search of the home and surrounding property of Grass for marijuana in any form and other items involved with the growth or sale of marijuana. The officers executed the search warrant and seized the marijuana plants from both the patio and the field. The defendant was charged with illegal cultivation of marijuana. The defense filed a motion to suppress all the marijuana.

140. How should the court rule on the motion to suppress?

(A) All of the marijuana should be suppressed because the officers relied on an anonymous tip.

(B) All of the marijuana is admissible because the officers did not violate the defendant's reasonable expectation of privacy.

(C) All the marijuana is admissible because the search was based on a valid search warrant and the search was within the scope of that warrant.

(D) All of the marijuana is inadmissible because Officer 1 violated defendant's privacy in the curtilage of his home and Officer 2 trespassed on Grass' posted and fenced field and the warrant was based on the illegal search by Officer 2.

Abby was lawfully stopped for speeding in a school zone during school hours. The police officer ordered Abby out of her car and ran a license and registration check. When the check turned up no outstanding warrants, the officer wrote out a traffic citation. After handing the completed traffic citation to Abby, the officer searched underneath the driver's seat of Abby's car and found a small quantity of marijuana. The officer also found a tiny marijuana pipe in her pants pockets. The officer then arrested Abby. She was charged with possession of an illegal substance and drug paraphernalia. The defense moved to suppress the marijuana and pipe.

141. The evidence is:

(A) admissible under the search incident to arrest doctrine if speeding in a school zone is an arrestable offense in the jurisdiction.

(B) admissible because the officer has the authority to order a legally stopped motorist from his or her vehicle and to frisk the motorist for the officer's safety.

(C) inadmissible because speeding is not an arrestable offense and an officer may not search incident to a speeding stop.

(D) inadmissible because the motorist, who was issued a citation, was not under arrest when the officer conducted the search, in violation of the Fourth Amendment.

Add the following facts to the foregoing question. When the officer ordered Abby to get out of her car, Abby was very surly, mumbled responses to the officer's questions, seemed to fidget inordinately, and indicated to the officer that she needed to get away from the area immediately. The officer responded to Abby's reaction by ordering her to sit in the back of the police cruiser. The officer, who knew Abby was a previously convicted felon, frisked Abby before placing her in the back of the cruiser but found no weapon. The officer checked Abby's license and registration and determined that there was no outstanding warrant for her arrest. The officer wrote the traffic ticket and walked Abby back to her car. Before allowing Abby to get in her car, the officer observed a gun handle protruding from the front seat. The officer arrested Abby for being a convicted felon in possession of a weapon. Prior to trial, Abby's lawyer moved to suppress the gun.

142. The gun is:

(A) admissible because it was found incident to a valid traffic arrest.

(B) admissible because it was found during a lawful search of the vehicle for weapons.

(C) inadmissible because the officer did not have probable cause to believe that there were weapons in the car.

(D) inadmissible because the officer had no authority to search the vehicle once he decided to release the motorist.

Tony O'Malley, an undercover police officer, purchased three rocks of crack cocaine from Tom Dunn, a street vendor. During the purchase, Dunn became suspicious and drew a gun on O'Malley who also drew his weapon. Both fired and Officer O'Malley was fatally injured. Dunn was wounded in the leg but managed to escape. Later, when Dunn was arrested, he was bleeding and taken to the hospital where doctors were able to stop the bleeding and dress the wound. At the request of the arresting officers, the hospital took Dunn to the operating room where he was anesthetized and had the bullet removed from his leg. The recovered bullet is critical evidence that Dunn was the drug seller who murdered the police officer. Dunn's attorney seeks to suppress the bullet.

143. The bullet should be:

(A) admitted at trial because it is essential to prove Dunn's guilt.

(B) admitted at trial because it was extracted incident to the arrest of Dunn.

(C) suppressed because it was seized without prior judicial approval.

(D) suppressed because the evidence taken from Dunn's body compels the defendant to incriminate himself in violation of the Fifth Amendment.

Tyrone Anderson was driving home from his job as a DJ at a local dance club at 3:30 a.m. He decided to stop at an all-night diner to get some food. He pulled into a public parking lot and started to get out of the car. Unfortunately, he got tangled up in his seat belt and fell out of the car onto the ground. His clumsy exit from the car was observed by Officer Krumpke who immediately ran over to Anderson. Krumpke smelled alcohol on Anderson's breath and believed Anderson was intoxicated. He helped Anderson to his feet and asked Anderson to perform a field sobriety test. Anderson refused, saying he had nothing to drink all night and had simply fallen.

Officer Krumpke then lawfully arrested Anderson on suspicion of driving while impaired. He told Anderson to stand next to the rear driver's door with his hands on the roof. Krumpke then searched the car. Under the driver's seat he found several credit cards in various names. Anderson was then taken to jail and his car was towed to the police impound lot. Consistent with the police department's impound regulations, the impound lot officer opened the trunk of the car and inventoried the contents, including a gold-rimmed vase. Later, the police confirmed that the credit cards and vase were stolen in a burglary a week before.

Anderson is eventually charged with receiving stolen property for possessing both the cards and the vase.

144. How should the judge rule on the motion to suppress the credit cards and vase?

ANSWER:

Guinness Stout drove his Ford pickup along the highway, weaving in and out of his lane, crossing both the lane and edge lines. Sheriff's Deputy Dogood saw Stout at 10:32 p.m. and pulled him over. The officer summoned back-up assistance and ordered Stout from the truck. Officer Dogood had his hand on his holstered pistol while waiting for assistance. Once the back-up officers arrived 20 minutes later, Dogood ordered Stout to perform certain field-sobriety tests. Not surprisingly, Stout performed very badly.

While clutching Stout's elbow and walking him to the police car, Dogood asked how much he had to drink. Stout answered, "Only six beers." Stout asked if he was under arrest and Officer Dogood said "you are now." At no time was Stout given *Miranda* warnings.

145. Is Stout's statement about his beer consumption admissible at his drunk driving trial?

(A) The statement is admissible because a traffic stop is not a custodial arrest and *Miranda* warnings need not be given.

(B) The statement is admissible because when asked if he was drinking, Stout had not yet been arrested.

(C) The statement is inadmissible because Officer Dogood conducted a *Terry* stop on reasonable suspicion of drunk driving which requires *Miranda* warnings.

(D) The statement is inadmissible because Stout was in custody and should have been given *Miranda* warnings prior to any questioning.

Charles ("Big") Deal was arrested and charged with a physical assault that lasted for almost 15 minutes. Shortly after the police were notified about the assault, an officer met with the victim to establish the identity of the assailant. The victim provided a detailed description of her attacker, which closely resembled Big. When asked to view slides that were selected by the police according to her description of the assailant, the victim selected Big and later confirmed this identification when she was shown a photo of him.

On the day trial began, a police officer and an assistant prosecuting attorney took the victim to the holding cell outside the courtroom where Big was being held prior to the commencement of the trial. The victim, again, identified Big as her attacker, picking him from a group of five men being held in the cell. This identification took place outside the presence of the defense attorney who was already in the courtroom. During the trial, the victim also identified Big as the man who assaulted her.

The defense challenged the victim's in-court identification. The trial court denied the defense motion to suppress, saying that the victim's in-court identification was not tainted by the holding cell viewing because of the detailed description which she had given the investigating officer shortly after the attack as well as her earlier identification of the defendant from the slide and picture. The defendant was convicted and appealed.

146. Should the in-court identification be suppressed and the conviction reversed?

(A) The conviction should be reversed because the final viewing of the defendant violated the defendant's Sixth Amendment right to counsel.

(B) The conviction should be affirmed because the victim's in-court identification was independent of the holding cell identification.

(C) The conviction should be reversed because the prosecutor's failure to notify defense counsel, who was nearby when the holding cell identification occurred, was a purposeful violation of the constitutional rule.

(D) The conviction should be affirmed because the holding cell viewing was casual and not a lineup.

Part II

Instructions: All of the remaining five short answer questions are based on the following facts.

On or shortly before May 30, 2020, law enforcement officials in Ann Arbor, Michigan, received a tip from a confidential informant, whose reliability had not yet been tested, that two Caucasian males from Las Vegas were traveling to Ann Arbor to distribute cocaine. The informant told the police that the two men intended to stay at the Hotel Motel in Ann Arbor and that a man named Arnold intended to deliver the proceeds of a drug sale to the two men at the motel. According to the informant, Arnold would be driving a white Toyota with a license plate number that the informant provided. A search of state motor vehicle records revealed that the license plate number identified by the informant was registered to Joe Arnold, 1002 E. Buckeye, Apartment No. 7, Ann Arbor, Michigan.

Police began surveillance of the Hotel Motel on May 31, 2020. During their surveillance, they discovered that a 1992 blue Ford Crown Victoria, parked in front of Room 17 of the motel, was registered to David Ram, whose address matched Arnold's except for the apartment number. At around 4:00 p.m. on June 1, Ram and Robert Smith, Caucasian males, exited Room 17 and departed in the Crown Victoria. Undercover officers followed the two men as they visited several locations, including an office supply store, where they purchased a set of digital scales of the type often used to weigh drugs. The two men then returned to the motel.

At around 8:15 a.m. on June 2, Arnold arrived at the motel driving the white Toyota described by the informant. After speaking with Ram who was outside working on the Crown Victoria, Arnold went into Room 17 with Ram. Police observed Arnold carrying a yellow plastic bag into Room 17. Arnold stayed in Room 17 for about 45 minutes before leaving in his white Toyota. The police could not tell whether he was still carrying the yellow plastic bag. Officers then followed Arnold, who was travelling on a two-lane highway, and eventually stopped him. When Arnold asked why he had been stopped, he was told that he had violated state law prohibiting a motorist traveling on a two-lane highway from crossing over the "fog line" adjacent to the road's right shoulder, in the absence of an emergency. The officer asked Arnold if he would provide consent to a search of his vehicle, which he readily provided. Upon searching the vehicle, police found an illegal sawed-off shotgun under the front passenger seat. No illegal drugs were discovered in the car. Arnold was taken into police custody.

Shortly after Arnold left the motel on June 2, Ram and Smith departed from the motel in the Crown Victoria and were followed by police. Four officers in two unmarked police cruisers thereafter activated their sirens and emergency lights and stopped the Crown Victoria. The four officers emerged, and with weapons drawn, ordered Ram and Smith to exit the Crown Victoria. The officers then handcuffed Ram and Smith and placed them in separate vehicles. The officers drove Ram and Smith from the scene of the stop to a convenience store parking lot, where they were removed from the vehicles. They were then read their *Miranda* rights, waived their rights, and were questioned separately.

The officer questioning Smith conducted a pat-down search of him and found the Room 17 Hotel Motel key (an actual key — not a key card — attached to a key ring with a small metal plate) in his pocket. The officer did not know what the key was until he removed it from Smith's pocket. Smith stated that the motel room was registered in his name. (Police had previously found that the room was registered to Smith.) The officers asked Smith for consent to search the motel room and presented him with a written consent form, which Smith signed within 10 to 15 minutes from the time police stopped the Crown Victoria.

A little more than 20 minutes from the time police stopped the Crown Victoria, Ram also gave the officer questioning him consent to search Room 17. He also had a key attached to a key ring to Room 17 in his pocket.

Police then searched Room 17 of the Hotel Motel and found a yellow plastic bag containing 25 individually wrapped packages of cocaine, a black notebook stuffed with $4,100 in cash, clear plastic wrappers containing cocaine residue, and two sets of digital scales. Ram and Smith were then taken into custody.

There are five separate questions to answer. The questions pinpoint various issues in a way so that you need not repeat yourself.

147. Can Ram and Smith challenge the surveillance and tracking by the police on June 1?

ANSWER:

148. Can Arnold challenge the stop and search of his car on June 2, resulting in the discovery of the shotgun? In answering, presume that the officer was technically incorrect, as a legal matter, in stating that it was a violation of state law to cross the fog line of the road on which Arnold was travelling.

ANSWER:

149. Can Ram and Smith challenge the stop of their car on June 2?

ANSWER:

150. Can Smith challenge the search of his person and the removal of the motel key from his pocket?

ANSWER:

151. Can Smith challenge the search of the hotel room because his consent was invalid?

ANSWER:

Answers

Incorporation

1. **Answer (C) is the correct answer.** In 1884, the U.S. Supreme Court held that the Due Process Clause of the Fourteenth Amendment is not a short-hand version of the rights contained in the Bill of Rights (the first ten amendments to the Constitution), and held that a defendant in a state criminal proceeding is not entitled to a grand jury indictment (ensured by the Fifth Amendment). *Hurtado v. California*, 110 U.S. 516 (1884). Through a process of "absorption" or "incorporation," undertaken since the 1920s, most, but not all, of the guarantees contained in the Bill of Rights have been applied to state criminal proceedings. A right is incorporated only if it is "fundamental ... to an Anglo-American regime of ordered liberty." *Duncan v. Louisiana*, 391 U.S. 145 (1968).

   Answer (A) is incorrect. Not quite all of the Bill of Rights has been incorporated into the Fourteenth Amendment and made binding on the states. The Fifth Amendment right to a grand jury indictment is not binding on the states. The Fifth Amendment right to a grand jury indictment remains binding upon federal prosecutions, but does not apply to state criminal prosecutions. States can, and do (e.g., New York), require use of grand juries in criminal cases.

   Answer (B) is incorrect. The Fifth Amendment guarantees that a defendant charged with "infamous crimes" has the right to a grand jury indictment. That right is binding on charges brought in federal courts. It is not binding on the states, and the states are free to adopt or reject the requirement.

   Answer (D) is incorrect. If the right to a grand jury indictment were deemed to be a fundamental right, the failure to accord the right could not be harmless error. One would assume that any right contained in the Bill of Rights is a fundamental right. While that applies to most rights contained in the Bill of Rights, the states are not required to commence prosecution with a grand jury indictment.

2. **Answer (A) is the correct answer.** In *Duncan v. Louisiana*, 391 U.S. 145 (1968), the U.S. Supreme Court held that the Sixth Amendment right to trial by jury was applicable to the states because "trial by jury in criminal cases is fundamental to the American scheme of justice." The Court further held that the right applies in "all criminal cases which — were they to be tried in a federal court — would come within the Sixth Amendment's guarantee." This was in keeping with the Supreme Court's established practice that the right is enforced against the states according to the same standards that protect those rights against federal encroachment. In all federal criminal cases, the right to a jury trial is guaranteed only to those charged with "serious offenses." A serious offense was later defined by the Court as one carrying a maxi-

mum authorized penalty of more than six months. *Baldwin v. New York*, 399 U.S. 66 (1970). That requirement would be met here.

Answer (B) is incorrect. Through a process of "absorption" or "incorporation," the Warren Court applied most, but not all, of the guarantees contained in the first eight amendments of the Bill of Rights to state criminal proceedings. Not all of the rights in the Bill of Rights are binding on the states — *e.g.*, the Fifth Amendment right to a grand jury indictment and the Seventh Amendment guarantee of a jury trial in civil cases. It is thus incorrect to say that the Sixth Amendment applies in "in all cases."

Answer (C) is incorrect. The Supreme Court's holding in *Duncan* applied the Sixth Amendment right to a jury trial to the states. The states are entitled to experiment and extend the rights beyond the minimum set by federal standards of due process. Here, the state could extend the right to trial by jury to an offense not covered by the federal right. The states may not, however, experiment below the minimum standard for due process binding on the states through the Fourteenth Amendment. The federal right guarantees a right to trial by jury for all serious offenses in state courts as well as in federal courts.

Answer (D) is incorrect. If the Sixth Amendment jury trial right is applicable, it would apply regardless of whether a case is "politically charged."

State Constitutional Protections

3. The Fourth Amendment standards of reasonableness and probable cause govern in federal and state criminal cases. The states may not violate these minimal standards, and evidence obtained in violation of the Fourth Amendment is subject to possible exclusion in state as well as federal criminal trials. *Ker v. California*, 374 U.S. 23 (1963). The U.S. Supreme Court has held that the Fourth Amendment does not prohibit police from arresting people for "very minor criminal offense." *Atwater v. City of Lago Vista*, 532 U.S. 318 (2001). In *Atwater*, the Court upheld the warrantless arrest of a motorist for failure to wear a seatbelt. Further, the Fourth Amendment allows for a search of the arrestee incident to a valid arrest. *United States v. Robinson*, 414 U.S. 218 (1973).

The Fourth Amendment, however, is not the end of the inquiry. Traditionally, the role of the U.S. Supreme Court in overseeing state criminal procedure is to impose the minimally acceptable standard below which a state may not venture. All that is required is that the states accord their citizens at least as much protection as is provided under the federal Bill of Rights provision. However, the state has the ultimate responsibility for administering its own system of criminal justice as long as it does not dip below the minimal standards of fairness imposed under the U.S. Constitution. The state constitution is a document enjoying independent force. Above and beyond the minimal federal standard, the states are free to offer greater protection under their own constitutions by imposing stricter standards upon state criminal justice actors. The state may do so by interpreting its own law as supplementing or expanding federal constitutional rights. *Michigan v. Long*, 463 U.S. 1032 (1983).

In the problem, the state is free to impose greater protection than the Fourth Amendment, and some states reject *Atwater* and prohibit police from arresting minor traffic offenders. However, state reliance upon the adequate state ground of its own constitution as the basis for greater protection of constitutional rights must be explicit and clear on its face or risk reversal by the U.S. Supreme Court. *Michigan v. Long*. By failing to explicitly rely solely upon the state constitution, the State Supreme Court risks reversal in holding that the police officer acted improperly. Absent this explicit reliance, the U.S. Supreme Court will presume that the state court relied on federal constitutional law and the federal court will decide the case on whether the state court correctly interpreted and applied federal constitutional law, not state constitutional law. As its interpretation of the Fourth Amendment was erroneous, per the *Atwater* decision, the U.S. Supreme Court, which has final say over the parameters of federal constitutional law, will reverse the State Supreme Court.

4. Answer (D) is correct. A warrantless arrest satisfies the Fourth Amendment so long as the officer has probable cause to believe that the suspect has committed or is committing a crime. *Atwater.* The U.S. Supreme Court has held "that when states go above the Fourth Amendment minimum, the Constitution's protections concerning search and seizure remain the same." *Virginia v. Moore*, 553 U.S. 164 (2008). The Supreme Court will not enforce the state's higher standards as part of the Fourth Amendment and will not reverse the conviction that complied with federal constitutional law. A violation of state law in and of itself does not equate to a violation of the Fourth Amendment. *California v. Greenwood*, 486 U.S. 35 (1988). Here, the State Supreme Court acted within its power to rely on the federal Fourth Amendment, which is controlled by *Atwater.*

Answer (A) is incorrect. The U.S. Supreme Court will not enforce state standards that exceed Fourth Amendment standards. The state is free to provide greater protections from unreasonable searches and seizures for its citizens under its own Constitution, but those greater protections do not become part of the Fourth Amendment. The police did not violate the Fourth Amendment when they made an arrest that was based on probable cause (and valid under federal constitutional law) but prohibited by state law.

Answer (B) is incorrect. The Supreme Court has held that an arrest based upon probable cause complies with the Fourth Amendment reasonableness command. *Atwater.* The state's statutory law embodying a more restrictive policy does not render less-restrictive ones unreasonable and unconstitutional based on the federal Fourth Amendment.

Answer (C) is incorrect. It is not the Supreme Court's role to enforce a state constitution's greater protection of Fourth Amendment rights than that afforded under the Fourth Amendment itself. Enforcement of the more restrictive policy rests with the state courts. Additional protections are treated "exclusively as matters of state law." *Virginia v. Moore*, 553 U.S. 164 (2008). Any state-based constitutional argument would need to be made to the state courts. The U.S. Supreme Court will simply not consider whether or not state law bars such arrests.

Fourth Amendment Right of Privacy

5. **Answer (A) is correct.** The Fourth Amendment protection of privacy that envelops a home is also applicable to the area surrounding the home, an area known as the curtilage. The U.S. Supreme Court applies four factors to determine whether an area close to a home is within the protected curtilage: (1) the proximity to the home of the area claimed to be curtilage of the home; (2) whether the area is included within an enclosure surrounding the home; (3) the nature of the uses to which the area is put; and (4) the steps taken by the resident to protect the area from observation by people passing by. *United States v. Dunn*, 480 U.S. 294 (1987). In weighing whether the shed is within the zone of privacy protected by the Fourth Amendment, the court would consider the fact that the shed is located only five feet from the house and lacks windows. Although the shed is not locked and anyone could enter the property and open it, the proximity of the shed to the house and the fact that it lacks windows weighs in favor of the homeowner. The warrantless entry of the shed within the curtilage of the home violates Muster's expectation of privacy and therefore the evidence should be suppressed. The warrant was based on an illegal observation that cannot be the basis of probable cause.

   Answer (B) is incorrect. The shed satisfies the *Dunn* test demonstrating that it is within the protected curtilage of the home. Anyone approaching a home or property is entitled to walk on the driveway but by using a windowless shed Muster took steps to shield the inside of the shed from view by persons lawfully on the driveway. Ollie could see the outside of the shed, but he could not see inside from where he was allowed to be.

   Answer (C) is incorrect. Based on the neighbor's complaint, Officer Ollie was permitted to enter the property and listen for loud music. However, opening the shed exceeded the scope of the license to enter the property. *Cf. Florida v. Jardines*, 569 U.S. 1 (2013).

   Answer (D) is incorrect. Officer Ollie was entitled to enter the property and listen for loud music. His entry onto the property in and of itself cannot be the basis for suppression of the evidence.

6. **Answer (C) is correct.** A police officer needs no predicate legal cause to walk up and talk to any person in a public place. The test for determining whether a person is seized is whether a reasonable person under the circumstances would feel free to walk away and ignore the police officer. *United States v. Mendenhall*, 446 U.S. 544 (1980). Under the prevailing test, the officer did not seize the defendant by walking up to him and asking, "May I speak with you." This would likely be viewed as a request, not an order, which is permissible, even in the absence of reasonable suspicion or probable cause to believe that the individual is engaged in

criminal activity. The Supreme Court has held that a dog sniff in itself is not a search. *See United States v. Place*, 462 U.S. 696 (1983) (holding that sniff by well-trained dog is *sui generis*, in that it reveals only the presence of illegal drugs). Here, similar to the facts of *Place*, the sniff would be deemed reasonable, validating the arrest and drugs found in the search conducted incident to arrest. That said, be mindful of more recent Supreme Court holdings regarding dog sniffs. *See Florida v. Jardines*, 569 U.S. 1 (2013) (invalidating warrantless dog sniff of porch of home); *Illinois v. Caballes*, 543 U.S. 405 (2005) (permitting warrantless dog sniff of lawfully stopped car).

When the dog sniff provided probable cause, the officer could arrest and search the defendant and his luggage.

Answer (A) is incorrect. Not every encounter between a person and a police officer is a seizure. The test for determining whether a person is seized by the police is whether a reasonable person under the circumstances would feel free to walk away and ignore the police officer. *United States v. Mendenhall*, 446 U.S. 544 (1980). The Supreme Court has relied on the belief that persons approached by an officer feel free to ignore the officer's requests to talk. In similar situations, courts have concluded that an on-the-street inquiry by a police officer is not a seizure and, therefore, requires neither probable cause nor reasonable suspicion. Nothing in the facts of this problem suggests that there was seizure; rather, it was a consensual encounter.

Answer (B) is incorrect. The officer did not have probable cause to justify an arrest or reasonable suspicion to justify a *Terry* stop. The defendant's change of direction did not constitute head-long flight. Head-long flight, alone, does not provide reasonable suspicion for a *Terry* stop but may be considered along with other factors such as when flight occurs in a "high-crime" neighborhood. *Illinois v. Wardlow*, 528 U.S. 119 (2000). However, the defendant was not seized before the dog sniff because the facts do not indicate anything other than a short, consensual encounter, which is not a seizure under the Fourth Amendment.

Answer (D) is incorrect. Even if the defendant was lawfully seized under *Terry* standards, police could conduct a frisk of outer clothing only if there was reasonable articulable suspicion to suspect that the defendant was armed. Here, the facts do not support such a finding.

7. **Answer (A) is the best answer.** In *Kyllo v. United States*, 533 U.S. 27 (2001), the Supreme Court held that a thermal scan of the outside of a home to detect the amount of heat escaping from the home is a search, even though the officers were situated in a public space outside the home. By deeming thermal imaging a search, the majority made the technique subject to judicial oversight and the requirements of the Fourth Amendment. The *Kyllo* Court stated that "obtaining by sense-enhancing technology any information regarding the interior of the home that could not otherwise have been obtained without physical 'intrusion into a constitutionally protected area' constitutes a search—at least where (as here) the technology in question is not in general public use." The question here is whether the use of night vision binoculars satisfied the not "in general public use" requirement in *Kyllo*. The actual intrusion in *Kyllo* was very slight: measuring the thermal quality of escaping heat. Here, the intrusion is greater: peering into the living room of a home, which militates in favor of considering the police activity a search.

Although night vision binoculars might be readily available to the public, *Kyllo* made clear that its test "assures preservation of that degree of privacy against government that existed when the Fourth Amendment was adopted." However, if the technology is seen simply as an enhancement of human sense, there is room to argue that the police behavior here was permissible. In *Dow Chemical Co. v. United States*, 476 U.S. 227 (1986), the Court upheld use of highly sophisticated surveillance cameras to take aerial photos, but there, police targeted an industrial complex, and the photos did not reveal "intimate details" associated with the home. This answer is the "best" answer if you convince the court (or your professor) that this technology is indeed "not in general public use" and/or permits a view of the inside of the home that otherwise would not be available to the officer under the circumstances.

Answer (B) is not correct. As *Kyllo* makes clear, police use of sense-enhancing technology to learn about activities within a home is potentially subject to Fourth Amendment oversight.

Answer (C) is not correct. The police can, if situated in a public vantage point, monitor a home regardless of whether they suspect the individual is engaged in criminal activity.

Answer (D) is not correct. Obviously, Tony could have better protected his privacy within his darkened home by completely closing the curtains. When one fails to take the necessary steps to protect one's privacy, it could be said that the person failed to manifest a subjective expectation of privacy. *Katz v. United States*, 389 U.S. 347 (1967). However, as this was Tony's home, a place of heightened privacy protection, and it was nighttime when one would not reasonably expect that one's private domain would be snooped on, a reviewing court would likely conclude that Tony's failure to completely close his curtains did not extinguish his expectation of privacy.

8. The answer turns on whether the police acquisition of the event data recorder information qualifies as a "search" under the Fourth Amendment. The precise question has yet to be decided by the U.S. Supreme Court. However, several of the Court's recent decisions are potentially relevant to answering the admissibility question posed.

In terms of what additional information might be useful, one might ask whether the police needed to trespass on an "effect" of Mott: did they need to enter his car and attach a device to secure the data from the recorder? In *United States v. Jones*, 565 U.S. 400 (2012), Justice Scalia and four other Justices found that police engaged in a search when they placed a GPS tracking device on the defendant's car and monitored its movements for twenty-eight days. Later, in *Florida v. Jardines*, 569 U.S. 1 (2013), the Court, with Justice Scalia writing, again invoked trespass to deem police conduct a search when they visited the front porch of a home with a drug detection dog. Here, trespass might be a basis for the defense to challenge police access of the information. *See Mobley v. State (Mobley II)*, 834 S.E.2d 785, 791–92 (Ga. 2019) (holding police entry of car passenger compartment and connecting device to an "airbag control module" to secure data was a search).

Alternatively, if the police accessed the data without a physical intrusion on an effect, the defense might try to apply the *Katz* reasonable expectation of privacy test, which remains viable as a basis to establish that a search occurred. *See Jones*, 565 U.S. at 409 (the *Katz* "test has been added to, not substituted for, the common-law trespassory test."). Under *Katz*, a search occurs when an individual manifests a subjective expectation of privacy and the expectation is regarded by society as reasonable. *See Katz v. United States*, 389 U.S. 347, 361 (1967) (Harlan, J., concurring). One doctrine that potentially affects the second prong is the "third party" doctrine, which dictates that an individual lacks a reasonable expectation of privacy in information voluntarily revealed to a third party. *See Smith v. Maryland*, 442 U.S. 735, 741 (1979) (no reasonable expectation of privacy in telephone numbers dialed by the defendant from his home that were in the possession of third party, a telephone company); *United States v. Miller*, 425 U.S. 435, 443 (1976) (no reasonable expectation of privacy in bank records held by third party, a bank). Although frequently criticized, the Court has expressly refused to jettison the third party doctrine. *See Carpenter v. United States*, 138 S. Ct. 2206 (2018).

In *Carpenter*, however, the Court held that government acquisition of seven days or more worth of historical "cell site location" information (CSLI) from a third party (a wireless cell phone provider) was a search. The third party doctrine did not apply, because Carpenter did not voluntarily provide the information to the companies (he simply carried his phone with him). Further, citing *Jones*, the Court held that the record of one's "physical movements" are a "qualitatively different category," compared to the bank records in *Miller* and phone records in *Smith*, because like in *Jones*, they can reveal many personal details about the life of the tracked individual. Whether police here invaded what the *Carpenter* majority called the "reasonable expectation of privacy in the whole of [defendant's] physical movements" is unclear. Unlike a cell phone, the data recorder in Mott's car was not carried into a home, for instance. We would also need to know more about the duration of the data tracked, even if it can be said that Mott (like Carpenter) did not voluntarily provide the data to a third party. Finally, another technical detail: where are the car data stored? In the data recorder box itself, to be downloaded, or held by a third party? If the former, the third party doctrine may not apply.

9. The admissibility of the evidence seized with the search warrants turns on the legitimacy of the information from the informant who provided the probable cause for the warrants. A warrant is valid if based upon probable cause that, in turn, must be based upon knowledge obtained by the police legally. The issue in this case is whether police could base search warrants on information provided by a visitor to the defendant's home who was working as an agent of the police (versus as a "private party"). The Supreme Court has upheld police use of an individual to whom the target voluntarily surrenders her Fourth Amendment privacy protection based on a "misplaced confidence." *Hoffa v. United States*, 385 U.S. 293 (1966).

With respect to the drug-related information, and the warrant issued, although Samantha went to Bob's house for the purpose of gaining information about Bob's drug dealing activities, it is Bob's conduct that controls. Bob allowed Samantha to enter the home and therefore eliminated his expectation of privacy. *On Lee v. United States*, 343 U.S. 747 (1952). Samantha, a former police officer, provided information based on her personal observation, and her identity is known by police (*i.e.*, she is not an anonymous source). The fact that Bob allowed Samantha to enter under a false pretense to discuss law school is irrelevant because, once inside, Samantha could see what there was to see and report that to the police. Also, Samantha simply followed Bob into the kitchen, where she readily viewed the contraband.

Information concerning the child pornography used to secure a warrant obliges a different analysis. Here, again, Samantha is lawfully on the premises and acting as a government agent. The analysis, however, turns on Samantha's, not Bob's, conduct. By opening the laptop and touching the space bar, Samantha engaged in a Fourth Amendment search. *See Arizona v. Hicks*, 480 U.S. 321 (1987). Also, the Court has held that a modern cell phone, because of the quantity and quality of the information it contains, differs from other containers. *See Riley v. California*, 573 U.S. 373 (2014). The laptop computer can therefore be said to enjoy particular Fourth Amendment protection. Moreover, concern exists that Samantha's viewing of the child pornography image occurred when she was exceeding the scope of her invitation. Bob's license to Samantha was to enter his apartment on a social/school visit. The license did not extend to Samantha opening and activating Bob's laptop, so her viewing of the pornography could not be the lawful basis of the search warrant. *See Gouled v. United States*, 255 U.S. 298 (1921) (invalidating search by business associate of defendant who when acting at police behest secured entry to defendant's home under pretense of social visit and rummaged through defendant's papers in his absence). *See also Florida v. Jardines*, 569 U.S. 1 (2013) (holding that entry onto front porch by officer with drug-detecting dog exceeded the license customarily allowing members of the general public to visit a front porch).

10. **Answer (D) is the best answer.** Under *Bond v. United States*, 529 U.S. 334 (2000), police engage in a search when they physically manipulate an object, such as the gym bag in the facts provided. In *Bond*, an officer acting without consent or probable cause of wrongdoing squeezed the soft luggage of the defendant and discerned a "brick-like" object that turned out to be methamphetamine, much as in the Durant facts. As in *Bond*, the search of Durant's bag would be unlawful.

Answer (A) is incorrect because Stano lacked probable cause simply on the basis that he "knew" Durant was in the drug business; his belief, even if correct, did not translate into probable cause that there were drugs in the gym bag at the time of the search.

Answer (B) is incorrect because Durant did not abandon the bag when he said nothing in response to Stano's query and tried to protect the bag. The facts are similar to *Smith v. Ohio*, 494 U.S. 541 (1990), where a defendant carrying a brown paper bag was approached by two plainclothes officers. When the officers identified themselves, the defendant threw the bag on the hood of a car. The officers asked what was in the bag and the defendant tried to grab it. The Court stated that "a citizen who attempts to protect his private property from inspection after throwing it on a car to respond to a police officer's inquiry clearly has not abandoned that property."

Answer (C) is incorrect because even if Stano was indeed engaging in racial/ethnic profiling, the Fourth Amendment does not provide a potential constitutional basis for relief; rather, the Fourteenth Amendment's Equal Protection Clause would be the vehicle. *See Whren v. United States*, 517 U.S. 806 (1996).

Private Searches

11. **Answer (A) is correct.** The Fourth Amendment limits official government behavior; it does not regulate private conduct. Courts have regularly declined to exclude evidence when it is obtained by private persons. *Burdeau v. McDowell*, 256 U.S. 465 (1921). For example, it has been held that no Fourth Amendment concern is raised when security officers with Federal Express, a private company, opened a package they believed might contain drugs and then turned the open package over to federal Drug Enforcement Administration agents. *United States v. Young*, 153 F.3d 1079 (9th Cir. 1998).

The exception applies only to private persons; the Fourth Amendment is applicable to all government officials, not just law enforcement officers. If a private person is acting as an agent of the police, the result is different. Official participation in the planning or implementation of a private person's efforts to secure evidence may taint the operation sufficiently as to require suppression of the evidence. *Coolidge v. New Hampshire*, 403 U.S. 443 (1971).

Walter was not an agent of the police when he entered the home. Although he was praised for his information gathering in the past, there is nothing in the problem that demonstrates that Walter was acting as an agent of the police: the police did not direct him to search, did not offer incentives for his actions, or otherwise make him an extension of the police. Therefore, the search would be considered a private search.

Answer (B) is incorrect. The test of government participation is whether under all of the circumstances the private individual must be regarded as an agent or instrument of the state. Walter was not an agent of the state when he broke into Larry's house. Agency requires more than the police getting information that is useful to them. It requires that the police direct or control Walter and cannot be created after the fact.

Answer (C) is incorrect. There is no such thing as an "unofficial agent." Walter either was or was not an agent of the police. As the facts demonstrate, the police did not control, direct, or otherwise exercise authority over Walter so he was not a police agent.

Answer (D) is incorrect because it only presents part of the key to this problem. Regardless of whether Walter's entry violated state trespass laws, the Fourth Amendment is only applicable against government actors. Before any issue of the manner of entry, trespass, or warrant requirement is addressed, you must first consider if a government actor is involved. Because Walter was a private individual, acting on his own, there is no need to go further in the analysis of his conduct. Because Walter acted as a private person, the evidence will not be suppressed.

Motion to Dismiss

12. The court of appeals will likely reverse the trial judge's ruling and reinstate the criminal case. The Supreme Court has held repeatedly that the manner in which a defendant comes before a court does not affect that court's jurisdiction to try the defendant in a criminal case. *United States v. Alvarez-Machain*, 504 U.S. 655 (1992); *Frisbie v. Collins*, 342 U.S. 519 (1952). Dismissal of charges is limited to gross governmental misconduct.

Absent extremely outrageous government behavior, if an arrest or search is illegal, the appropriate remedy is suppression of evidence that may have been obtained incident to the search or seizure. Any relief to which the defendant may be entitled would come on the motion to suppress. Here, if the pornography is suppressed, the court or prosecution may eventually dismiss the charges because of lack of proof. Dismissal with prejudice, however, is reserved for far more egregious cases involving substantial government misconduct. *See, e.g., United States v. Chapman*, 524 F.3d 1073 (9th Cir. 2008) (upholding dismissal of indictment with prejudice for government's failure to provide the defendant *Jencks* and *Brady* materials; prosecution acted "flagrantly, willfully, and in bad faith").

In this case, there was no government misconduct. Walter was a private citizen acting on his own without police encouragement or involvement. *Cf. United States v. Williams*, 504 U.S. 36 (1992) (improper for district court to dismiss an otherwise valid indictment because the government failed to inform the grand jury of substantial exculpatory evidence).

Search Warrants

13. **Answer (A) is the best answer.** The Fourth Amendment provides that "no Warrants shall issue, but upon probable cause, supported by oath or affirmation, and particularly describing the place to be searched, and the persons or things to be seized." Here, assuming probable cause existed to support the search, and that the particularity requirement is satisfied by the address, the warrant only vaguely stated that the police were authorized to search for "evidence of any felonies." The warrant needed to specify the crimes so that the warrant was not so open-ended to authorize a search for evidence of any crimes. In part, this requirement is meant to let not only the officers know what they can do but also the subject of the search so that she can limit the scope if the officers start to stray. This warrant is in effect a general warrant that the Fourth Amendment was designed to prohibit.

    Answers (B) and (D) are not correct because the officer "described the varied suspected illegal activities of Abigail," and the fact that the warrant that was issued lacked particularity regarding the items to be targeted by the search. While conclusory statements are not sufficient to support a warrant, an officer's statements describing illegal conduct can be sufficient to support a warrant application. The magistrate must be able to evaluate the evidence that leads to the conclusion, not just the conclusion.

    Answer (C) is not the best answer because the facts contained in the affidavit, especially the officer's eyewitness observation of drug dealing, likely would have been sufficient to create probable cause for the search for drugs.

14. Probable cause at its most basic level is simply that there is reasonable cause to believe that the items sought by the police will be at the place specified in the warrant when the police want to search. *Zurcher v. Stanford Daily News*, 436 U.S. 547 (1978). The warrant was invalid because the judge should have been given information about when the robberies took place. Whether probable cause exists for a search warrant depends upon the time frame for the information creating the probable cause and the nature of the object. Information that evidence existed in the past may or may not help determine whether the evidence is still present at the same location. An affidavit in support of a search warrant must contain some information that would allow the magistrate to independently determine that probable cause presently exists — not merely that it existed at some time in the past. Thus, a supporting affidavit that does not give any time frame for the events it describes fails, as a matter of law, to demonstrate probable cause, and a search warrant issued based solely on that affidavit is invalid.

There is no hard and fast rule to determine when the information becomes stale. It depends, as with all probable cause questions, upon the totality of the circumstances. Factors to be considered include the nature of the object sought, the purpose of the object, and the type of criminal activity involved. For example, one court has held that four weeks is a guideline for staleness in drug cases, absent evidence of long-term continued activity. *People v. Hulland*, 110 Cal. App. 4th 1646 (2003). Staleness would be less of an issue if the police were searching for a stolen piano, for instance.

In the problem, the affidavit failed to state when the robberies occurred. The affidavit could have been supplemented by sworn testimony of the affiant stating the dates of the robberies. Without that information, the issuing magistrate had no basis for concluding that evidence of the robberies was presently located in the hotel room.

15. **Answer (B) is the correct answer.** The warrant was a valid anticipatory search warrant. Different probable cause issues arise when the evidence to be seized is not yet at the place to be searched. The difficult question is how a magistrate can make a finding of *present* probable cause which anticipates the *future* arrival of evidence at the place to be searched. All search warrants must: (1) be based on facts that establish probable cause; (2) particularly describe the place to be searched; (3) particularly describe the things to be seized; and (4) be issued by a neutral and detached magistrate. An anticipatory search warrant must meet two additional criteria. First, an affidavit in support of an anticipatory search warrant must show that the evidence is on a sure and irreversible course to its destination. Additionally, an anticipatory search warrant must provide adequate judicial control of the warrant's execution. The issuing court should list clear, narrowly drawn conditions in the warrant controlling the discretion of the police executing the warrant. *United States v. Grubbs*, 547 U.S. 90 (2006). In this case, because the probable cause was predicated on the delivery of the package, the warrant could not be executed until the package was actually delivered.

Answer (A) is incorrect. In *Grubbs*, the Court held that the fact that the object sought is not at the house at the time the warrant was issued is irrelevant: "Because the probable cause requirement looks to whether evidence will be found when the search is conducted, all warrants are, in a sense, 'anticipatory.'"

Answer (C) is incorrect. Although the police created a "controlled delivery" of the package containing the illegal substance, this does not invalidate the probable cause. In fact, because the police were going to deliver the package, the triggering event was nearly certain to occur. To comply with the probable cause requirement: (1) there must be a fair probability if the triggering condition (delivery of the package) occurs "that contraband or evidence of a crime will be found in a particular place," and (2) "there is probable cause to believe that the triggering condition will occur. The supporting affidavit must provide the magistrate with sufficient information to evaluate both aspects of the probable-cause determination." *Grubbs*, 547 U.S. at 96. The triggering event need not be specified in the warrant provided it is presented to the court in the supporting affidavit.

Answer (D) is incorrect simply because it ignores the triggering event. The probable cause requirement for an anticipatory warrant must include that it is probable that the object will be at the place to be searched when the warrant is executed.

16. **Answer (D) is correct.** A cornerstone of the warrant requirement is that judges, and not police officers, determine the existence of probable cause. For judicial participation in the probable cause determination to be meaningful, the judge must serve as more than a rubber stamp for the police. Therefore, those seeking a warrant must present enough underlying facts and circumstances to allow a judge to draw his or her own conclusions about the existence of probable cause. An affidavit couched only in conclusions, *i.e.*, that probable cause exists to believe that evidence of a crime will be found, denies the judge the opportunity to draw those conclusions and robs the Fourth Amendment of its essence. *Johnson v. United States*, 333 U.S. 10 (1948).

In the problem, Detective Roberts failed to inform the issuing magistrate about any of the underlying facts and circumstances which gave rise to the belief that the drugs would be found at Smith's home. The facts in the affidavit do not provide the magistrate with any information about how the affiant knew that the drugs were present or how the police knew that Smith was operating a drug operation out of his home. Without this information, the magistrate could not independently conclude that probable cause existed.

Under *United States v. Leon*, 468 U.S. 897 (1984), police can rely on and execute a search warrant if they have a "good faith" (*i.e.*, objectively reasonable) belief that the warrant is valid, even if later it proves not to be, for instance because it is actually lacking in probable cause. The *Leon* Court, however, made clear that the exception does not apply when police rely on a probable cause affidavit that is "so lacking in indicia of probable cause as to render official belief in its existence entirely unreasonable." Such would appear to be the case here.

Answer (A) is incorrect. The answer suggests that even though the warrant may be invalid, it should be saved by the "good faith exception" to the exclusionary rule. However, as just noted, the exception is not available when the warrant is issued on a "bare bones" affidavit containing no facts allowing the magistrate to make an independent judgment. *United States v. Leon*, 468 U.S. 897 (1984).

Answer (B) is incorrect. Police may rely upon information supplied by a confidential informant and they need not disclose the identity of the informant as long as the judge is assured of the reliability of the informant. *McCray v. Illinois*, 386 U.S. 300 (1967). However, maintaining the secrecy of the informant's identity does not extend to failing to provide the magistrate with the underlying facts on which the informant based his conclusion or that there was an informant giving information to the police. All Detective Roberts presented to the magistrate was his own conclusion; the result would be the same even if Roberts had said, "I know this to be true because an informant told me so." There are still no underlying facts presented to allow the magistrate to make an independent determination.

Answer (C) is incorrect. While Detective Roberts may have had probable cause to believe the drugs would be found at Smith's home, he failed to present the facts and circumstances that would allow the magistrate to judge the correctness of Detective Roberts' conclusions. The test focuses on whether the magistrate could find probable cause, not on whether the police believe they had probable cause.

17. **Answer (D) is correct.** In *Shadwick v. City of Tampa*, 407 U.S. 345 (1972), the Court held that a non-lawyer serving as a municipal clerk could issue arrest warrants for minor offenses (there, offenses prescribed in the municipal code). As a consequence, the fact that Tammy was out of compliance with his professional obligation as a lawyer was of no constitutional significance.

    Answer (A) is incorrect. Although a common law an officer was required to personally observe a minor non-breach of the peace offense, here the requirement was immaterial because the arrest was based on a valid warrant.

    Answer (B) is incorrect. See above — Tammy was constitutionally qualified under *Shadwick*.

    Answer (C) is incorrect. In *Atwater v. City of Lago Vista*, 532 U.S. 318 (2001), the Court held that police can arrest an individual for commission of a non-jailable, non-breach of the peace offense committed in public (in *Atwater*, the officer's observance of the defendant's failure to wear a seat belt while driving).

Searches without Warrants

18. **Answer (D) is the best answer.** In the case of a warrantless arrest or search, probable cause must be measured by objective facts known to the police officer prior to a warrantless arrest or search. Here, it appears that the officer had probable cause to arrest the defendant, based on the prior drug sale. Evidence gathered as the result of a search or arrest may not be used retroactively to establish probable cause. *Smith v. Ohio*, 494 U.S. 541 (1990). In the problem, however, again, probable cause existed prior to and independent of the contents of the bag. The Supreme Court has held that a search incident to an arrest can occur before the actual arrest, with the search encompassing the arrestee's body and "grab area," if the probable cause materializes before the arrest. *Rawlings v. Kentucky*, 448 U.S. 98 (1980). This is the case under the facts presented.

    Answer (A) is incorrect. There are no grounds for a court to find reasonable suspicion to support a *Terry* stop in the problem. The statement of facts provides no reasonable articulable suspicion of illegal activity, at least at the outset of the police-citizen encounter. *Terry v. Ohio*, 392 U.S. 1 (1968). Also, a *Terry* "frisk" can occur only if there are facts and circumstances giving rise to a reasonable belief that the suspect is armed. Here, it is unlikely that suspicion would exist simply because it is a "high-crime" area and the defendant is believed to have sold drugs two weeks before. Finally, even if such reasonable suspicion existed, the officer could have patted the paper bag to see if it contained a weapon. What he could not do was open the bag.

    Answer (B) is incorrect. The earlier drug buy would not provide probable cause to search the bag, as the buy occurred two weeks before and defendant's carrying it has no apparent nexus.

    Answer (C) is incorrect. This answer is correct, as indicated in the above discussion of Answer (A), but Answer (D) provides the best answer.

19. The trial court should deny the defense motion to suppress the drugs found on Holt's person because the officer did have probable cause to make an arrest. Probable cause is not a scientific term. The hearing court must determine whether, based on the totality of the circumstances, the reasonable police officer could fairly determine that a crime had occurred, is occurring, or is about to occur. Facts and circumstances that seem innocent to the average person might be viewed quite differently by an experienced police officer. While a judge cannot rely solely on an officer's conclusions, a judge evaluating information provided by police should respect an officer's common sense conclusions about human behavior. *United States v. Cortez*, 449 U.S. 411 (1981). While a court should respect a police officer's common sense judgments, as well as inferences drawn by an experienced police officer, the court must draw its own con-

clusion whether at the moment before the arrest the facts and circumstances known to the officer were sufficient to conclude that there is a fair probability that a crime was occurring. *Illinois v. Gates*, 462 U.S. 213 (1983).

Although Officer Matterly did not see Holt engage in illegal behavior, the report of the one woman that Holt was her pimp and had just given them their work assignments was sufficient to provide probable cause to arrest Holt. The woman reported direct, personal knowledge of criminal activity and Matterly possessed independent knowledge that the women were in fact prostitutes. The totality of the circumstances was sufficient to give Officer Matterly probable cause that Holt was involved in a crime. Police officers have the authority to arrest an individual in public without a warrant if they have probable cause to believe that the suspect committed, is committing, or is about to commit an offense. *Atwater v. City of Lago Vista*, 532 U.S. 318 (2001).

Because Officer Matterly had probable cause to arrest Holt, her order to him to remove his hands from his pockets was valid. Seeing the drugs fall from his pocket was likewise valid and the drugs could be seized as the fruits of a search incident to a valid arrest.

The fact that Holt was never charged with a promoting prostitution is irrelevant to this question. The only issue is whether Officer Matterly had probable cause to arrest Holt when she did. As the answer to this question is "yes," the resulting search was also valid.

20. **Answer (A) is correct.** Probable cause is a factual determination based upon facts and circumstances known to the police officer immediately before the arrest. "In dealing with probable cause, however, as the very name implies, we deal with probabilities. These are not technical; they are the factual and practical considerations of everyday life on which reasonable and prudent men, not legal technicians, act." *United States v. Ventresca*, 380 U.S. 102 (1965).

Here, the officer observed the men on the sidewalk in front of the post office shortly before police received notice of the silent alarm. The officer reasonably drew the conclusion that the men had been at the post office and that they were closer to the post office than the other people indicating that they were more likely than the others to have tripped the alarm. Location is especially significant because the location in question was the vicinity of an actual crime. It was not a general, amorphous claim that the defendants were in a "high crime" area, justifying the stop. This fact, as well as the evasive post-stop behavior of the defendants, provided probable cause to arrest the men, and the evidence was found during a search incident to a lawful arrest.

Answer (B) is incorrect. Location is significant in this case because there was a crime report and there were few other people in the area. Additionally, probable cause was based on the evasive answers provided. A reasonable police officer would have concluded that Wilson and his companion had committed the break-in.

Answer (C) is incorrect. The facts and circumstances do give rise to reasonable suspicion to justify a temporary seizure of the suspects, and as discussed, the additive effect of the suspects' evasive behavior gave rise to probable cause. With the probable cause-based arrest occurring before the officer placed the suspects in the patrol car, the search of Wilson's pocket was a lawful search incident to arrest.

Even with reasonable suspicion alone, however, police can move a suspect for purposes of safety and security. *Florida v. Royer*, 460 U.S. 491 (1983). The question thus becomes whether the officer could frisk Edwards and his companion before placing them in her patrol car. Here, there was reasonable justification to order the suspects to sit in the police car because the officer was alone, and *Terry* permits this degree of safety precaution. Some courts have held that police can conduct a pat-down frisk to ascertain whether suspects are armed before putting them in a police car. *See, e.g., State v. Lozada*, 748 N.E.2d 520 (Ohio 2001) (deeming frisk reasonable when necessary to protect suspect or officer from a dangerous condition). Here, however, searching a pants pocket, leading to discovery of paint chips, went far beyond the scope of a permissible *Terry* frisk.

Answer (D) is incorrect. Although the officer may have had reasonable articulable suspicion to stop Wilson under *Terry*, because the officer arrested Wilson, this is not a *Terry* situation. Nor do the facts suggest that the officer had reasonable suspicion to justify a frisk for weapons. Rather, the issue will turn on probable cause for the arrest, which as discussed existed, and served as a lawful basis for the search incident to arrest.

21. The drugs are the product of a legal search and are likely admissible. Several approaches are possible.

    There is a hierarchy of dependability surrounding information from informants. Law enforcement officers who personally observe criminal activity or suspicious circumstances are obviously good sources of information. A magistrate may accept a police officer's sworn accounting of facts and circumstances without inquiring into the officer's veracity. Based on the "collective knowledge" doctrine, police officers may also reasonably rely on information provided by other officers when proceeding with a warrantless search or arrest. This occurred here when Officer Huey received a radio call indicating other officers had witnessed Newton rob a convenience store. Based on this information, Officer Huey had probable cause to arrest Newton and to conduct a search of Newton and his car incident to an arrest. However, the arrest would not justify the search of the trunk as a search incident to the arrest. *New York v. Belton*, 453 U.S. 454 (1981).

    In order to justify the search of the trunk, police would invoke the automobile exception (*i.e.*, that there was probable cause to believe that evidence, fruits or instrumentalities of the robbery were in the trunk). Considering the recent robbery observed by fellow officers, Huey likely had probable cause to search the car and trunk for evidence (weapons and stolen items). The marijuana in plain view would have been the product of a legal search and admissible.

    Another theory is that the drugs found in the trunk would have been inevitably discovered based on the vehicle's impoundment and inventory.

    Here, probable cause likely existed to stop and arrest Newton for the convenience store robbery.

22. **Answer (B) is the correct answer.** The taking of a blood sample, which entails physical intrusion beneath the skin, qualifies as a search under the Fourth Amendment. Therefore, police needed to get consent from Dalton, obtain a search warrant, or identify an exception to the

warrant requirement (such as exigency). Here there was no consent to taking the blood sample and there was no warrant. In *Missouri v. McNeely*, 569 U.S. 141 (2013), the Court held that there is no per se exception to the warrant requirement, based on exigency, to take a blood draw. An exigency is to be assessed on a case-by-case basis per the totality of the circumstances. *See Schmerber v. California*, 384 U.S. 757 (1966) (finding exigency based on totality of the circumstances). Here no exigency was apparent: Officer Harris, for instance, could have taken steps to secure a warrant while Shelton drove the patrol car taking Dalton to the hospital. Of note, the Court more recently held that the exigency exception "almost always" allows police to take a blood sample, without consent or a warrant, when a DUI arrestee is unconscious. *Mitchell v. Wisconsin*, 139 S. Ct. 2525 (2019). The only exception would be if the defendant can show that his blood would not otherwise be drawn at the hospital and that police were unreasonable in the judgement that securing a search warrant was not feasible.

Answer (A) is incorrect. Although consent would allow for a warrantless search, it need not have been in writing. Also, even absent consent, a valid search warrant would allow for taking the blood sample.

Answer (C) is incorrect. That state law allowed for taking a blood draw "under the circumstances" does not decide the Fourth Amendment question, resolved in *McNeely*.

Answer (D) is incorrect. Dalton's refusal to comply with the less intrusive technique of a breath test is irrelevant to the constitutionality of the warrantless blood draw. Also, the Court held in *Birchfield v. North Dakota*, 136 S. Ct. 2160 (2016) that the Fourth Amendment permits warrantless breath tests incident to arrest for drunk driving, but police must secure a valid warrant for a blood draw (absent consent or exigency).

23. **Answer (C) is correct.** In *Carpenter v. United States*, 138 S. Ct. 2206 (2018), the Court held that police needed a search warrant to obtain "cell site location information" from a cellular phone provider. The Court reasoned that the data, which reflected the location of the defendant over a period of seven days or more, was deserving of Fourth Amendment privacy protection because it was capable of revealing private aspects of the defendant's life (*e.g.*, a trip to the doctor). Although the Court has yet to address a pole camera scenario, *Carpenter*'s rationale would support (although not be dispositive of) the defense contention that filming the front door of a home is worthy of similar if not greater privacy protection, given the heightened privacy concern raised by the home.

Answer (A) is incorrect. *Illinois v. Gates*, 462 U.S. 21 (1983), held that probable cause can be based on an anonymous tip of criminal wrongdoing, if sufficient corroborating details are provided by the tipster. Here, an anonymous tipster alerted the police to the killing, but the tip itself played no role in the development of probable cause.

Answer (B) is incorrect. *Brigham City, Utah v. Stuart*, 547 U.S. 398 (2006) held that police need not obtain a warrant before entering a residence wherein they have an objectively reasonable belief that a person inside is seriously injured or is threatened with such injury. Here, the time of exigency, sadly, had passed, and the police did not even enter the residence.

Answer (D) is incorrect. In *Collins v. Virginia*, 18 S. Ct. 1663 (2018), the Court held that the automobile exception to the search warrant requirement did not justify police warrantless entry onto the curtilage to gather evidence (there, lifting a tarp draped over a motorcycle parked on a partially enclosed top portion of the driveway of a home). *Collins*, while an important decision, is irrelevant in the Sellers case.

Probable Cause: Police Truthfulness

24. Ordinarily, it does not matter if an affidavit in support of a search warrant contains factual errors. The critical issue is whether the affidavit provided a substantial basis upon which the magistrate could make an independent determination that probable cause existed for the search. *Illinois v. Gates*, 462 U.S. 213 (1983).

One narrow exception, however, allows the defendant to focus on misinformation in the affidavit when a warrant was issued. This exception, discussed in greater detail in the answer to the next question, was retained as part of the objective good faith doctrine of *United States v. Leon*, 468 U.S. 897 (1984). It holds that the reliance on a warrant does not shield a search from the exclusionary rule if the affiant knew or should have known the affidavit was false except for the reckless disregard of the truth. The *Leon* exception was based on the earlier case, *Franks v. Delaware*, 438 U.S. 154 (1978). *Franks* held that while an affidavit supporting a search warrant is presumed valid, a defendant can challenge the affidavit if she makes a "substantial preliminary showing" that (1) a false statement was included by the affiant; (2) the affiant made the false statement "knowingly and intentionally" or with reckless disregard for the truth; and (3) the false statement was necessary to the finding of probable cause.

This substantial preliminary showing must be more than mere identification of the errors in the affidavit. Instead, the defendant must show by a preponderance of the evidence that the misstatements were made knowingly or with a reckless disregard for the truth. Yet, even if this is established, evidence is not automatically suppressed. The affidavit, after the false portion is excised, must be scrutinized to determine whether there are sufficient facts and circumstances remaining to establish probable cause. The prosecution has the opportunity to demonstrate that the false statement was not material to the probable cause finding. If the remaining content is sufficient to establish probable cause, the motion to suppress will be denied, notwithstanding the falsehood.

In the problem, the information withheld from the magistrate went to the very claim that the evidence sought was presently at Angel Smith's home. The legal issue was not simply a battle of informants, but that Detective Roberts withheld the contradictory information from the magistrate. The second informant's report that no drugs would be at the house for at least two weeks eliminated any foundation for probable cause. Roberts' statement that he believed the drugs are present "now" was simply false. The misinformation was material to the probable cause, and the evidence should be suppressed irrespective of the existence of a search warrant.

25. **Answer (C) is correct.** The good faith exception will not save evidence that would be suppressed because of police material misinformation in an affidavit. The goal of the exclusionary rule is to deter illegal police conduct by taking away the fruits of the illegal conduct — that is the evidence found during an illegal search. The good faith exception overrides the exclusionary rule when police officers reasonably rely upon a search warrant because the deterrence value of exclusion of evidence is negated when the police reasonably believed they were conducting a lawful search. The presumption that warrantless searches are *per se* unreasonable and therefore unconstitutional supports the principle that police should seek a warrant prior to conducting a search. When the police comply with this mandate, they should be permitted to rely upon the validity of a warrant issued by a judge. The police should not have to be in the business of second guessing the correctness of the warrant judge's decision because the warrant specifically authorizes them to do the search. However, the *Leon* Court said that suppression remains an appropriate remedy where the warrant is invalid because of a *Franks* violation. *United States v. Leon*, 468 U.S. 897 (1984). More particularly, *Leon* holds that the reliance on a warrant does not shield a search from the exclusionary rule if the affiant knew or should have known the affidavit was false except for the reckless disregard of the truth.

Answer (A) is incorrect. As just noted, suppression remains an appropriate remedy where the warrant is invalid because of a *Franks* violation.

Answer (B) is incorrect because as indicated the omitted information undercut probable cause to believe that the contraband would be present in the apartment.

Answer (D) is incorrect. While at one time the exclusionary rule was thought to ensure that courts not be complicit in police wrongdoing, this "majestic conception" of the rule is no longer operative. *Herring v. United States*, 555 U.S. 135, 141 n.2 (2009). Rather, as *Herring* and other recent cases make clear, deterrence of police misconduct is the goal sought to be achieved. Answer (C) is the best choice.

Search Warrants: Particularization

26. **Answer (D) is the best answer.** The Fourth Amendment requires that a warrant specify the person and place to be searched or seized. "The requirement that warrants shall particularly describe the things to be seized makes general searches under them impossible and prevents the seizure of one thing under a warrant describing another. As to what is to be taken, nothing is left to the discretion of the officer executing the warrant." *Marron v. United States*, 275 U.S. 192, 196 (1927).

   A search of Smith at his place of employment was not supported by probable cause. The probable cause was tied to Smith's residence. The warrant listed no particular place where the search of Smith was to occur, but probable cause existed only for a search at Smith's residence. Hence, the government may not rely on the existence of the warrant which was so facially deficient with regard to probable cause to search Smith's person anywhere but in Smith's home that the executing officers cannot reasonably presume it to be valid. *United States v. Leon*, 468 U.S. 897 (1984).

   Answers (A) and (B) are incorrect. The probable cause established that Carl Smith was operating a fencing operation out of his home. The warrant ordered a search of his home and his person. Police had no reason to believe that evidence of the crime would be found on his person away from his home.

   Answer (C) is incorrect because a warrant ordering that a person be searched ordinarily does not specify where that search should take place. In the problem, however, police did not have probable cause to believe that evidence of the crime would be on Smith's person outside of the home.

27. **Answer (C) is correct.** As noted above, the particularity requirement is designed to avoid "general warrants," which would provide police free rein to search and seize whatever they like. Here, police searched and seized the tablet computer, which was not specified in the warrant, requiring that the child pornography found on the tablet be suppressed. The warrant's authorization to search for "physical photos" refers to hard copy photos rather than digital images on a computer and, therefore, did not authorize search of the tablet computer that may or may not have contained digital images of pornography.

   Answer (A) is incorrect. As noted above, warrants must satisfy the particularity requirement and the execution of a warrant must respect the warrant's limitations. Here, even if police had probable cause to believe that Peters possessed pornographic images, the search warrants limited the search to the laptop computer and hard copy images. When a warrant limits a search, the warrant authorizes an invasion of privacy only to the extent outlined in the warrant. Irrespective of probable cause, the warrant here severely constrained the search; the tablet computer was beyond the scope of this authority. The fact that child pornography is a very serious crime does not negate the particularity requirement.

Answer (B) is incorrect. A warrant must specifically describe the item to be searched. Here, the warrant only specified that the laptop, not the tablet computer, could be searched.

Answer (D) is incorrect. The warrant made clear that police also had authority to search for "physical photos" of child pornography in Peters' home. This permitted the search to continue after the two files were found on the laptop computer, but the search was limited to places were "physical photos" could be found. This did not include the tablet computer.

Execution of a Search Warrant

28. Answer (C) is correct. The Fourth Amendment requires that, absent exigent circumstances, police knock and announce and wait a reasonable time before entering a residence to execute a search warrant. *Wilson v. Arkansas*, 514 U.S. 927 (2002). The Supreme Court has held, however, that failure to comply with that Fourth Amendment requirement does not trigger the exclusionary rule if the search warrant was supported by probable cause. *Hudson v. Michigan*, 547 U.S. 586 (2006). Rather, redress, if any, will come as a result of a federal civil rights claim challenging the failure to properly knock and announce before entry.

Answer (A) is incorrect. The Fourth Amendment does require that police knock and announce and wait a reasonable time before entering a residence to execute a search warrant, but the failure to comply with the requirement does not require the evidence found with the valid search warrant be excluded. *Hudson*.

Answer (B) is incorrect. Failure to comply with the Fourth Amendment's requirement that police knock, announce and wait before entering might "shock the conscience" of many, but it is unlikely that the Due Process Clause standard would be applied by the Court. It would instead apply the reasonableness standard of the Fourth Amendment.

Answer (D) is incorrect. Exigent circumstances cannot rest simply upon a claim of exigency. Exigent circumstances must be supported by facts giving rise to the exigency in the case before the court. Narcotics can be destroyed simply by flushing down the toilet but there are no facts that establish this risk in this search. There was no exigency established in the problem.

29. Answer (D) is correct. In *Michigan v. Summers*, 452 U.S. 692 (1981), the Court held that it is permissible to detain individuals found on the premises to be searched. The Court explained that a limited detention served the legitimate interests of "preventing flight in the event that incriminating evidence is found," "minimizing the risk of harm" to both "the police and the occupants" of the premises, and facilitating "the orderly completion of the search" by ensuring that the occupants of the premises are available to "open locked doors or locked containers to avoid the use of force that is not only damaging to property but may also delay the completion of the task at hand." *Id.* at 702–03. More recently, the Court held in *Bailey v. United States*, 568 U.S. 186 (2013) that police unlawfully detained an individual located about one mile away from the search site, beyond the "beyond the immediate vicinity" of the search, reasoning that the detention did not promote the safety and efficacy of the search. The Court stated that "[i]n closer cases [not a mile away] courts can consider a number of factors ... including the lawful limits of the premises, whether the occupant was within the line of sight of his dwelling, the ease of reentry from the occupant's location, and other relevant factors." *Id.*

at 201. Here, the detention of Dillard in the convenience store would not likely support the foregoing criteria. Also, the detention of Dillard occurred before, not during, the search. Therefore, the police seizure of Dillard and demand that he empty his pockets was unlawful.

Answer (A) is incorrect. As noted above, although the convenience store was seemingly less than a mile away from the search site, it is very unlikely that it fell within the scope of the criteria identified by *Bailey*.

Answer (B) is incorrect. While it is true that the convenience store was not specified in the warrant, Answer D is a narrower, more accurate basis for why the detention and search of Dillard were unlawful.

Answer (C) is incorrect. The officer did not conduct a *Terry* frisk, nor do the facts indicate that a frisk would be justified. Rather, the officer simply ordered Dillard to empty his pockets, which revealed the revolver.

30. **Answer (B) is correct.** Recently courts have begun to recognize that people do have a reasonable expectation of privacy in the emails that they send. *United States v. Warshak*, 631 F.3d 266, 288 (6th Cir. 2010). However, this is only the first step in answering the question because the police did in fact get a warrant. The valid warrant protects the expectation of privacy by placing a neutral and detached magistrate between the government and the person. Therefore, the search was valid and the evidence will not be suppressed.

Answer (A) is incorrect. As noted, the defense has room to argue that the defendant had a privacy expectation in the content of his email.

Answer (C) is incorrect. Snicker does have an expectation of privacy in his email communications. The warrant requirement of the Fourth Amendment protects that expectation of privacy. The fact that the emails were obtained from the ISP instead of Snicker does not violate Snicker's expectation of privacy because the warrant was valid, predicated on probable cause.

Answer (D) is incorrect. The private contract between Snicker and the ISP is part of the equation of reasonable expectation of privacy and supports the need for Fourth Amendment protection but it cannot and does not operate as a shield against a valid warrant. *See Zurcher v. Stanford Daily*, 436 U.S. 547 (1978). The ISP must comply with the warrant regardless of the contractual relationship with Snicker.

Plain View

31. Answer (B) is the correct answer. Objects in the plain view of an officer are subject to seizure and may be introduced in evidence. *Horton v. California*, 496 U.S. 128 (1990). The "plain view" exception to the warrant requirement applies when: (1) the officer is in a lawful vantage point when observing an object; (2) the officer has a right to physically access the object; and (3) it is immediately apparent to the officer that the object is contraband or constitutes evidence, fruit or instrumentality of a crime.

The underlying theory is that police do not have to avert their eyes, or other senses, and ignore what they see when lawfully doing their job. A police officer may view evidence from a location that she has the right to be. In this case, the officer's presence in the bathroom was permissible under the warrant. Her view into Kimberling's room was in plain view. The observation, however, did not justify entry of the room absent a warrant or exigent circumstances. "Incontrovertible testimony of the senses that an incriminating object is on the premises belonging to a criminal suspect may establish the fullest possible measure of probable cause. But even where the object is contraband … the police may not enter and make a warrantless seizure." *Coolidge v. New Hampshire*, 403 U.S. 443 (1971). What the officer observed provided probable cause for issuance of a warrant to search Kimberling's room and seize the contraband. However, there was no need to enter the dorm room because the police could have secured the premises including detaining Kimberling while a search warrant was obtained. *Illinois v. McArthur*, 531 U.S. 326 (2001).

They may also have obtained Kimberling's consent to search.

Answer (A) is incorrect. Certainly, the contents of Kimberling's room were in open view or plain view. However, the plain view exception does not authorize an officer to enter a residence to seize the evidence simply because the evidence was in open or plain view. Possession of a small quantity of marijuana is not a serious offense and would not justify an immediate entry under exigent circumstances. Police may secure the premises so that the evidence is not destroyed while a search warrant is obtained.

Answer (C) is incorrect. A dorm room is a residence and is entitled to full protection of the Fourth Amendment. Police may not enter a dorm room for purposes of inspection for contraband. The dorm room is just as protected under the expectation of privacy as a home or apartment. Just as landlords reserve the right to enter a lessee's apartment for safety or repair purposes, dorm rooms may be subject to periodic inspections by college officials for safety or maintenance purposes. That fact does not allow either a landlord or college officials to permit police to conduct warrantless searches.

Answer (D) is incorrect. A person who leaves a door open to a house, an apartment, or a dorm room runs the risk that someone — including a police officer — who is lawfully present outside may see into the house, apartment, or dorm room and see evidence of a crime. The warrant authorized the officer to search Broadley's room and from that vantage point the officer could view Kimberling's room. The officer, however, did not have authority to enter Kimberling's room.

32. **Answer (A) is correct.** An officer is entitled to conduct a protective sweep for weapons of the passenger compartment of vehicle based on a reasonable belief "that the vehicle contain[s] weapons potentially dangerous to the officers." *Michigan v. Long*, 463 U.S. 1032, 1034 (1983). Here, even presuming that the bumper sticker raised such a suspicion, Officer O'Shea's search of the wallet exceeded his authority as the wallet was not likely to contain a firearm. Nor would the "plain view" exception to the search warrant requirement be at play, as it was not "immediately apparent" that the wallet was contraband. *Horton v. California*, 496 U.S. 128 (1990). It was only after opening the wallet that O'Shea was able to discern that the wallet was in fact stolen property. Probable cause must exist without moving the object to examine it. *Arizona v. Hicks*, 480 U.S. 321 (1987).

    Answer (B) is incorrect. Under *Michigan v. Long*, O'Shea arguably had a basis to enter the car to verify or dispel his concern about a weapon being present.

    Answer (C) is incorrect. There are absolutely no facts provided that would allow Officer O'Shea to conclude that the wallet constituted contraband.

    Answer (D) is incorrect. The plain view exception requires probable cause to seize an item in plain view. As noted, O'Shea had no reason to think that the wallet was stolen — until he opened (*i.e.*, searched) it. Therefore, this was not a valid plain view search.

33. The court should grant the motion to suppress. Relying upon the same rationale that underlies the plain view doctrine, the U.S. Supreme Court held that a "plain feel" corollary to the plain view exception should be recognized. The Court held that the seizure of nonthreatening contraband or evidence, detected through the sense of touch during a *Terry* protective pat-down search, is permitted, so long as it is immediately apparent to the officer that the object is contraband or evidence. *Minnesota v. Dickerson*, 508 U.S. 366 (1993). The pat-down in *Dickerson* did not stay within those bounds. The frisking officer felt a small lump in the suspect's front pocket, and immediately determined that it was not a weapon, but continued to probe the object with his fingers and then determined that it was crack cocaine. The Court ruled that the seizure of drugs was unlawful because the officer exceeded the bounds of *Terry* by squeezing, sliding, and manipulating the object.

    The issue is whether, at the time the officer concluded that the object in the suspect's pocket was not a weapon, the officer had probable cause to believe that the object was contraband or evidence of a crime. Here, the officer equivocally stated that the objects "might be used to carry crack cocaine." Moreover, as a threshold matter, there is a question whether reasonable articulable suspicion existed to support the initial *Terry* stop and the ensuing weapons frisk by the officer.

Custodial Arrest for Petty Offenses

34. **Answer (C) is correct.** The Fourth Amendment does not prohibit custodial arrests for minor, trivial offenses when supported by probable cause. *Atwater v. City of Lago Vista*, 532 U.S. 318 (2001) involved a custodial arrest for not wearing a seat belt, an offense that carried a $50 fine and no jail time. The Supreme Court held that neither English common law nor United States law at the time of the adoption of the Constitution prohibited arrests for any offenses. The Court rejected the defendant's request to create a "modern arrest rule … forbidding custodial arrest, even upon probable cause, when conviction could not ultimately carry any jail time and when the government shows no compelling need for immediate detention." Incident to a custodial arrest valid under the Fourth Amendment, a police officer may search the arrestee's person. *United States v. Robinson*, 414 U.S. 218 (1973).

    Answer (A) is incorrect. The Fourth Amendment does not prohibit custodial arrests for minor, trivial offenses even when no valid purpose is served by an arrest rather than a summons.

    Answer (B) is incorrect. Following a custodial arrest, police may search the arrestee's person even though no evidence of the crime for which the person was arrested may exist and there was no reason to suspect the arrestee was armed and dangerous. *Robinson*. Despite the fact that there is no need for additional supportive evidence of jaywalking, the officer may conduct a full search incident to arrest, not merely a pat-down search for weapons.

    Answer (D) is incorrect. In *United States v. Robinson*, 414 U.S. 218 (1973), the Court held that there need not be any relationship between the basis for the arrest and the evidence or contraband discovered during the search conducted incident to the arrest.

Arrest

35. **Answer (C) is correct.** Warrantless arrests, based on probable cause, for serious and non-serious offenses alike, are valid when made in public. *Atwater v. City of Lago Vista*, 532 U.S. 318 (2001) (arrest for non-jailable, fine-only offense); *United States v. Watson*, 423 U.S. 411 (1976) (arrest for felony). Whether a person is in a public place is determined at the moment the police begin the process of making the arrest. *United States v. Santana*, 427 U.S. 38 (1976). Here, Ms. Hanson was in public, so the arrest, based on probable cause, was lawful. Furthermore, an officer can search the body of an arrestee (and their "grab area") incident to a lawful arrest, and any contraband or evidence discovered can be used in a prosecution. *United States v. Robinson*, 414 U.S.218 (1973).

    Answer (A) is incorrect. An arrest in public is lawful if supported by probable cause. *See Atwater.* The subjective motivation of an officer, including personal animosity, is irrelevant. *Whren v. United States*, 517 U.S. 806 (1996).

    Answer (B) is incorrect. As noted, both the public arrest and the search incident to arrest revealing the cocaine, were lawful.

    Answer (D) is incorrect. Whatever the seriousness of the weapons violation, the arrest and search incident were valid.

36. **Answer (C) is correct.** There was probable cause to arrest given what was reported to the officers, what they saw, and their knowledge of Mallory's ex-felon status. That probable cause, coupled with the attempt to arrest Mallory for a felony when he was outside of the house, permitted the officers to continue the chase into the house. *Warden v. Hayden*, 387 U.S. 294 (1967). Hot pursuit of a suspected felon, as here, is a recognized exception to the warrant requirement and the entry into the home was a continuation of the chase of Mallory that began outside and ended inside the home. *United States v. Santana*, 427 U.S. 38 (1976).

    It bears mention that if the offense in question is a misdemeanor (as opposed to a felony, as here), there is no per se "hot pursuit" exigency justifying warrantless entry of a suspect's home to effectuate an arrest. Rather, "[a]n officer must consider all the circumstances in a pursuit case to determine whether there is a law enforcement emergency. On many occasions, the officer will have good reason to enter—to prevent imminent harms of violence, destruction of evidence, or escape from the home. But when the officer has time to get a warrant, he must do so—even though the misdemeanant fled." *Lange v. California*, 141 S. Ct. 2011 (2021).

    Answer (A) is incorrect. Generally, an arrest inside a home must wait until the police obtain a warrant. *Payton v. New York*, 445 U.S. 573 (1980). There are several exceptions to the warrant requirement, and one is hot pursuit. Because the police were chasing Mallory for a felony before he ran into the house, the entry to arrest him was lawful.

Answer (B) is incorrect. It is true that Mallory could somehow have been authorized to carry the gun (for instance, as stated, because it was a facsimile). But the standard for probable cause does not require an elimination of all innocent explanations before a finding of probable cause can be made. *Illinois v. Gates*, 462 U.S. 213 (1983). There is enough evidence to support the conclusion that Mallory was committing a crime by possessing the gun. That Mallory might be innocent does not eliminate the probable cause evidenced by the facts.

Answer (D) is incorrect. Probable cause is the requisite determination before any arrest can be made but that fact alone does not end the evaluation in this case. The police needed more than just probable cause to arrest Mallory inside the house and therefore this answer is incorrect and incomplete because it does not require an exception to the warrant requirement.

37. No, the actions of the officers did not jeopardize the prosecution of Dudd. This is so even though the arrest occurred in his home without a warrant. The facts provided closely resemble those in *New York v. Harris*, 495 U.S. 14 (1990), where the Court held that even though police violated *Payton v. New York*, 445 U.S. 573 (1980), because they did not secure an arrest warrant, the confession later obtained at the station was admissible. As the Court stated with respect to the arrestee in *Harris*, "[b]ecause the officers had probable cause to arrest Harris for a crime, Harris was not unlawfully in custody when he was removed to the station house, given *Miranda* warnings, and allowed to talk. For Fourth Amendment purposes, the legal issue is the same as it would be had the police arrested Harris on his doorstep, illegally entered his home to search for evidence, and later interrogated Harris at the station house. Similarly, if the police had made a warrantless entry into Harris' home, not found him there, but arrested him on the street when he returned, a later statement made by him after proper warnings would no doubt be admissible" *Id.* at 18. Moreover, nothing in *Payton*'s reasoning "suggests that an arrest in a home without a warrant but with probable cause somehow renders unlawful continued custody of the suspect once he is removed from the house. There could be no valid claim here that Harris was immune from prosecution because his person was the fruit of an illegal arrest." *Id.*

38. An arrest warrant adequately protects the Fourth Amendment interests of the person to be arrested, whether the arrest occurs in his home or that of another when he has a privacy expectation there (*e.g.*, is an overnight guest). Here, so far as James Falco goes, all police needed was a valid arrest warrant to justify his arrest and the drugs found incident to the search can be used by the government.

If, however, police found evidence in Grandma Falco's home that implicated her in a crime, and wished to prosecute her on that basis, police would need a search warrant that specified that James Falco was present in the home. *Steagald v. United States*, 451 U.S. 204 (1981). The *Steagald* Court found it unreasonable that police could enter a third person's home to search for another without a judicial evaluation of the facts that led them to believe that the nonresident would be found at that home. The Court saw too great a potential for abuse if an arrest warrant sufficed, as this could result in generalized searches of homes.

Judicial Review of an Arrest

39. The warrrantless arrest of a person in public is constitutionally acceptable if there is probable cause for the arrest. *United States v. Watson*, 423 U.S. 411 (1976). However, the Fourth Amendment requires any arrest without a warrant to be validated by a magistrate ordinarily within 48 hours of the arrest. *County of Riverside v. McLaughlin*, 500 U.S. 44 (1991). In this case, Quill was held for a period far in excess of that.

Although Quill's right to a probable cause hearing was violated, this in and of itself does not require suppression of the statement. The Supreme Court has not addressed this issue, *Powell v. Nevada*, 511 U.S. 79 (1994), but the lower federal courts have consistently required a causal connection between the violation of the 48 hour rule and the statement obtained. *See, e.g., United States v. Fullerton*, 187 F.3d 587 (6th Cir. 1999); *United States v. Morrison*, 153 F.3d 34 (2d Cir. 1998). In this case, Quill's statement was obtained after the magistrate found probable cause, thereby terminating any influence of the Fourth Amendment violation. Additionally, there is no causal connection between the failure to take Quill's case to a magistrate and the statement obtained, coupled with the apparent good faith on the part of the police. Because of these factors, the statement will be admitted.

Pretextual Stops and Arrests

40. Answer (D) is correct. The Supreme Court has held that a traffic stop can be motivated by pretext so long as there is a legal basis to justify the stop. *Whren v. United States*, 517 U.S. 806 (1996). Here, because there was probable cause to support the traffic stop, the motive of the police officer may not be considered in determining the legality of the stop under the Fourth Amendment. After the stop, Trooper Jacks was permitted to look inside the purse when Dukes opened it. When he smelled marijuana and saw the marijuana in Dukes' purse, he had probable cause to arrest her and search the car.

Answer (A) is incorrect because there was a lawful basis for the stop, making the pretext claim irrelevant. The subjective motivation of the officers is irrelevant if in fact probable cause existed.

Answer (B) is incorrect. In making its broad ruling in *Whren*, the Court rejected the "reasonable officer test," finding it unworkable in determining which traffic stop based on probable cause would have been made by a reasonable police officer and which would not have been made.

Answer (C) is not the best answer. Seeing the marijuana in the purse and smelling the marijuana would give Officer Jacks probable cause to arrest Dukes and then search the bag for the marijuana, but the issue in this question is the validity of the stop to put Officer Jacks in position to see inside the purse. If the stop was valid then seeing and smelling the marijuana would be possible under the plain view/smell doctrine.

Protective Sweep of a Home

41. **Answer (C) is correct.** An arrest in a home is dangerous because the officer is on his or her adversary's home turf. As a precautionary matter, a police officer may, incident to arrest, look in closets and other spaces "immediately adjoining" where the arrest takes place, from which an attack by another individual could be launched. This is not a search for evidence, but solely a "quick and limited search of the premises," a "cursory inspection of those spaces where an individual may be found." The sweep can last "no longer than is necessary to dispel the reasonable suspicion of danger." Moreover, in addition to this limited area, police can conduct a warrantless protective sweep elsewhere in the residence if reasonable suspicion exists "that the area [to] be swept harbor[s] an individual posing a danger to the officer or others." *Maryland v. Buie*, 494 U.S. 325 (1990). Evidence that is in plain view in those areas will be admissible at a subsequent trial. Here, because police knew this to be the hangout of the gang, either *Buie* basis entitled police to open the closet door and to check the rooms and closets adjacent to the room where the arrest occurred in order to protect their safety, as these were physical spaces that could contain a potential attacker. When the officers saw the automatic weapons in plain view, they had probable cause to believe that the weapons were illegal to possess and were used in burglaries and robberies.

    Answer (A) is incorrect. Even if Break was handcuffed before the officers opened the closet door, under *Buie* they have authority to look into "immediately adjoining" areas to make sure that there was no hidden threat to their safety.

    Answer (B) is incorrect. When the police officers opened the closet door, they were not searching for evidence. They acted to ensure their safety. Police may look into "immediately adjoining" areas without a warrant in the interest of self-protection from others possibly posing a threat. When they opened the closet door, the weapons were in plain view, allowing the police to seize them.

    Answer (D) is incorrect. Probable cause is not an alternative to a search warrant, which was not obtained in this case. Probable cause allows police to obtain a search warrant. However, the search of the closet was valid because it was conducted as a protective sweep that does not require a search warrant.

42. Under *Maryland v. Buie,* police can only look in physical spaces "where a person may be found" who could present a threat to the safety of the officers. A police officer may conduct a limited protective sweep of the entire dwelling in conjunction with an in-home arrest if there are "articulable facts which, taken together with the rational inferences from those facts, would warrant a reasonably prudent officer in believing that the area to be swept harbors an indi-

vidual posing a danger to those on the arrest scene." *Maryland v. Buie*, 494 U.S. 325 (1990). The Supreme Court cautioned, though, that it was not sanctioning a "top to bottom search" and stressed that the authority to conduct a protective sweep of the entire house is not automatic, but only available when there is reasonable suspicion to believe that the house is harboring a person posing a danger.

Here, the police had information from an undercover officer that the gang could be in Break's home, although they lacked probable cause at the moment that any gang member was in fact present. However, it is likely that police could establish the necessary reasonable suspicion to support such a belief. This allowed them to conduct a protective sweep of the entire house to look for Break's confederates, based on the second *Buie* option noted *supra*. Here, in conducting the sweep the police opened the small cabinet and found the jewelry. The officer did not have reason to believe that one or more of Break's confederates was hiding in the small cabinet. Consequently, opening the cabinet was not part of the lawful sweep but an illegal warrantless search. The evidence in the cabinet must be suppressed. Police should have secured the house and obtained a search warrant to extend the search beyond a protective sweep.

Search of a Person or Item Incident to Arrest

43. **Answer (D) is correct.** Incident to a lawful custodial arrest of a motorist, a police officer is empowered to conduct a full search of the motorist's person. *United States v. Robinson*, 414 U.S. 218 (1973). All of the evidence is admissible.

    Answer (A) is incorrect. Incident to a custodial arrest, a police officer is not limited to searching the arrestee for weapons. Even if the offense is one where there could be no evidence, *e.g.*, driving with a suspended license, the officer can conduct a full search of the person at the scene of the arrest. *See Robinson.*

    Answer (B) is incorrect. A police officer may, incident to a lawful custodial arrest, search the arrestee at the scene of the arrest. The search is reasonable because it provides for officer safety and prevents the destruction of evidence. Although a delayed inventory search is possible and would have occurred at the jail, there is no requirement that an officer delay a search until reaching the police station.

    Answer (C) is incorrect. Whether the officer knew or did not know when he felt the pockets that Freeman had contraband on his person, the authority to make a full search of the arrestee automatically flowed from the lawful custodial arrest. The officer did not need probable cause to conduct the search.

44. **Answer (D) is correct.** The predicate for a search incident to arrest is an actual valid arrest. *United States v. Robinson*, 414 U.S. 218 (1973). The Supreme Court has expressly held that no authority to search arises when the officer issues a citation or summons. *Knowles v. Iowa*, 525 U.S. 113 (1998). Because Officer Smythe issued Henry a citation and did not arrest Henry, he could not conduct a search when he did.

    Answer (A) is incorrect. A full search of a motorist's person is permissible following a custodial arrest. *United States v. Robinson*, 414 U.S. 218 (1973). The underlying justifications that allow for a warrantless search of a person following a custodial arrest — the need to disarm a suspect or discover and preserve evidence — do not exist when as here the person is simply ticketed before the search. *Knowles v. Iowa*, 525 U.S. 113 (1998).

    Answer (B) is incorrect. A traffic stop does not eliminate Fourth Amendment protections. Because Officer Smythe decided not to arrest Henry, and no other exception permitting the search exists, his order to empty her pockets was an unconstitutional search.

Answer (C) is incorrect. A search incident to arrest may occur before a formal arrest so long as there is probable cause for the arrest (that is preexistent and independent of any contraband or evidence found in the search) and the arrest happens shortly after the search. *Smith v. Ohio*, 494 U.S. 541 (1990). This answer is incorrect because the facts demonstrate that Officer Smythe did not arrest Henry before he conducted the search; he merely issued her a ticket.

45. Incident to the arrest of a person, a police officer may use reasonable force to secure evidence on the arrestee's person. Here, presuming the arrest was lawful, the court's ruling will depend upon the reasonableness of the force used based on the situation the officer faced at the time of the search. The issue was addressed by the U.S. Supreme Court prior to imposition of the Fourth Amendment exclusionary rule on the states under the Fourteenth Amendment. In *Rochin v. California*, 342 U.S. 165 (1952), the "stomach pumping" case, the Supreme Court found the state's attempts to retrieve evidence swallowed by the arrestee to "shock the conscience" of the Court and violate the Due Process guarantee of the Fourteenth Amendment. In *Rochin*, police officers jumped upon the defendant and unsuccessfully attempted to extract the drug evidence. When that effort failed, the officers handcuffed the defendant and took him to a hospital where a doctor forced an emetic solution into the defendant's stomach against his will, forcing the defendant to vomit two capsules containing morphine. Since *Rochin*, it seemingly takes a great deal more to shock the Supreme Court's and other courts' consciences.

Today, the court will likely determine the legality of the officer's behavior according to Fourth Amendment reasonableness principles looking at the totality of the circumstances. Incident to the arrest of a person, a police officer may use reasonable force to secure the evidence on the arrestee's person. Reasonableness will turn on whether the method used was life threatening and whether there were less intrusive means available to obtain the evidence. *Winston v. Lee*, 470 U.S. 753 (1985). It is relevant, as well, that the objects, if swallowed, may have been life threatening to the arrestee. Officer Jenson seemingly had probable cause to arrest Apten based on his personal knowledge of Apten's past and the behavior he witnessed. When Officer Jenson first observed Apten attempt to swallow the item, he took reasonable steps to prevent the destruction of the item. Additionally, it was not unreasonable for Officer Jenson to surmise that the item was drugs. His hitting of Apten as a second step to retrieve the item likely will be found to be reasonable as it was a non-lethal use of force, there was no less intrusive method available, and the risk of harm to Apten if the item was in fact drugs was quite real. The evidence likely will not be suppressed.

Search of a Home Incident to Arrest

46. **Answer (A) is correct.** The police had a warrant to arrest the defendant, and had reason to believe he was at home when the warrant was executed, which was all they needed for the defendant's arrest. *Payton v. New York*, 445 U.S. 573 (1980). Incident to a lawful arrest, police may search the arrestee's person and the area under the arrestee's "immediate control." The area within the arrestee's control has been defined as the area from which the arrestee can reach and grab weapons to use to escape or threaten the police officers or to grab evidence that the arrestee might wish to destroy. *Chimel v. California*, 395 U.S. 752 (1969). A warrantless search incident to arrest is not necessarily a search for evidence. Such searches incident to arrest are solely for the purposes of protecting the officers and preventing the arrestee from destroying evidence.

Here, the search of the defendant's person was clearly permissible. Determining the physical scope of the "grab area" of a person is more complicated, however. If the space is determined by the defendant's location at the moment of arrest, the search incident to arrest would extend to all objects the arrestee could reach at that moment. Thus, an officer can search an area after the arrestee has been removed from the area, serving to expand the physical scope of police search authority. *See, e.g., United States v. Abdul-Saboor*, 85 F.3d 664 (D.C. Cir. 1996).

Over time, some courts have adopted a narrower view, instead using the place where the arrestee is at the time of the search, limiting the physical scope of search on the rationale that the area from which an arrestee is removed posed neither a risk of evidence destruction nor a threat to police. In contrast, the place where the arrestee was physically located at the time of the search may pose significant risk to the officers and the evidence. *See, e.g., United States v. Blue*, 78 F.3d 56 (2d Cir. 1996).

The former approach appears to be the majority view, favoring the government position here. At the moment of defendant's arrest, he was inside the closet. Even though he continued to struggle after being pulled from the closet, the closet falls within the reach and grab area. Therefore, this search was a proper search incident to arrest and the evidence likely is admissible.

Answer (B) is incorrect. There is nothing in the record that would demonstrate probable cause for any search. However, this search was conducted as a result of the arrest, not because of probable cause that anything was present. Absent the search incident to arrest, the arrest warrant would not serve as a search warrant for the closet.

Answer (C) is incorrect. As noted above, the police needed only an arrest warrant for defendant. If, however, defendant had no relation to the home, and police found evidence in the home that resulted in the prosecution of the actual homeowner, police would have needed to have a search warrant specifying that defendant would be present in the home in order to admit the evidence against the actual homeowner. *Steagald v. United States*, 451 U.S. 204 (1981).

Answer (D) is incorrect. As noted, the facts of the problem place the search within the accepted parameters of a search of the reach and grab area of a person subject to a lawful arrest.

47. Incident to a lawful custodial arrest, with or without a warrant, police may search the body of the arrestee and the area within the immediate control of the arrestee, meaning the "reaching or grabbing" distance. *Chimel v. California*, 395 U.S. 752 (1969). Until recently, a search of the passenger compartment of a car pursuant to *Chimel* was well established and was permitted even if the person was not near the car at the time of the search. However, in *Arizona v. Gant*, 556 U.S. 332 (2009), the Court limited the search of a car to situations in which the person is "within reaching distance of the passenger compartment at the time of the arrest or it is reasonable to believe the vehicle contains evidence of the offense of arrest." Since there is no reasonable belief that evidence of soliciting prostitution will be found in the car, the search is only valid if Zimmer was within reaching distance of the passenger compartment at the time of the search.

    In *Gant*, Gant was handcuffed and was locked in the back seat of the police car when his car was searched. Because Gant could not actually reach his car the search exceeded the power to conduct a search incident to arrest. In Zimmer's case however, Zimmer arguably could get to the passenger compartment because he was not secured and was near the back of his car. As such, the search of the car will be permitted as a search incident to arrest and the pill will not be suppressed.

48. **Answer (A) is correct.** Because Joinder was under arrest, it was necessary for her to get dressed. Since she asked to get dressed prior to being transported to the station house, the police could reasonably remain in her presence while she did so. *Washington v. Chrisman*, 455 U.S. 1 (1982). In *Chrisman*, defendant was arrested outdoors on suspicion of underage drinking and the arresting officer followed defendant to his dormitory room to get his identification. As the defendant entered his dorm room, the officer initially remained in the open doorway but soon entered after the defendant's roommate appeared nervous, whereupon the officer observed marijuana seeds and a smoking pipe. The *Chrisman* Court upheld the entry and visual inspection, reasoning that the arresting officer "had a right to remain literally at [the arrestee's] elbow at all times." The purpose is to protect the officer and prevent destruction of evidence.

    Here, the officer had the right to follow Joinder into her bedroom and he saw the gun in plain view. The search is consistent with the *Chimel* test because Joinder's control has extended to areas beyond her reaching or grabbing distance at the time of the arrest.

Answer (B) is incorrect. Allowing Joinder to dress does not rise to the level of exigent circumstances in and of itself. That Joinder might want to get dressed, and even that the police might want her to get dressed as well, does not create an exigency. Exigency is reserved for situations where real necessity or emergency exists and there is still the requirement that the police have probable cause before the search is conducted. Since getting dressed was not critical to facilitate Joinder's arrest but was instead an accommodation to her request, it was not an exigent circumstance.

Answer (C) is incorrect. The fact that there was an alternative, perhaps less intrusive, method to the one the police officers chose does not make the method used unreasonable under the Fourth Amendment. Further, the fact that the officers were men and Joinder was a woman does not eliminate the policy consideration of protecting police officers. The gun was just as dangerous to the police whether Joinder was a man or a woman.

Answer (D) is incorrect. This search is not based on an exigent circumstance as we traditionally view that term. While there was no time to secure a warrant, no warrant could issue because the police had no probable cause to obtain a warrant to search the area in question. Joinder does have an expectation of privacy in her bedroom dresser but the search incident to arrest doctrine permits this search in spite of that expectation of privacy.

Exigent Circumstances

49. Answer (A) is correct. The 911 call with no one on the other end and the repeated failed efforts by police to follow up on the call justified a visit to the residence based on what is known as the emergency aid doctrine. Under the "emergency aid" exception to the warrant requirement, police can enter a home without a search warrant when they have an objectively reasonable basis to believe that their entry is needed to "assist persons who are seriously injured or threatened with such injury." *Brigham City v. Stuart*, 547 U.S. 398, 403 (2006); *see also Michigan v. Fisher*, 558 U.S. 45, 49, (2009) (per curiam) (warrantless entry justified where "there was an objectively reasonable basis for believing that medical assistance was needed, or persons were in danger"). Some courts have allowed police to invoke the exception based on a 911 call hang-up when the operator was unable to reach anyone when the operator called back repeatedly. *See, e.g., Hanson v. Dane Cty., Wis.*, 608 F.3d 335 (7th Cir. 2010). Here, the defendant actually came to the door and refused entry. But in such a circumstance precedent also exists to afford police authority to enter. *See, e.g., United States v. Najar*, 451 F.3d 710 (10th Cir. 2006). Consistent with this position, Answer (A) posits that the entry based on the facts provided was permissible, but the discovery of the marijuana inside the dresser drawer would nonetheless be improper. The emergency aid exception is justified by the need to intervene to protect against imminent serious harm to persons; searching the drawer did not serve this goal. The marijuana found inside the dresser drawer should be suppressed even if the entry was legal.

Answer (B) is incorrect. The right to grant consent includes the right to refuse consent. The mere fact that consent is withheld serves as neither a basis for probable cause nor an objectively reasonable belief that someone is in danger. Recently, the Supreme Court held that no "community caretaking" exception exists allowing police to enter a home without a warrant, consent, or the need to render "emergency aid" to an inhabitant. *Caniglia v. Strom*, 141 S. Ct. 1596 (2021).

Answer (C) is incorrect. As noted, searching the dresser drawer exceeded the authority of police based on the emergency aid exception, requiring that the marijuana found therein be suppressed.

Answer (D) is incorrect. If the circumstances justify police to enter based on the emergency aid exception, they need not discharge their duty by merely peering into the windows of a residence from outside (which itself was likely a search). Their responses must be reasonable under the circumstances to satisfy the Fourth Amendment. As here, this may well permit them to enter without permission and look around to see if someone needs assistance.

50. **Answer (B) is correct.** Because police had a lawful arrest warrant for the defendant, they were entitled to execute the in-home arrest. *Payton v. New York*, 445 U.S. 573 (1980). Furthermore, the government can argue that the "hot pursuit" exigency justified the entry of the girlfriend's home. When the police have probable cause to arrest a suspect and begin chasing him outside of a home, they are permitted to continue the chase into the home rather than having to break off the chase in order to obtain a warrant. *United States v. Santana*, 427 U.S. 38 (1976). The police in this case were allowed to arrest the suspect when he was outside the home and began their chase before he entered the home. The entry into the home was a continuation of the chase and therefore the entry was valid. The handgun was then found incident to a lawful arrest.

Answer (A) is incorrect. The arrest warrant and exigency justified defendant's in-home arrest. Police would need a search warrant only if they secured evidence in the home of another person and wished to use the evidence to prosecute that person. *Steagald v. United States*, 451 U.S. 204 (1981).

Answer (C) is incorrect. Again, the police had probable cause (indeed, an arrest warrant) to arrest the suspect for a felony and commenced their effort to arrest outside the home, with the arrest culminating in the home.

Answer (D) is incorrect. Whether or not a search warrant for the home would be issued does not affect the authority of police to arrest and search the defendant under the facts.

51. The presence of the first officer was reasonable under the facts of the situation and in compliance with the Fourth Amendment. Although the warrant to search was ultimately denied, the officers believed they had probable cause. In *Illinois v. McArthur*, 531 U.S. 326 (2001), the Court recognized that some interference with a person's right to move about the house is reasonable when the police have probable cause, have a good reason to fear that evidence might be destroyed, "the police made reasonable efforts to reconcile their law enforcement needs with the demands of personal privacy" (for instance, remaining at a doorway), and the interference was for a limited time.

The facts in this case are very similar to those of *McArthur*, where the Court upheld the actions of police. Unlike *McArthur*, however, the magistrate here denied the warrant because of a lack of probable case. Nevertheless, the conduct of the police was reasonable given the suspect's statement about the "stash" and concern that evidence could be destroyed by the girlfriend. And while two hours is a long time, there is nothing in the facts that show the police delayed in seeking the warrant. *Segura v. United States*, 468 U.S. 796 (1984). Under the totality of the circumstances, the conduct of the police was reasonable, and the continued presence of the officer did not violate the Fourth Amendment.

52. The facts provided closely resemble those in *United States v. Ramirez*, 676 F.3d 755 (8th Cir. 2012). The Eighth Circuit held that the circumstances did not justify the officers' warrantless entry, noting that the officers had neither seen nor heard anything indicating that the occupants of a room, who were suspected of possessing drugs, might imminently destroy evidence. The Court observed that there was "no dead bolt lock being engaged, no toilet flushing

or a shower or faucet running, and no shuffling noises or verbal threats emanating from the room; nor did the officers have any information that an occupant…had attempted to escape through a window, nor any indication that these individuals were armed or dangerous." *Id.* at 763. The Court explained that "when the police knock on a door but the occupants choose not to respond or speak, or maybe even choose to open the door and then close it, or when no one does anything incriminating, the officers must bear the consequences of the method of investigation they've chosen." *Id.* at 762. The Court observed that, even assuming the officers were "conducting a run-of-the-mill attempt to simply knock and gain entry," the occupant was not obligated to allow them to enter and was "within his bounds in his attempt to close the door." *Id.* The Court concluded that the occupant's attempt to shut the door in response to the officers' knock did not support finding exigency and "[t]hat he did so, without more, does not bolster the claim that it was reasonable to conclude that the destruction of evidence was imminent." *Id.*

Community Caretaking Function

53. **Answer (C) is correct.** In performance of their caretaking function, police may stop vehicles or inquire of people who appear to be having difficulties. *South Dakota v. Opperman*, 428 U.S. 364 (1976); *Cady v. Dombrowski*, 413 U.S. 433 (1973). These searches and seizures are reasonable under the Fourth Amendment. Police here exercised that authority when checking on Maluck and neutralizing the community risk presented by the car being in "drive" mode under the circumstances. When performing this duty, they were in a lawful vantage point to see the contraband. *Horton v. California*, 496 U.S. 128 (1990). The plain view doctrine would then apply.

Answer (A) is incorrect. Nothing in the facts suggests that Maluck possessed a weapon that presented a safety risk to the officers or Maluck.

Answer (B) is incorrect. The officer had authority and even duty to inquire and make sure that the person slumped over the wheel of the car did not need assistance and that the car was safe (the gear was in "drive" and Maluck's foot was on the brake though he may be unconscious). Whether or not there was probable cause is immaterial. The officer's actions were reasonable under the Fourth Amendment.

Answer (D) is incorrect. The officer did properly invoke the caretaking function to make sure that the person slumped over the wheel did not need assistance and the vehicle was safe. The caretaking function allows the police to provide assistance and even stop people. The function permits limited searches in furtherance of that caretaking. *South Dakota v. Opperman*, 428 U.S. 364 (1976). These searches are reasonable under the Fourth Amendment. Here, again, the marijuana was discovered in plain sight while discharging this function.

Search of an Automobile Incident to an Arrest

54. **Answer (D) is the best answer.** Incident to the custodial arrest of a motorist, a police officer may, depending on the circumstances, search the interior compartment of the vehicle. A search incident to arrest, however, does not extend to the trunk of the vehicle. *New York v. Belton*, 453 U.S. 454 (1981). The prosecution should have argued that the search was an inventory of the vehicle, assuming that the police department had policies for vehicle impoundment and inventory searches in such a situation, and that the policies were followed.

    Answer (A) is incorrect. Police can search the passenger compartment when the arrestee is within reaching distance of it or it is reasonable to believe that evidence relevant to the crime of arrest is inside the vehicle. *Arizona v. Gant*, 556 U.S. 332 (2009). Here, neither exception exists because Laval was handcuffed in the police car and had been arrested for driving without a license. Even if the search was permissible under *Gant*, a search incident to arrest does not extend to the trunk of a vehicle. *Belton*.

    Answer (B) is incorrect. A search of the trunk would have been lawful under the automobile exception if the officer had probable cause to believe that evidence of a specific crime would be found in the car. *California v. Carney*, 471 U.S. 386 (1985). Nothing in the facts reveals that the officer had probable cause to search the trunk of the vehicle.

    Answer (C) is incorrect. A custodial arrest for a traffic offense does not violate the Fourth Amendment. *Atwater v. City of Lago Vista*, 532 U.S. 318 (2001).

55. **Answer (C) is the best answer.** The cocaine is admissible under *Arizona v. Gant*, 556 U.S. 332 (2009), because the burglary arrest warrants, the basis for the arrest, provide a basis for the officer to believe that there might be related evidence in the car. The cocaine found under the front seat was therefore lawfully secured in plain view. The cell phone image, however, can be subject to suppression under *Riley v. California*, 573 U.S. 373 (2014), which held that absent consent or exigency (neither is evident under the facts), police must obtain a warrant to search a cell phone. The officer's accessing of the cell phone by entering the code, revealing the photo, constituted a search, which *Riley* does not allow.

    Answers (A), (B) and (D) are incorrect for reasons noted.

Automobile Exception

56. **Answer (B) is the best answer.** Police may search a vehicle without a warrant under the automobile exception when the officer has probable cause to believe that evidence of a specific crime or contraband will be found in the vehicle. Police "may search an automobile and the containers within where they have probable cause to believe contraband or evidence is contained." *California v. Acevedo*, 500 U.S. 565 (1991). This exemption from the warrant requirement originally rested on exigent circumstances because it was likely that the evidence would be gone before police could obtain a search warrant. *Carroll v. United States*, 267 U.S. 132 (1925). Ultimately, the "general mobility of a vehicle" and the "diminished expectation of privacy that one has in an automobile" became the basis for the exception, and police no longer need prove exigent circumstances. *Maryland v. Dyson*, 527 U.S. 465 (1999). The critical issue here is whether Trapper's lawful discovery (in plain view) of the machine gun in the passenger compartment provided probable cause to believe that another gun (or perhaps ammunition) would be found in the trunk. Although a very close call, this not likely the case, so the marijuana found in the trunk will be suppressed. Trapper could have secured the car while a search warrant was obtained or impounded it and waited for an inventory search of the trunk.

    Answers (A) and (C) are incorrect for reasons just noted.

    Answer (D) is incorrect. While an accurate statement of the law concerning the scope of police searches incident to arrest, the question asked where the automobile exception would permit the search of the trunk. The auto exception does allow for search of a trunk, but *Acevedo*, for reasons noted, would not likely permit the search of the trunk here.

57. **Answer (B) is correct.** The automobile exception authorizes a warrantless search of the vehicle when there is probable cause to believe that contraband or evidence of a specific crime will be found in the vehicle. *See California v. Acevedo*, 500 U.S. 565, 580 (1991) ("The police may search an automobile and the containers within it where they have probable cause to believe contraband or evidence is contained."). Tango's alert to the vehicle is not a search under the Fourth Amendment and can serve as grounds for probable cause. *Illinois v. Caballes*, 543 U.S. 405 (2005). As in *Caballes*, the sniff occurred without unduly extending the duration of the stop. *Cf. Rodriguez v. United States*, 575 U.S. 348 (2015) (invalidating dog sniff because it extended an otherwise-completed traffic stop). Because the alert was on the trunk, Officer Trapper now had probable cause to search the trunk of the car and any containers in the trunk where drugs could be found.

Answer (A) is incorrect. A lawful arrest does not permit the search of a car trunk. *New York v. Belton*, 453 U.S. 454 (1981).

Answer (C) is incorrect. The proposition stated in Answer (C) does not state the current law. The automobile exception was originally based upon exigent circumstances, allowing police to search a vehicle at the scene because delay to obtain a warrant risked loss of evidence due to the mobility of the vehicle in question. The requirement of exigent circumstances no longer exists. The ability to search a car is based on having probable cause to search a vehicle.

Answer (D) is incorrect. A search, supported by probable cause, under the automobile exception extends to the entire vehicle and containers within the vehicle that could house the object sought. *United States v. Ross*, 456 U.S. 798 (1982). The expectation of privacy of an automobile is diminished throughout the automobile and the standard for an automobile exception search is the same whether the search is of the passenger compartment or the trunk.

58. **Answer (B) is correct.** Under the automobile exception, police with probable cause may search all containers within a vehicle that could contain the objects sought. Consequently, the automobile exception extends to a passenger's belongings. *Wyoming v. Houghton*, 526 U.S. 295 (1999). In *Houghton*, an officer had probable cause to believe that drugs were in a car based on his observation of a hypodermic needle in the shirt pocket of the male driver of the vehicle and his acknowledgment that he used the needle to shoot drugs. The officer thereafter saw a woman's purse lying on the backseat, searched the purse, and discovered drugs, which resulted in the prosecution of the female-passenger owner of the purse. The *Houghton* Court utilized a balancing test to conclude that the government's interest in searching "a passenger's personal belongings when there is reason to believe contraband or evidence of criminal wrongdoing is hidden in the car" outweighs the "[p]assenger's, no less than the driver's, ... reduced expectation of privacy with regard to the property that they transport in cars."

Moreover, a passenger "will often be engaged in a common enterprise with the driver," and have a common "interest in concealing contraband or evidence." It is also possible that a driver might place, unbeknownst to the passenger, contraband in the passenger's belongings. The police officer is not required to first ascertain if the passenger is involved in the driver's illegal enterprise. Here, despite the fact that the Judge otherwise perhaps enjoyed a reputation of law abidingness, the search of both suitcases, as to one or both police had probable cause to believe contained the money, was valid.

Answer (A) is incorrect. A police officer does not need probable cause to link a passenger to the driver's illegal enterprise in order to search a passenger's belongings. The only limitation is that the officer may not search containers which could not hold the object which is sought. Here, police had probable cause to believe the cash was in the back of the car, and both suitcases were identical and could contain the cash that Officer Williams has probable cause to believe was in the suitcase.

Answer (C) is incorrect. When probable cause focuses generally on a vehicle, police may search any container within the vehicle where the object sought could be hidden. The officer lawfully detained Judge Russo while he sorted out the situation. There was no probable cause to implicate Judge Russo in the illegal operation, but the police could lawfully detain him for a short period of time until he searched the suitcases.

Answer (D) is incorrect. Probable cause did not exist to implicate Judge Russo in James's criminal syndicate. Therefore, the search of Judge Russo's suitcase was not incident to a valid arrest. However, his suitcase was subject to search under the automobile exception because probable cause focused on the back of the vehicle where the suitcases were found. Police, with probable cause, may lawfully search any container in the vehicle that could contain the object sought. *United States v. Ross*, 456 U.S. 798 (1982). Again, as *Acevedo* stated, "[t]he police may search an automobile and the containers within it where they have probable cause to believe contraband or evidence is contained."

Search of Containers

59. **Answer (C) is correct.** Incident to arrest, police may search the arrestee and objects within the "area of immediate control" of the arrestee. A search incident to arrest without a warrant is permitted to prevent the arrestee from gaining access to weapons that might threaten the safety of the arresting officers or to evidence which the arrestee might seek to destroy. *United States v. Robinson*, 414 U.S. 218 (1973). In this case, Albion was in custody of the police. She was formally arrested and in a secured location. The officer lawfully searched her incident to the arrest and found the luggage claim ticket. However, the search of a container incident to an arrest is limited to the containers in the grab area of the person at the moment of arrest. *Chimel v. California*, 395 U.S. 752 (1969). Because the luggage was not near Albion at the moment of her arrest, police needed a search warrant or an exception (*e.g.*, exigency or consent) to allow the search. The contraband was discovered as the result of an illegal search and must be suppressed.

   Answer (A) is incorrect for the reasons set forth above. The luggage was not within her grab area at the time of arrest.

   Answer (B) is incorrect. Even if the officer had probable cause, the facts do not provide any basis to find exigency. The luggage could have been secured while a search warrant was obtained.

   Answer (D) is incorrect. The answer option is correct in stating that the facts do not support a lawful search incident to arrest, and is correct in stating that no probable cause existed to search the luggage. However, it misstates why the search was not a valid search incident to arrest. The search was improper because it exceeded the "grab area" limit of the exception.

60. The drugs are admissible. Under the automobile exception to the warrant requirement, police may search a vehicle and any container found in the vehicle that might hold the object of the search. All that is necessary for a valid search under the automobile exception is independent probable cause to believe that evidence of a specific crime will be found in the automobile. *California v. Acevedo*, 500 U.S. 565 (1991). Even though there might be no reason to suspect wrongdoing on the part of the delivery vehicle driver, police had probable cause to believe that the package contained illegal drugs and therefore the seizure and search of the package was within the automobile exception. The police limited the scope of the search to the container that they had probable cause to search.

Author's Note: The purpose of this question and the previous question is to focus on the different rules that apply when a container is seized in public and when it is seized from an automobile. If the container is being carried in a public place, police may seize it on probable cause and hold it while a warrant is obtained. If the container is seized from an automobile, police acting on probable cause may search it without a warrant solely because it was in an automobile.

Impoundment and Inventory Search of a Vehicle

61. **Answer (B) is correct.** An inventory search that satisfies the Fourth Amendment is not a search for evidence; it is a search intended to protect the owner's property, protect the police from false claims of loss, and protect the police and public from dangerous items. Inventory searches are valid under the Fourth Amendment if reasonable under the circumstances.

    As an initial matter, the legality of the inventory search depends upon a lawful impoundment. Generally, police may impound a vehicle when it is evidence of a crime, if it is abandoned, if the driver has been arrested, or there would be a traffic hazard if the car were left where it is found. An illegally parked vehicle may be impounded, especially in this situation where it is parked in a no parking zone. Because the car was lawfully impounded, based on a policy that was followed, it was subject to an inventory search. *Colorado v. Bertine*, 479 U.S. 367 (1987). Additionally, the scope of the inventory must also be based on a valid policy, conceived in terms of one or more of the three concerns noted *supra* (*e.g.*, a policy cannot allow for vacuuming of the microfibers of the car's carpet, because doing so does not serve the aforementioned policy interests), that is in fact followed by police. In this case, removing the door panel likely exceeded the scope of a reasonable inventory search and therefore the cocaine must be suppressed. *United States v. Best*, 135 F.3d 1223 (8th Cir. 1998).

    Answer (A) is incorrect. Because the impoundment of the vehicle was lawful, this answer is incorrect. The inventory was invalid, as outlined above.

    Answer (C) is incorrect. The car was illegally parked and subject to towing. The vehicle was properly impounded but, as noted above, the scope of the search exceeded the proper scope of a valid inventory search.

    Answer (D) is incorrect. A properly impounded vehicle is subject to a reasonable inventory search. *Colorado v. Bertine*, 479 U.S. 367 (1987). As noted, the problem with the inventory search in this case is that it exceeded the scope of a proper inventory search.

62. **Answer (A) is correct.** During a lawful inventory, police may open closed compartments of the vehicle and any containers found in the vehicle. *South Dakota v. Opperman*, 428 U.S. 364 (1976). However, inventory searches must be governed by standardized departmental procedures restricting the untrammeled discretion of police officers. The Fourth Amendment does not prohibit inventory searches of vehicles that extend to closed containers if there is a written

standard policy governing such inspections. *Florida v. Wells*, 495 U.S. 1 (1990). The key in this question is that there was such a standardized policy authorizing police officers to open and inventory the contents of closed containers. Although the policy here was discretionary, in that it turns on whether a container's contents can be discerned from the exterior, the *Wells* Court suggested that such a policy would be permissible. The inventory of the interior of the vehicle, the glove compartment where the officer found the watch, and the trunk where the opaque package was found, which contained marijuana inside, were lawful.

Answer (B) is incorrect. The departmental policy authorized an inventory of the passenger compartment and the trunk after a serious automobile collision. The officer was authorized to open the trunk, inventory its contents, and open the opaque package containing the marijuana.

Answer (C) is incorrect. A lawful inventory is not restricted to objects that are visible within the interior compartment of a vehicle.

Answer (D) is incorrect. Although inventory searches are to be conducted pursuant to a policy, the Court does not require a formal, mandatory policy, instead authorizing officers to exercise discretion under a policy in terms of when to search, the scope of the search, and the thoroughness of the search. *Florida v. Wells*, 495 U.S. 1 (1990). Additionally, the subjective motivation of the officer is irrelevant to the validity of the inventory search so long as the inventory was otherwise valid. *United States v. Hawkins*, 279 F.3d 83 (1st Cir. 2002).

Comparing Different Justifications for the Search of an Automobile

63. In this question, you should analyze the various searches and potential justifications for each search. First, the officer reached into Maluck's pocket and removed his license. In *United States v. Hensley*, 469 U.S. 221 (1985), the Court authorized a stop to check identification under *Terry v. Ohio*. At a minimum, the officer had reasonable articulable suspicion that Maluck was intoxicated in public (and perhaps driving while impaired), and therefore, a stop to check his identification was reasonable. Reaching into Maluck's pocket was more invasive than simply asking Maluck his name or asking him to produce his identification but was likely reasonable under the circumstances.

The first search issue concerns the viewing of the heroin protruding from the unzipped backpack, the removal of the backpack from the passenger compartment of the car, and its subsequent search. The officer could look into the passenger compartment from the outside of the car, since the interior is in plain view and open to the public. There is no expectation of privacy preventing the police, or anyone, from looking inside a car. This allowed the officer to see the white powder sticking out of the backpack. Based on his objectively reasonable belief that the substance was heroin, the officer acted within his authority to seize the clear plastic bag containing the heroin.

The lawfulness of seizing and then searching the backpack, however, is somewhat less clear. The government could argue that Maluck was under lawful arrest when the pill bottle was found based on the public drunkenness or discovery of what appeared to be heroin. If Maluck was under lawful arrest, the officer could conduct a search incident to arrest. Under *Arizona v. Gant*, 556 U.S. 332 (2009), police can search a car's passenger compartment and any containers inside it, if at the time of a search, the arrestee is within reaching distance of the compartment or it is reasonable to believe that the vehicle contains evidence of the offense of arrest. Here it could be argued that the search of the backpack might reveal evidence relating either to an arrest for public drunkenness or heroin possession. On this basis, the "rummaging" (*i.e.*, search) of the backpack and discovery of the pill bottle would be permissible.

Alternatively, the government could argue that the automobile exception permitted the securing and search of the backpack. The exception allows police to search a car without a warrant when probable cause exists to believe that evidence of a crime will be found in the automobile. *California v. Acevedo*, 500 U.S. 565 (1991). Here, discovery of the heroin provided police that justification, allowing for search of the backpack located in the car's passenger compartment, and the ultimate discovery of the pill bottle found inside the backpack.

The officer's viewing of the stolen red Camaro, however, was likely improper. The facts provided closely resemble those before the Court in *Collins v. Virginia*, 138 S. Ct. 1663 (2018). In *Collins*, the Court was asked to address, in effect, whether the automobile exception trumps the expectation of privacy in a home's curtilage. In *Collins*, police walked up a driveway next to a home, located in much the same place as the facts recounted here, removed a tarp covering what was believed to be a stolen motorcycle, and confirmed their belief. The Court held that, despite having probable cause to believe the motorcycle was stolen, the police intruded upon the defendant's curtilage without a warrant or consent, which rendered the police conduct unconstitutional. Citing *Collins*, Maluck could successfully move to suppress the information about the Camaro obtained by the police.

Finally, although we are getting ahead of ourselves here, the government could possibly mount a successful argument that, even presuming that the backpack was unlawfully secured at the scene, its contents would have been inevitably discovered post-arrest as a result of Maluck's car being impounded and inventoried, because it was located in the middle of a public street. *See* discussion of the inevitable discovery doctrine in "Derivative Evidence: Exceptions," *infra*.

Stop and Frisk

64. Answer (D) is the best answer. Police may detain and talk to a person without having reasonable suspicion or probable cause to believe that the person is engaged in criminal activity. Matters change, however, if a reasonable person would not feel free to refuse to terminate the interaction or walk away from the officers. Rather than being a "consensual encounter," not implicating the Fourth Amendment, a person in such a situation is "seized," triggering Fourth Amendment protection. *United States v. Mendenhall*, 446 U.S. 544 (1980). The difference between a consensual encounter and a seizure (a "*Terry* stop") is not always easy to discern. Police persistence does not necessarily transform a consensual encounter into a *Terry*-stop. Here, the facts state that Glick "realized that [the police] would not let him ignore them and leave," which would tend toward a finding that Glick was seized; however, the demeanor of the officers cuts the other way. If Glick was in fact seized at this point, based on an objective assessment of the totality of the circumstances, police would need reasonable articulable suspicion to believe that he was engaged in criminal activity. *Terry v. Ohio*, 392 U.S. 1 (1968). Nothing in the facts suggests that this standard was met.

Assuming, however, that he was not seized, the question becomes whether the officer's subsequent retention of Glick's license was a seizure, which it likely was: a reasonable person in this situation would not feel free to walk away and forfeit his or her driver's license. However, at this point police likely had reasonable suspicion that Glick was involved in drug activity based on the report of drug activity and Glick's lying to the officers about where he lived. None of the possible answers, however, refers to the legality of the stop. Answer (D), which concerns the legality of the backpack search, is therefore the best choice.

Incident to a lawful *Terry*-stop, police may conduct a limited frisk for weapons if facts and circumstances give rise to a reasonable belief that the suspect is armed or represents a threat to them. A legitimate frisk is only a search for weapons, not for evidence. *Terry v. Ohio*, 392 U.S. 1 (1968). There is no evidence to support any reasonable articulable suspicion that Glick was carrying a weapon and so no search of the backpack would be permissible. In addition, the officer's statement that Glick could regain his license only if he consented to a search of the backpack makes it unlikely that the government could successfully argue that Glick consented to a search of the backpack. The drugs are not admissible at Glick's trial.

Answer (A) is incorrect. Glick did not voluntarily consent to a search of his backpack. His consent was the product of police coercion: they told him he could leave only if he consented to a search and they had his driver's license. The consent to search was not voluntary.

Answer (B) is incorrect. Whether Glick was lawfully in the hallway does not determine the lawfulness of the officers' behavior in the fact pattern. The key issues are whether the officers had reasonable suspicion, probable cause, or consent to search the backpack.

Answer (C) is incorrect. The search of Glick's backpack was not a limited search for weapons. A limited search would not have involved opening the bag. It appears that the officers opened the bag looking for evidence of drug dealing. Also, the search for weapons was not justified under *Terry* as there was no reasonable articulable suspicion that Glick was armed.

65. **Answer (A) is the best answer.** In determining whether the facts and circumstances known to a police officer prior to the *Terry* seizure rise to the level of reasonable suspicion, a court must make the determination based on the totality of the circumstances. That totality must be evaluated "through the eyes of a reasonable and cautious police officer on the scene, guided by his experience and training." *United States v. Cortez*, 449 U.S. 411 (1981). *Terry* requires the court to distinguish between inarticulable hunches and articulable facts and circumstances giving rise to reasonable suspicion of criminal activity. Here, no *Terry* stop occurred until Starkie submitted to his command to place his hands on the car. *California v. Hodari D.*, 499 U.S. 621 (1991). At that point, it is likely that the stop was supported by reasonable articulable suspicion of criminal activity, given the time of night, the nature of the area, Starkie's clothing (heavy coat and winter hat during the summer), and his behavior (*e.g.*, unsuccessfully trying to enter a closed business at 11 p.m. and "fiddling with something in his waistband").

Assuming the lawfulness of the *Terry* stop, the question next becomes whether the *Terry* frisk was lawful. Under *Terry*, a frisk is justified if the officer has reasonable articulable suspicion that the suspect possesses a weapon that might pose a safety threat to the officer. Here, given Starkie's initial refusal to show his hands, the fact that Officer Sammie was outnumbered late at night in a high-crime area, the sound of metal hitting the ground, Sammie's inability to locate the object on the ground, and Starkie's quick retrieval of and placement of an unknown object in his coat, Officer Sammie had reasonable articulable suspicion that Starkie had a weapon. Although Sammie "did not think the items were weapons, his training and experience immediately caused him to believe that they were burglary tools." The aforementioned language would support what is known as the "plain feel" exception under *Minnesota v. Dickerson*, 508 U.S. 366 (1993). With respect to "tactile discoveries of contraband," if an officer "lawfully pats down a suspect's outer clothing and feels an object whose contour or mass makes its identity immediately apparent," the item (i.e., contraband) can be seized and used by the government. *Id.* at 375.

Answer (B) is incorrect. The validity of a *Terry* stop is reviewed under the totality of the circumstances as known to the officer at the time the interaction is initiated. Here the totality of the circumstances supports a reasonable suspicion that Starkie was about to commit a crime and therefore the stop was valid.

Answer (C) is incorrect. As noted, the facts provided support the conclusion that both a *Terry* stop and frisk were justified.

Answer (D) is incorrect. The facts do not rise to the level of probable cause supporting an arrest.

66. The cocaine is admissible. Police must have reasonable suspicion that a crime is occurring, has occurred or is about to occur to make a *Terry* stop. Prior to a *Terry* stop, a police officer needs no justifiable predicate to engage a citizen on the street. An officer may talk to anyone and request information; such an encounter rises to the level of a *Terry* stop only when a reasonable person would not feel free to walk away or otherwise terminate the encounter. *United States v. Drayton*, 536 U.S. 194 (2002); *United States v. Mendenhall*, 446 U.S. 544 (1980). However, a reasonable person's perception of the situation is not the only measurement of whether a seizure has occurred. Rather, the suspect's response to the police conduct matters.

Here, Warble was not seized until he was tackled by the officer. *California v. Hodari D.*, 499 U.S. 621 (1991). Reasonable suspicion will not be evaluated until the moment Warble was seized (here, by being tackled). Moreover, Warble's flight when he saw Officer Carbonari is a fact that may be considered by a court reviewing whether reasonable suspicion justified the seizure: "Headlong flight — wherever it occurs — is the consummate act of evasion: it is not necessarily indicative of wrongdoing, but it is certainly suggestive of such." It is important to note that flight alone does not provide sufficient reasonable suspicion for a *Terry* stop; however, it is a factor that can be combined with the fact that the suspect is in a "high-crime" area. *Illinois v. Wardlow*, 528 U.S. 119 (2000). The facts state the neighborhood was a high crime area. When Warble was running away, as noted, he was not seized but his flight in the high-crime area, combined with his discarding several objects, likely qualified as reasonable suspicion, justifying his seizure.

As in *Hodari D.*, the objects he jettisoned during his flight could be recovered and examined by police. They were not the product of a Fourth Amendment seizure, which had not yet occurred.

67. Answer (A) is the correct answer. Police must have at least reasonable suspicion to justify a traffic stop. *United States v. Brignoni-Ponce*, 422 U.S. 873 (1975). A reviewing court must consider the tipster's veracity and basis of knowledge, "although allowance must be made in applying [the criteria] for the lesser showing required [regarding reasonable suspicion.]" *Alabama v. White*, 496 U.S. 325 (1990). With anonymous tips, as here (as in *White*), it typically is not possible to verify the tipster's veracity, so analysis of a tipster's basis of knowledge is key.

The fact pattern in the question closely resembles that of the Supreme Court's decision in *Navarette v. California*, 572 U.S. 393 (2014). In *Navarette*, a five-member majority upheld a traffic stop when an anonymous 911 caller reported that she had been "run off the road by a reckless driver," and provided information on the truck that allegedly had done so, along with a description and license number. The *Navarette* Court held that while an anonymous tip "alone seldom" provides a basis for reasonable suspicion, the call "bore adequate indicia of reliability for the officer to credit the caller's account." Naming a particular vehicle at a certain location that allegedly committed a specific wrongful act provided the "basis of knowledge" supporting the tip's reliability. The caller's veracity was bolstered by the officer's observation of the described truck in the area that coincided with the tipster's account; so too was the fact that 911 calls possibly can be traced, which can deter false allegations. Altogether, the tipster's report of being run off the road provided reasonable suspicion of an ongoing crime such as "drunk driving as opposed to an isolated episode of past recklessness."

The facts in the question differ insofar as the caller stated that she was "almost" (not actually, as in *Navarette*) run off the road, which a reviewing court would not likely deem a material difference. Moreover, here the caller alleged that the Bronco was "driving erratically," but in both *Navarette* and here the officer himself did not see the motorist break any laws. Because the traffic stop was lawful, the smelling of the burnt marijuana and plain view observation of the marijuana in the glassine bag were lawful.

Answer (B) is incorrect. In *Navarette*, police similarly followed the motorist for five minutes yet failed to detect any wrongdoing. The detailed tip itself with the subsequent corroboration provided reasonable suspicion for the *Terry* stop.

Answer (C) is incorrect. Information provided by an anonymous tipster can in fact serve as a basis to create reasonable suspicion. *See Navarette; Alabama v. White*, 496 U.S. 325 (1990). The question is whether the report of alleged wrongdoing has "adequate indicia of reliability" for the officer to credit the account, which a court would likely find here.

Answer (D) is incorrect. Assuming the lawfulness of the traffic stop, the officer had authority to order Harris out of the car. *Pennsylvania v. Mimms*, 434 U.S. 106 (1977). When Harris exited the car, the marijuana on the driver's seat was in plain view.

68. **Answer (C) is the correct answer.** Following a lawful stop of a vehicle to issue a traffic citation, police may walk a drug dog around the vehicle to check for drugs. There need be no factual justification for using the drug dog beyond the lawful stop for a traffic violation. The use of the drug dog does not constitute a search, and the positive alert provided probable cause to search the trunk of the car under the automobile exception to the warrant requirement. The only limit on the police behavior is the time required for the drug dog to reach the scene of the traffic stop may not unreasonably extend the time required to issue a traffic citation. *Illinois v. Caballes*, 543 U.S. 405 (2005).

The dog sniff of the vehicle occurred 15 minutes after the justification for the traffic stop ended. The Court recently reaffirmed that officers may conduct unrelated checks for things like warrants during a traffic stop but any checks that extend the duration of the traffic stop beyond that necessary to fulfill the purpose of the stop must have a separate justification. *Rodriguez v. United States*, 575 U.S. 348 (2014). Because the 15 minute period after issuing the warning served no apparent purpose other than to detain Wells until the drug dog arrived, the continued stop and subsequent dog sniff were invalid.

Answer (A) is incorrect. A drug dog alert to a lawfully stopped car can provide probable cause for the search of the car. *Caballes*. But, as just noted, here the car was not lawfully stopped at the time of the dog sniff. The traffic stop was unreasonably extended to await the dog's arrival.

Answer (B) is incorrect. There is nothing improper about a dog sniff of a car during a lawful traffic stop. But again, the dog sniff here that led to the search of the car occurred after the authority to detain Wells expired and this renders the dog sniff invalid.

Answer (D) is incorrect. Police need neither probable cause nor reasonable suspicion to use a drug dog to check out an automobile following a lawful traffic stop. The only issue is whether the time police need to get the drug dog to the scene unreasonably extends the time to write the traffic citation. *Rodriguez.* Here, the officer observed the defendant run a red light and lawfully stopped Wells. Police may use a drug dog to check any vehicle lawfully stopped, but because the wait for the dog extended the traffic stop beyond the time period needed to complete the reason for the stop, the dog sniff was invalid.

Checkpoint Stops

69. The motion to suppress should be denied. The answer turns on the legality of the checkpoint stop for information pertaining to a past crime. A police order to a motorist to stop is a Fourth Amendment seizure of the vehicle and all of its occupants. The stop must meet the reasonableness standard of the Fourth Amendment. The Supreme Court has upheld checkpoint stops to ensure that the motorist is properly licensed and the vehicle properly registered. Checkpoint stops may include testing the safety of the vehicle. These checkpoints are related to ensuring safety on the highway. Checkpoint stops are lawful, provided that police discretion is limited, and who is stopped is not left to the arbitrary exercise of discretion by the officers manning the checkpoint. *Delaware v. Prouse*, 440 U.S. 648 (1979). The same reasoning that led to license and safety checks now permits roadblocks to check for drunk drivers. *Michigan Dept. of State Police v. Sitz*, 496 U.S. 444 (1990). Although safety concerns are paramount here as they are in safety checks, the immediate result of a violation is a criminal charge. The Supreme Court disallowed a checkpoint stop for illegal drugs: "We have never approved a checkpoint program whose primary purpose was to detect evidence of wrongdoing." *City of Indianapolis v. Edmond*, 531 U.S. 32 (2000).

The Court, however, permitted a roadblock stop designed to obtain information from motorists about a fatal hit-and-run accident that occurred at the same location exactly one week earlier, very similar to the stop in the question. The Court used a balancing test to uphold the stop, finding that the importance of soliciting citizen information outweighed the defendant's Fourth Amendment right not to be seized without individualized suspicion. *Illinois v. Lidster*, 540 U.S. 419 (2004).

Once a checkpoint passes Fourth Amendment muster, the issue then focuses on the facts and circumstances which support singling out a particular motorist for further inquiry. Once a motorist is diverted from the regular flow of traffic past the checkpoint, the routine standardized stop of all vehicles becomes an investigative stop of a single vehicle for which particularized suspicion is required. Field sobriety tests may be administered only if reasonable suspicion to believe that the motorist is impaired develops from the initial minimal encounter. In turn, the results of the tests themselves can provide a basis for probable cause to arrest.

The police officer noticed Evans' impaired condition during the minimal and reasonable intrusion involved in handing each driver a handbill. Those facts and circumstances rose to the level of reasonable suspicion to allow for further inquiry. When Evans failed field sobriety tests, probable cause arose for the arrest and Breathalyzer test. The evidence pertaining to the field sobriety tests is admissible because the first officer had reasonable suspicion to believe that Evans was driving while impaired, justifying the order to the side of the road. The second officer had reasonable grounds to order the field sobriety tests, and then based on those test results, to arrest Evans. The Breathalyzer result is admissible because the field sobriety tests gave rise to probable cause.

Traffic Stops:
Duration and Scope of Inquiry

70.   **Answer (A) is the correct answer.** This question explores whether police can ask questions unrelated to the basis for a traffic stop and whether police may ask for permission to search a
stopped car for contraband. The seminal decision is *Ohio v. Robinette*, 519 U.S. 33 (1996). In
Robinette, the defendant was lawfully stopped for speeding and given a warning. After the officer
returned his license, he asked Robinette "One question before you get gone: Are you carrying
any illegal contraband in your car? Any weapons of any kind, drugs, anything like that?" After
Robinette said no, the officer asked to search his car, Robinette consented, and the ensuing
search revealed drugs in the car. The *Robinette* Court held that the stop was over and that Robinette was actually free to leave when his license was returned and that the officer did not need
to inform him that he was free to leave in order for his consent to a car search to be voluntary.
The facts in the question track those of *Robinette*. Whether the motorist knew it or not, he was
free to leave, as he was engaged in a consensual encounter with the officer. *Robinette*. Moreover,
even during a stop, police can ask unrelated questions so long as the inquiries "do not measur-
ably extend the duration of the stop." *Arizona v. Johnson*, 555 U.S. 323, 333 (2009).

Moreover, use of the drug-sniffing dog was constitutional both per *Illinois v. Caballes*, 543 U.S.
405 (2005), which allowed the use of dogs during car stops generally, and because the arrival of
the dog and its alert to Morgan's trunk did not extend the duration of what had become a constitutionally valid a police-motorist encounter (as noted above). In *Rodriguez v. United States*,
575 U.S. 348 (2015), the Court held that police may not extend an otherwise-completed traffic
stop, absent reasonable suspicion, in order to conduct a dog sniff. Under the facts presented, however, the stop was over (per *Robinette*), and Anderson's preliminary request of the drug dog and
its arrival when the consensual search was about to be undertaken did not extend the encounter.

Answer (B) is incorrect. As noted, the *Robinette* Court held that an officer need not expressly
tell an individual that a traffic stop is completed and that the motorist is free to leave (*i.e.*, that
the stop has evolved into a consensual encounter). Because the seizure had been transformed
into a consensual encounter, the officer was free to continue speaking with Morgan and request consent.

Answer (C) is incorrect. As noted, use of the dog was proper per *Caballes* and *Rodriguez*.

Answer (D) is incorrect. Although probable cause will allow a search of a vehicle without a
warrant or consent, the facts do not support a finding of probable cause. This was not an automobile exception search. Generalized beliefs that Frisbee golf players use marijuana, even

when combined with observed nervousness, do not equal probable cause that Morgan possessed marijuana.

Administrative Searches

71. **Answer (D) is correct.** The facts reveal that the housing inspector was conducting a routine safety inspection of the apartment. *Camara v. Municipal Court of City and County of San Francisco*, 387 U.S. 523 (1967). It is an "administrative search," undertaken for purposes other than to "search[ ] for evidence of crime." *Michigan v. Tyler*, 436 U.S. 499, 511–12 (1978). The Supreme Court initially held, in *Frank v. Maryland*, 359 U.S. 360, (1959), that the Fourth Amendment did not apply to municipal housing inspections. In *Frank*, the Court upheld the conviction of a resident who refused entry of inspectors who did not possess a warrant of any kind. *Camara* overruled *Frank*, at once finding that a resident can refuse a warrantless inspection (*contra Frank*) and that a warrant-based inspection is lawful and cannot be refused by a resident.

In *Camara*, a resident refused an inspector access to his premises multiple times, demanding that the inspector obtain a warrant. He was charged with refusing to permit a lawful inspection. Camara sued, arguing that the search had been unlawful without a warrant and that he could not be prosecuted for blocking an illegal warrantless search. The Supreme Court agreed. Although acknowledging that civil searches and seizures need not satisfy the Warrant Clause requirements governing criminal searches, the Court held that the inspectors were required to obtain an administrative warrant that satisfied a relaxed standard of probable cause. *See Camara*, 387 U.S. at 538 (holding that probable cause exists to support issuance of administrative warrant where "reasonable legislative or administrative standards for conducting an area inspection are satisfied with respect to a particular dwelling"). The Court in *Camara* emphasized that the availability of "individualized review" before a neutral decision-maker is vital to making an administrative search reasonable, as such pre-compliance review guards against the unconstrained exercises of "discretion of the official in the field." *Id.* at 532. The Court determined that while the standards for probable cause "will vary with the municipal program being enforced, [they] may be based on the passage of time, the nature of the building (e.g., a multifamily apartment house), or the condition of the entire area, but they will not necessarily depend upon specific knowledge of the condition of the particular dwelling." *Id.* at 538. The Court explicitly modified the probable cause test from the standard applied in criminal cases, reasoning that "[t]he warrant procedure is designed to guarantee that a decision to search private property is justified by a reasonable government interest. But reasonableness is still the ultimate standard. If a valid public interest justifies the intrusion contemplated, then there is probable cause to issue a suitably restricted search warrant." *Id.* at 538–39. A judge need only conclude that an established inspection policy exists and that the inspection sought fits within that program. Here, the inspector advised O'Malley that the inspection was pursuant to the established rules and policies of the city and pursuant to a set schedule and an administrative search warrant. O'Malley was required to grant access for this search even if the warrant lacked individual probable cause or reasonable suspicion of a safety violation.

Answer (A) is incorrect. Although the stress of exams is enough to push any law student over the edge, personal circumstances, inconvenience, or other reasons are not sufficient excuses to prohibit entry pursuant to a valid warrant. Because the safety inspection was authorized pursuant to the safety inspection warrant, O'Malley was required to allow the entry.

Answer (B) is incorrect. The standard for probable cause for safety inspections is different than a warrant to search for evidence for a crime. The question is not whether there is probable cause to believe that there is a housing code violation (or that evidence of criminal activity would be found). Rather, the question is whether there is probable cause to believe that the apartment is covered by the regulatory structure. *Camara.* Here, the test appears to be satisfied, requiring that the motion to dismiss should be denied.

Answer (C) is incorrect. Although Baldus's history could create suspicion that any of his apartments could be in violation of the housing code, such evidence is not necessary to justify an inspection. *Camara.* Specific probable cause for an administrative housing code search that the apartment is in violation is not the standard for probable cause, so this answer is incorrect.

Topic 30 | Answers

Special Needs Searches

72. The Fourth Amendment prohibits "unreasonable searches and seizures" by the government, and its protections extend to brief investigatory stops of persons or vehicles that fall short of traditional arrest. *Delaware v. Prouse*, 440 U.S. 648 (1979). Under the "border search" exception to the Fourth Amendment, however, government authorities situated at fixed (rather than roving) checkpoints on the nation's borders or the "functional equivalent" of a border can conduct routine warrantless stops and searches without any individualized reasonable suspicion or probable cause of wrongdoing. These searches and seizures are reasonable under the Fourth Amendment. *United States v. Martinez-Fuerte*, 428 U.S. 543 (1976). The rationale is that border checkpoints are designed to serve special needs, beyond the normal need for law enforcement, associated with monitoring the movement of people and items at the border. Here, the checkpoint is 42 miles from the Mexican border, but in *Martinez-Fuerte*, the Supreme Court upheld routine border checkpoint activity over 50 miles from the Mexican border. Later, in *United States v. Flores-Montano*, 541 U.S. 149 (2004), the Court held that a vehicle directed by border officials to a secondary inspection station could be searched (there, disassembling an auto gas tank), without reasonable suspicion or probable cause.

Agent Chokan specifically identified the red Explorer as having crossed the border based on the radio report and his training and experience justified the diversion of the Explorer to the secondary inspection site. Therefore, both the initial stop at the checkpoint and the move to and search at the secondary inspection site are constitutionally sound and the motion to suppress should be denied.

73. **Answer (B) is correct.** The validity of the food service worker testing program is linked entirely to those workers' proximity to the prisoners where a drug problem has been proven. Drug testing is a search under the Fourth Amendment because there is an expectation of privacy in one's body. Ordinarily, particularized suspicion is required for such an extensive intrusion. However, the "special needs" searches are valid as reasonable under the Fourth Amendment, even though there is no particularized need to search any individual.

The Supreme Court upheld special needs drug testing of customs agents where the testing was: (1) limited to specific positions of persons involved in the interdiction of illegal drugs at the borders; (2) employees were notified of the drug-testing requirement; and (3) test results were used for very limited purposes. *National Treasury Employees Union v. Von Raab*, 489 U.S. 656 (1989).

In the case at hand, the testing is limited to food service workers in prisons who, by definition, had or could have contact with prisoners, there was a specifically identified problem, and it was reasonable for the Department of Corrections to suspect the food service workers were the root of the problem. In *International Union Workers v. Winters*, 385 F.3d 1003 (6th Cir. 2004), the Sixth Circuit upheld a suspicionless drug testing program targeting non-custodial prison employees when, as in the facts, there was no demonstrated drug use among the targeted employees.

Answer (A) is incorrect, for reasons noted above.

Answer (C) is incorrect. The Supreme Court has upheld suspicionless drug testing of specific groups or class of people such as student athletes and students involved in extra-curricular activities. *Bd. of Educ. v. Earls*, 536 U.S. 822 (2002). The legality of such testing is not dependent upon its extension to other groups.

Answer (D) is incorrect. The Equal Protection Clause does not demand similar treatment for persons in different groups. Not extending the testing to other prison workers does not violate the Equal Protection Clause of the Fourteenth Amendment because the classification is rational. The Department of Corrections reasonably concluded that the food service workers were the likely cause of the drug problem and therefore the Equal Protection Clause was not violated by limiting testing to the problem group.

Consent Searches

74. **Answer (B) is correct.** Hutton voluntarily consented to a search of her purse. A court reviewing a government claim of consent must determine, on the totality of the circumstances, whether the consent was an act of free will, voluntarily given, and not the result of duress or coercion, express or implied. Although Hutton felt under pressure, this pressure did not come from the officer. Consent must be free from official coercion. *Schneckloth v. Bustamonte*, 412 U.S. 218 (1973). In this case, the pressure came from sources outside of the officer and therefore Hutton's consent was voluntary. Moreover, the officer did not need to inform Hutton that she had a right to refuse consent or that any refusal of consent on her part could not be used to create reasonable suspicion or probable cause of criminal wrongdoing. *United States v. Drayton*, 536 U.S. 194 (2002).

    Answer (A) is incorrect. Although Hutton felt pressured by her circumstances to consent and may even have complied in reflex to the question, her consent was not involuntary under Fourth Amendment standards. This does not require the same showing necessary to demonstrate a waiver of constitutional rights (as in *Miranda*) but simply a showing by the state that the consent was voluntary and free from express or implied coercion or duress. *Bustamonte*.

    Answer (C) is incorrect. Under the facts, the officer had no reasonable suspicion to stop Hutton under *Terry*. Even if he did, the belief that law students use marijuana would not justify a search of the contents of her purse since a *Terry* search is limited to a "frisk" for weapons.

    Answer (D) is incorrect. The Court has never imposed a Fourth Amendment warning akin to *Miranda* warnings. And, in particular, it has not required that police advise an individual that they have a right to refuse consent. Also, "[w]hile knowledge of the right to refuse consent is one factor to be taken into account, the government need not establish such knowledge as the sine qua non of an effective consent." *Bustamonte*. 412 U.S. at 227.

75. **Answer (A) is correct.** Mr. Dixon voluntarily gave consent to the search. The police can rely on consent as long as it was reasonable to believe the person had authority to consent to the search. *Illinois v. Rodriguez*, 497 U.S. 177 (1990). Because Officer Smaltz knew that Mr. Dixon was the spouse, Smaltz could rely on his apparent ability to give consent. *Rodriguez*. Indeed, it would appear that Mr. Dixon had actual authority to consent to a police search of the family home, and he could consent to the search without need to get consent from the absent Mrs. Dixon. *Fernandez v. California*, 571 U.S. 292 (2014).

    Answer (B) is incorrect. There is no evidence of an exigency that would eliminate the need for a warrant to search the home. But police do not need a warrant to search a home when an occupant voluntarily consents to the search.

Answer (C) is incorrect. The only questions in consent cases are (1) were the police reasonable in relying on the authority of the person giving consent, (2) was the consent voluntarily given, and (3) was the scope of consent given exceeded. Generally, the motivation of the person is irrelevant to the validity of the consent. *See Massachusetts v. Upton*, 466 U.S. 727 (1984) (reliability of tip not negated by expressed motivation of informant).

Answer (D) is incorrect. Although the home receives strong protection under the Fourth Amendment, a warrant is not always required to enter and search a home. Consent is a valid and accepted doctrine to permit a search even in cases in which a warrant could not be obtained. *Schneckloth v. Bustamonte*, 412 U.S. 218 (1973). In this case, Officer Smaltz had no basis to seek or obtain a warrant. This fact does not invalidate the consent given by Mr. Dixon.

76. The evidence found in the basement is inadmissible. When police rely on consent to search, they are limited by any conditions, express or implied, attached to the consent. *Florida v. Jimeno*, 500 U.S. 248 (1991). This includes limitations based on the scope of authority to grant consent. *United States v. Matlock*, 415 U.S. 164 (1974).

Because Mr. Dixon denied having actual authority to consent to the search, the question is whether it was reasonable for Officer Smaltz to rely on Mr. Dixon's consent when Mr. Dixon clearly stated that he did not have authority to enter the room. *Illinois v. Rodriquez*, 497 U.S. 177 (1990). Given Mr. Dixon's express statement that he was excluded from this area of the home and that only his wife had a key, the reasonable police officer would not rely on his consent since there was no claim of authority to give consent. *See Moore v. Andreno*, 505 F.3d 203 (2d Cir. 2007). Because Mr. Dixon lacked actual authority to consent and it was unreasonable for Officer Smaltz to rely on any claimed apparent authority to consent, the antiquities must be suppressed.

77. **Answer (B) is correct.** The police asked Ms. Coleman for permission to enter her home and talk with her in the living room. Her consent to enter was valid whether or not she knew she could refuse. However, she was not asked to consent to a search of her bedroom. If the police while lawfully present in the living room saw the drugs, the plain view exception would apply and allow for the drugs to be used in the government's case. However, by wandering into the bedroom and looking under the bed the officer exceeded the scope of the consent provided.

Answers (A) and (C) are incorrect. In this question, the state relies upon the defendant's consent to support the warrantless home entry and search. Whether a defendant knows that he or she may refuse a police request to conduct a search is one factor to be considered when determining the validity of any consent to search. The validity of consent to search should be determined on the totality of the circumstances, and a defendant's ignorance of his or her rights will not cause an otherwise valid consent to fail. *Ohio v. Robinette*, 519 U.S. 33 (1996); *Schneckloth v. Bustamonte*, 412 U.S. 218 (1973).

The concern presented by the question is whether the scope of the consent provided was exceeded. Thus, Answers (A) and (C) are both incorrect. Knowledge of the right to refuse is not irrelevant, but it is only one fact to consider in the analysis. As there are no other facts that support a conclusion that Ms. Coleman's consent to enter was otherwise involuntary, her consent to enter the home was valid but this does not equate to consent to search the bedroom.

Answer (D) is incorrect. Ordinarily, police need both probable cause and a search warrant to enter a home to conduct a search, absent a valid consent or exigent circumstances. Probable cause and the warrant requirement are not alternative requirements; a warrant should not issue but upon probable cause. Therefore, the existence of probable cause, without some exigency, would not support a warrantless search. Additionally, the report probably would not rise to the level of probable cause without additional supporting information. *Illinois v. Gates*, 462 U.S. 213 (1983).

78. **Answer (A) is correct.** The question turns upon whether the apartment manager had actual or apparent authority to consent to a search of Dennis' apartment. As a general rule, a landlord or manager lacks authority to consent to the search of a tenant's residence, absent abandonment, contract, termination of the lease, or eviction. *Chapman v. United States*, 365 U.S. 610 (1961); *United States v. Elliott*, 50 F.3d 180 (2d Cir. 1995). A reasonably trained police officer would know this, and it was unreasonable for the officer to search based on the manager's consent. *Cf. Stoner v. California*, 376 U.S. 483 (1969) (holding that hotel clerk lacked authority to consent to search of defendant's hotel room).

Answer (B) is incorrect. While police did lack probable cause, even if they had probable cause, they would still need lawful consent or assert an exigency of some kind that would excuse the search warrant requirement.

Answer (C) is incorrect. The fact that the property manager had access to the apartment and even had authority to enter it under limited circumstances (*e.g.*, to make repairs) does not grant him legal authority to allow the police to enter and search the apartment.

Answer (D) is incorrect. Dennis was renting the apartment, but this does not eliminate his expectation of privacy. The apartment is his home and is protected to the same degree that it would be protected if he owned the home. Dennis did not have an expectation of privacy that would keep the property manager from entering the apartment within the scope of the need to manage the property, but this did not eliminate Dennis' expectation of privacy that the police would not enter and search the apartment.

79. In *Georgia v. Randolph*, 547 U.S. 103 (2006), the Court held that a refusal of consent by a physically present resident trumped the grant of another physically present resident who consented. In *Fernandez v. California*, 571 U.S. 292 (2014), the Court addressed the different situation where a physically present spouse objects to a house search, but police thereafter remove the objector from the premises on an "objectively reasonable" basis, and then conduct a search based on the consent of a fellow resident. The Court upheld the search because of both the language of *Randolph* requiring presence and the practical realities of creating a rule to guide police in determining when the refusal to consent would expire.

Here, as in *Fernandez*, Mr. Masten was lawfully arrested (per the arrest warrant) and police had a valid medical reason to transport him from the scene. The evidence of sexual abuse found in the closet is admissible. (Note: conceivably, in the absence of consent, a *Maryland v. Buie* "protective sweep" of the premises, including the bedroom closet, would be permissible but would not permit police to look inside the small rectangular box in the closet. No person posing a potential threat to police could hide in the small box.)

Electronic Eavesdropping

80. The Fourth Amendment provides protection to communications including electronic communications. *Katz v. United States*, 389 U.S. 347 (1967). Because of the unique nature of electronic communications Congress provided enhanced protections in 18 U.S.C. § 2510 et seq, Title III of the Omnibus Crime Bill and the Electronic Communications Privacy Act. This statute imposes increased procedural and substantive requirements on wiretap warrants beyond the base requirements of the Fourth Amendment. Title III warrants must still be predicated on probable cause but also require a showing of necessity to intercept the communication, that is, that other investigative means have been unsuccessful in obtaining the information, and interception is allowed only so long as is necessary and in no event for longer than 30 days.

Title III is implicated because it applies not only to telephone calls but to all communication over interstate networks. Also, the "mirror" computer actually captured the communications as they were being transmitted rather than simply reviewing the image or communication after receipt. Communications that are obtained from means other than interception while being transmitted are exempt from Title III limits. *See Goldman v. United States*, 316 U.S. 129 (1942) (addressing a statute similar but predating the Wiretap Act).

The hacking into the kidconnexion server was not expressly authorized by the warrant. While it might be better policy for the issuing court to authorize specific conduct in intercepting the communication, the Court found it "implicit" in the warrant that covert entry into the target area is authorized in order to execute the warrant. *Dalia v. United States*, 441 U.S. 238 (1979). The hacking into kidconnexion is similarly implicit in executing the warrant in this case.

Under the facts presented, the Title III warrant was justified and search was conducted within the scope of the warrant. Also, the 15 day duration was well within the time limit imposed by Title III. The evidence is admissible.

Exclusionary Rule

81. The Supreme Court will deny the defendant's appeal. The Fourth Amendment requirements are limited to requiring warrants (when applicable) and the probable cause or reasonable suspicion standards. The police officer did not violate the Fourth Amendment when she arrested the defendant on probable cause even though the arrest was prohibited by state law. The Fourth Amendment does not impose jurisdictional restrictions on the authority of police. When a state chooses to impose such a limit, and provide its citizens more protection, the limit does not attach to the Fourth Amendment. *Virginia v. Moore*, 553 U.S. 164 (2008).

The Supreme Court has held that the federal Constitution requires the exclusion of evidence only when a particular search or seizure violates the Fourth Amendment. States remain free to fashion their own remedies when a particular procedure violates only state law. They may choose to exclude evidence in such cases, but exclusion flows from the state law and is not mandated under the United States Constitution. "While a State is free as a matter of its own law to impose greater restrictions on police activity than those this Court holds to be necessary upon federal constitutional standards, it may not impose such greater restrictions as a matter of federal constitutional law when this Court specifically refrains from imposing them." *Arkansas v. Sullivan*, 532 U.S. 769 (2001).

The trial judge erred when deciding that the arrest violated the defendant's Fourth Amendment rights. The officer violated the higher standard imposed by state law. The state courts are free to decide, but are not compelled, to exclude the evidence under state law. Because the state court applied the Fourth Amendment (not its own Constitution), the Supreme Court will reverse based on *Virginia v. Moore* and an erroneous application of federal Fourth Amendment law.

Good Faith Exception

82. **Answer (C) is correct.** The Court has limited the reach of the exclusionary rule by adopting a good faith exception. Under the exception, evidence may not be excluded from a criminal trial if exclusion would not deter the illegal police practice in question. *Herring v. United States*, 555 U.S. 135 (2009). "To trigger, the exclusionary rule, police conduct must be sufficiently deliberate that exclusion can meaningfully deter it, and sufficiently culpable that such deterrence is worth the price paid by the justice system ... [T]he exclusionary rule serves to deter deliberate, reckless or grossly negligent conduct, or in some circumstances recurring or systemic negligence." *Herring*, 555 U.S. at 144. *Herring* states that the key is whether a reasonably well trained officer would have known that the search was illegal in view of all the circumstances at the time.

In *Herring*, as in the question, police arrested and then searched an individual on the basis of a faulty arrest warrant in a negligently maintained database, which did not satisfy any of the aforementioned exceptions. Officer Alzahabi, acting as a reasonably well-trained police officer, was entitled to rely on the records check that revealed the arrest warrant and, therefore, the heroin found as a result of the search conducted incident to arrest is admissible.

Answer (A) is incorrect. Officer Alzahabi lacked probable cause to believe that the woman at the bus stop was engaged in or had been engaged in criminal activity. The sole basis for arrest was the (faulty) arrest warrant.

Answer (B) is incorrect. The issue is not whether the warrant was valid or invalid, but whether Officer Alzahabi's reliance on the warrant was reasonable.

Answer (D) is incorrect. As noted, the *Herring* Court held that some degree of law enforcement culpability in failing to maintain records greater than negligence might render reliance on a record inappropriate. *Herring v. United States*, 555 U.S. 135 (2009). If the police were reckless or maybe even grossly negligent in maintaining the records, then the exclusionary rule would apply. Also, if for some reason Officer Alzahabi had reasonable basis to not rely on the accuracy of the records, then the arrest would be invalid. But that is not the situation in this case. His reliance was reasonable under the good faith exception to the exclusionary rule.

83. The evidence is inadmissible. The Fourth Amendment exclusionary rule will not be applied to bar the use in the prosecution's case-in-chief of evidence obtained by officers acting in objectively reasonable reliance on a search warrant issued by a detached and neutral magistrate but ultimately found to be unsupported by probable cause. However, a police officer may not rely on "a warrant based on an affidavit so lacking in indicia of probable cause as to render

official belief in its existence entirely unreasonable." Moreover, "a warrant may be so facially deficient — *i.e.*, in failing to particularize the place to be searched or the things to be seized — that the executing officers cannot reasonably presume it to be valid." *United States v. Leon*, 468 U.S. 897 (1984). The test for the good-faith exception is "whether a reasonably well trained officer would have known that the search was illegal despite the magistrate's authorization."

Here, the "good faith" exception would not apply. The first issue is whether the search warrant was supported by adequate probable cause. In reviewing a lower court's conclusion of probable cause, the duty of the appellate court is to ensure that the issuer of the warrant had a "substantial basis" to determine that probable cause existed. "The task of the issuing magistrate is simply to make a practical, common-sense decision whether, given all the circumstances set forth in the affidavit before him, including the 'veracity' and 'basis of knowledge' of persons supplying hearsay information, there is a fair probability that contraband or evidence of a crime will be found in a particular place. And the duty of a reviewing court is simply to ensure that the magistrate had a 'substantial basis for conclud[ing]' that probable cause existed." *Illinois v. Gates*, 462 U.S. 213 (1983). Similarly, reviewing courts may not substitute their own judgment for that of the issuing magistrate by conducting a *de novo* determination as to whether the affidavit contains sufficient probable cause upon which the reviewing court would issue the search warrant.

Here, the officer's affidavit sets out information supplied by the informant. Other than the allegation of "possibl[e]" possession of drugs and "is dealing" cocaine from the house, the information related only to the identification of the defendant and his address. Both of these facts were verified by observation of the officer. Further, the informant's information regarding a vehicle driven by appellant was confirmed by observation of the officer. These facts do not provide verification of drug activity or support the veracity of the informant. The fact that an ounce of cocaine was seized at the same location two years before does not bolster a finding of probable cause that current drug activity was afoot.

Even if the affidavit's conclusory representation that the informant had provided reliable information in the past satisfies the informant veracity requirement, the affidavit lacks supporting evidence of the informant's basis of knowledge of the suspected criminal activity in the home (for instance, having seen cocaine in Washington's home during a visit). The affidavit was so deficient that the magistrate did not have a substantial basis for finding probable cause.

The fact that no drugs were found is irrelevant to the analysis. A review of the sufficiency of a warrant is made looking at the time the warrant was issued. Hindsight cannot be used to justify probable cause or to remove it.

84. The court will need to assess whether the government agents acted with an objectively reasonable good faith belief that their conduct was lawful. After the Court's landmark decision in *Leon*, applying the good faith exception to an invalid search warrant, the exception has been applied to evidence obtained from warrantless searches later held to be unconstitutional. In *Illinois v. Krull*, 480 U.S. 340 (1987), for example, the Court applied the exception where officers had "act[ed] in objectively reasonable reliance upon a statute authorizing warrantless administrative searches, but where the statute [was] ultimately found to violate the Fourth Amendment." *Id.* at 342. The Court reasoned that if a "statute is subsequently declared unconstitutional, excluding evidence obtained pursuant to it prior to such a judicial declaration will not deter future Fourth Amendment violations by an officer who has simply fulfilled his responsibility to enforce the statute as written." *Id.* at 350. More recently, the Court applied the good faith exception to a warrantless search that complied with then-binding appellate precedent that was later overruled. *See Davis v. United States*, 564 U.S. 229 (2011). In *Davis*, police conducted a vehicle search in reasonable reliance on binding precedent (*Belton v. New York*), but several years later—while the defendant's criminal appeal was still pending—the Court held that such searches were unconstitutional (in *Arizona v. Gant*). The Court applied the good faith exception, reasoning that the deterrence function of the exclusionary rule would not be served when police act on the basis of settled precedent.

Here, of the two aforementioned exceptions, that announced in *Krull* would seem most fitting. As in *Krull*, law enforcement relied on a statute later deemed unconstitutional. And, much as in *Krull*, the investigators who obtained Rungun's CSLI in 2016 conducted a warrantless search authorized by a statute that was not deemed unconstitutional until after the search—indeed, two years later. In short, as courts have held on the question, the court here will be justified in rejecting the motion to suppress based on the good faith exception. *See, e.g., United States v. Beverly*, 943 F.3d 225 (5th Cir. 2019).

Interrogation and Confession: Custody

85. *Miranda* requires that a suspect be given warnings prior to custodial interrogation: and that he has a right to remain silent; that anything he says can and will be used against him; and that he has a right to the presence of an attorney, either retained or appointed. The purpose of the warnings is to alleviate the inherent coerciveness of custodial interrogation. If a suspect is not in custody or is not being interrogated, the warnings need not be given. Donald was not given *Miranda* warnings prior to the interview. If the interview was "custodial interrogation," *Miranda* was violated and the statements inadmissible.

The issue is whether he was in "custody" at the time he made the statements at issue. A reviewing court considers all the circumstances surrounding the interrogation. The relevant inquiry is whether a reasonable person would have believed during the interrogation that he was in custody. *Miranda* defines custody as occurring when a person "is taken into custody or otherwise deprived of his freedom of action in any significant way." The analysis is an objective one, which is not dependent on the subjective view of the suspect or the officer(s). Neither the subjective belief of the suspect nor the interrogator is relevant in this analysis. *J.D.B. v. North Carolina*, 564 U.S. 261 (2011); *Stansury v. California*, 511 U.S. 318 (1994). *See also Thompson v. Keohane*, 516 U.S. 99, 112 (1995) ("the court must apply an objective test to resolve the ultimate inquiry: was there a formal arrest or restraint on freedom of movement of the degree associated with formal arrest").

In this case, several factors point in opposite directions. Donald was told that he was not under arrest and was free to go. He and his family went to the social worker's office (rather than to the police station); his wife was present in the room during the interrogation; and he was permitted to leave and return home at the conclusion of the interview. The last fact is often considered critical and suggests the interview was not custodial.

However, other facts support an argument that Donald was in custody. Donald and Mrs. Daffo did not wish to go to the office in the first place: they were compelled to show up upon threat that Sandra might be removed from their home if they did not attend the interview. The atmosphere during the interview was physically intimidating.

While the fact that Donald was not arrested and was permitted to return home at the conclusion of the interview weighs against a finding of custody, a stronger case can be made for custody. Everything about this interview reasonably conveyed to Donald that he had no choice but to submit to the meeting and questioning. The atmosphere prior to the interview and during the interrogation was coercive. During the interrogation, a reasonable person in Donald's position likely would not have believed that he could terminate the interview and leave. *Miranda* warnings should have been given. Donald's statements are therefore inadmissible. *Howes v. Fields*, 565 U.S. 499 (2012); *Stansbury v. California*, 511 U.S. 318 (1994).

86. **Answer (D) is correct.** The *Miranda* warnings are intended to alleviate the coercive atmosphere that arises when a person in custody is subject to police interrogation. Although Carrie undoubtedly felt coerced when she was detained and questioned by the store detective, the *Miranda* rights are not applicable. The store detective is not a government employee and is not subject to the *Miranda* requirements. *See, e.g., Paige v. State*, 126 A.3d 793, 804 (Md. App. 2015) ("as many courts recognize, private security guards are not required to give the *Miranda* warnings when interrogating individuals").

    Answer (C) is incorrect. The facts presented would support a plausible claim that Carrie was in fact in custody. *Stansbury v. California*, 511 U.S. 318 (1994). However, it remains the case that the store detective was not a government agent.

    Answer (A) is incorrect because the store detective was not a government agent and is not limited by the *Miranda* requirements. *Miranda* was designed to prevent pressure by government personnel, not by private employees.

    Answer (B) is incorrect also because there was no government or police behavior. The store detective was a private employee not subject to the same restrictions that would apply to a police officer. This result does not seem fair when often private security guards are licensed by the state. However, the store detective's behavior was certainly coercive, and could trigger due process scrutiny if he had been a state actor. *Cf. Colorado v. Connelly*, 479 U.S. 157 (1986).

Interrogation and Confession: Public Safety Exception

87. Answer (B) is the correct answer. Following an arrest police may question an arrestee without first giving *Miranda* warnings when they face "overriding considerations of public safety." *New York v. Quarles*, 467 U.S. 649 (1984). The public safety exception to *Miranda* applies when an objectively reasonable police officer would believe that danger to members of the public or to the police warrants immediate action. In *Quarles*, police responded to a report of a woman being sexually assaulted by a man with a gun. When they found the suspect and arrested him, in a grocery store, they immediately asked him where the gun was located. The suspect so indicated and his response was admitted in the government's case-in-chief. In the facts here, police similarly asked Charles where his gun was, and in going to that location found contraband, which is admissible under the "plain view" exception to the warrant requirement.

Answer (A) is incorrect. A search of the trunk incident to arrest would not be permitted both because of the delay and because police cannot use the exception to search the trunk of a car. Although the arresting officer possibly could have searched the passenger compartment of the vehicle incident to the arrest of the driver, the authority to conduct the search no longer existed once the driver was removed from the scene of the arrest. Moreover, a search of the vehicle incident to the arrest of the driver or passenger does not extend to the trunk of the vehicle. *New York v. Belton*, 453 U.S. 454 (1981).

Answer (C) is incorrect because the officer was operating under the public safety exception to *Miranda*.

Answer (D) is incorrect because whether Officer Charles was legally entitled to possess the gun does not bear on whether its location in a public area posed an immediate safety risk. The search of the trunk of the vehicle was lawful. Officer Charles' admission that the gun was in the trunk of the car provided probable cause for police to search the trunk, under the automobile exception, to find and remove the gun. Once they had legal authority to search the trunk, evidence found in the trunk in plain view became admissible at trial. This was not an inventory search under standardized procedures because the car was not impounded. This was a search for a specific item.

Interrogation

88. **Answer (D) is correct.** Police must give *Miranda* warnings prior to interrogating a person who is in custody. *Miranda v. Arizona*, 384 U.S. 436 (1966). However, answers to questions that are asked as part of a standardized booking process are admissible without prior administration of *Miranda* warnings. Videotaped answers to basic background matters (so-called pedigree questions — names, address, height, weight, etc.) are not rendered inadmissible simply because the slurred nature of the defendant's speech is incriminating. The line, which is not altogether clear, is crossed when a defendant's response is incriminating, not just because of delivery but because the content of the answer demonstrates the defendant's cognitive impairment, an element of the offense. The Supreme Court held that the line was crossed when a defendant, arrested for drunk driving, could not provide police with the correct date of his sixth birthday, and the content of his answer supported an answer that his mental state was confused. *Pennsylvania v. Muniz*, 496 U.S. 582 (1990). Here, police asked Brewster when he would turn a certain age, a question that seeks to discern mental impairment, which would likely be subject to suppression.

    Answer (A) is incorrect. Even though drunk driving certainly poses a serious threat to public safety, the police were not motivated by exigency. Standardized booking questions are exempted from the *Miranda* warning requirement. It is only when a question is asked that is not a standardized booking question that *Miranda* comes into play. Here, when the officer asked Brewster when he would turn age 52, the officer was not seeking booking information. He was attempting to demonstrate the confused nature of Brewster's mind, later used as evidence of intoxication rather than for ordinary booking purposes. That question would not be exempted from the *Miranda* requirement.

    Answer (B) is incorrect. The question concerning the date of Brewster's 52nd birthday would likely be beyond the scope of permissible routine booking questions. It was not a pedigree question exempted from the *Miranda* requirement. The question was intended to demonstrate that Brewster was impaired.

    Answer (C) is incorrect. The questions regarding name and address were within the permissible scope of the routine booking question exception. Police are not required to issue *Miranda* warnings immediately following an arrest. Warnings must be issued following an arrest and prior to police interrogation. If police never interrogate an arrested person, they need not give *Miranda* warnings.

89. **Answer (A) is correct.** The *Miranda* warnings were intended to alleviate the inherent coerciveness of custodial interrogation. "The fundamental import of the privilege while an indi-

vidual is in custody is not whether he is allowed to talk to the police without the benefit of warnings and counsel, but whether he can be interrogated.... Volunteered statements of any kind are not barred by the Fifth Amendment and their admissibility is not affected by our holding today." *Miranda v. Arizona*, 384 U.S. 436, 478 (1966). Police are not obligated to stop a suspect who volunteers an incriminating statement. Here, Danny offered the incriminating information of his own volition, without prodding or questioning by police. No *Miranda* warnings were needed because Danny, though under arrest, was not interrogated.

Answer (B) is incorrect. If Danny's statement had been in response to a police officer's question, the statement would be inadmissible even if prosecutors could prove that Danny had prior knowledge of the *Miranda* warnings. *Miranda* warnings must be provided even when police have reason to believe that the person they have in custody is aware of the contents of the *Miranda* warnings. The Supreme Court believed that the inherent coerciveness of custody must be mitigated by the warnings prior to any interrogation. Here, of course, there was no interrogation when Danny confessed.

Answers (C) and (D) are incorrect. *Miranda* requires that a suspect be warned prior to custodial interrogation. Unlike on television, police are not obligated to issue the warnings at the time of arrest or while transporting an arrestee to the jail. Warnings must be given prior to interrogation. If, as here, the arrestee is never interrogated, police need not administer the *Miranda* warnings.

90. The confession is likely admissible. First, we must analyze whether Hothead was subjected to a custodial interrogation in violation of *Miranda*. As Hothead was under arrest, he was in custody, but the defense would have a harder time convincing a court that the berating qualified as police interrogation. Warnings must be given prior to any custodial interrogation. *Miranda v. Arizona*, 384 U.S. 436 (1966). The defendant was not advised of his *Miranda* rights until after he had confessed to the crime. But was he interrogated by police?

Interrogation is defined as "express questioning or its functional equivalent." *Rhode Island v. Innis*, 446 U.S. 291 (1980). Functional equivalent was further defined as "any words or actions on the part of police (other than those normally attendant to arrest and custody) that the police should know are *reasonably likely to elicit an incriminating response* from the suspect." *Id.* at 301 (emphasis added). In determining whether police conduct constitutes interrogation, the courts apply an objective standard.

Hothead would argue that there was no reason to subject him to the victim's family's abuse other than to provoke an emotional response. He was forced to sit close to the family for 20 minutes. Unlike *Innis*, where the Court held that a reasonable officer would not have anticipated that the defendant would respond to a worried general statement about handicapped children finding a gun used in a cabdriver's killing, here police were aware of the abusive situation that they allowed to unfold.

However, *Arizona v. Mauro*, 481 U.S. 520 (1987), cuts the other way and is arguably more on point. In *Mauro*, the Court focused on the absence of police conduct in doing the interrogation. The police allowed a husband and wife to talk, with an officer in the room with a tape recorder, and the husband made incriminating statements. The statements were admissible because, even though the police knew that statements were likely, the conduct of police did not constitute an interrogation. It is likely the same result will be found here because the police did not interrogate Hothead and there is no evidence the victim's family was in any way acting as a government agent during their encounter with Hothead. Therefore, the first confession ("I will tell you how and why I murdered my girlfriend") is likely admissible.

Now, as to the second confession. Surely, if the officer asked a question, perhaps even a general one such as "So tell me about the murder of your girlfriend," *Miranda* warnings should have been given since it was likely custodial interrogation. Under that scenario, the second incriminating statement would be inadmissible. Here, however, the officer seemingly did nothing of the sort. Hothead might argue that his first confession was involuntarily secured in violation of due process and that the second confession should be excluded if it were derived from the first. *Oregon v. Elstad*, 470 U.S. 298 (1985); *Spano v. New York*, 360 U.S. 315 (1959). If that is the case, his second statement would be inadmissible. *Oregon v. Elstad*, 470 U.S. 298 (1985). However, a reviewing court would not likely find that the circumstances experienced by Hothead violated due process. No one touched Hothead and the police were nearby to protect him if necessary. There is no evidence that the second confession was the product of coercion or the result of interrogation by police.

91. **Answer (A) is correct.** *Miranda* is intended to alleviate the inherent coercion associated with custodial interrogation. Hothead was in custody and was being interrogated by the police, but he did not know it. The Supreme Court has said that when a person does not know he is being interrogated by a police officer, even while in custody, there is absent the inherent coercion attendant upon interrogation by a person known to the defendant to be a police officer. Therefore, the questioning lacks the pressure brought to bear when a suspect is facing a police officer who demands answers. Even though Hothead was questioned by a police officer while in a jail cell, he thought he was dealing with someone in the same situation as he. Consequently, there was no police interrogation that would have required *Miranda* warnings. *Illinois v. Perkins*, 496 U.S. 292 (1990). Rules for jail house snitches under the Sixth Amendment's right to counsel are discussed below.

Answer (B) is incorrect because Hothead did not volunteer his confession but rather made the confession in response to questioning by his cellmate. It was not a spontaneous statement.

Answers (C) and (D) are incorrect. Because the defendant did not know he was being questioned by the police, there was no need to inform him of his *Miranda* rights before the questioning, and the deceit and trickery by the undercover officer did not create a coercive custodial environment requiring the protection of *Miranda* warnings.

Miranda Warnings

92. The Supreme Court in *Miranda v. Arizona* stated that "when an individual is taken into custody or otherwise deprived of his freedom by the authorities in any significant way and is subjected to questioning, the privilege against self-incrimination is jeopardized. Procedural safeguards must be employed to protect the privilege." These safeguards require that the suspect be advised prior to any questioning "that he has the right to remain silent, that anything he says can be used against him in a court of law, that he has the right to the presence of an attorney, and that if he cannot afford an attorney one will be appointed for him prior to any questioning if he so desires." *Miranda v. Arizona*, 384 U.S. 436, 479 (1966).

The warnings given to the defendant in the question are unclear, but likely adequate. While the detective informed the defendant that he had the right to seek a lawyer's advice prior to answering any questions, the language also suggests that he was not entitled to appointed counsel until charges are filed against him and he appeared in court. Although the *Miranda* warnings are easy enough to read precisely as they were written, the Supreme Court said, "This Court has never indicated that the 'rigidity' of *Miranda* extends to the precise formulation of the warnings given a criminal defendant." Rather, the Supreme Court has been satisfied if the police officer giving the warnings touches all the bases. *Florida v. Powell*, 559 U.S. 50 (2010); *California v. Prysock*, 453 U.S. 355 (1981).

In a decision involving essentially the same warnings as in the question, the Supreme Court concluded that the warnings, as a whole, conveyed the information required by *Miranda*. *Duckworth v. Eagan*, 492 U.S. 195 (1989).

93. **Answer (C) is correct.** A *Miranda* waiver must be knowingly, voluntarily, and intelligently made. The relinquishment of the right must be voluntary, not the result of intimidation, coercion, or deception. Here, the question turns on whether the defendant made a "knowing" and "intelligent" waiver when the officer failed to educate him regarding the full scope of questioning that was to ensue. He did make a valid waiver of his *Miranda* rights.

Waiver must be made with a full awareness of both the nature of the right being abandoned and the consequences of that decision. The defendant was aware that he could remain silent and that anything he said could be used against him. The knowingly requirement is limited to knowledge of constitutional rights, not every possible consequence of a waiver of the privilege. Police need not inform a suspect of all of the crimes they will question him about. *Colorado v. Spring*, 479 U.S. 564 (1987). *Miranda* is a general protection and the warnings and waiver apply to any and all areas of an interrogation.

Answer (A) is incorrect. Unless the suspect limits the scope of the interrogation, the scope of the waiver extends to any and all criminal activity of possible interest to interrogating officers. A waiver of *Miranda* rights is not offense specific. *See, e.g., United States v. Soliz*, 129 F.3d 499 (9th Cir. 1997).

Answer (B) is incorrect because this kind of trickery and deceit is clearly permissible. The legitimacy of a *Miranda* waiver is not affected by police trickery in luring a suspect into believing that the interrogation is about one crime when, in reality, they are most interested in a different crime.

Answer (D) is incorrect because the statement is too broad. Deceit and trickery in not informing the defendant of the subject matter of the interrogation are permissible, but deceit and trickery would not be permissible in advising a suspect about his *Miranda* rights, such as by telling him he had no right to counsel during the interrogation. The latter could render the waiver involuntary.

Waiver of *Miranda* Rights

94. **Answer (D) is correct and the best answer.** The Supreme Court has held that a suspect need not be informed that counsel has been retained for him and has sought to speak to him. *Moran v. Burbine*, 475 U.S. 412 (1986). According to the Court, "[n]o doubt the additional information would have been useful to [the suspect].... But we have never read the Constitution to require that the police supply a suspect with a flow of information to help him calibrate his self interest in deciding whether to speak or stand by his rights." *Id.* at 422. Stone waived counsel when he replied, "I guess so" after being asked whether he was prepared to waive his rights.

    Answer (A) is incorrect because Stone's half-hearted "I guess so" waiver of *Miranda* rights was a valid waiver. *Berghuis v. Thompkins*, 560 U.S. 370 (2010); *Davis v. United States*, 512 U.S. 452 (1994); *North Carolina v. Butler*, 441 U.S. 369 (1979). Had Stone wanted to invoke his Fifth Amendment right to counsel, he would have had to do so unambiguously, which did not occur here. Again, a suspect need not be told that counsel has been retained and wishes to speak with him in order for a waiver to be valid. *Moran v. Burbine.*

    Answer (B) is correct but not the best answer because it did not indicate he waived his *Miranda* rights.

    Answer (C) is incorrect based on *Moran v. Burbine*. Stone did not unambiguously assert his right to counsel until it was too late. He had already received and waived his *Miranda* warnings and confessed.

95. The motion to suppress likely will be granted. Dealer clearly invoked his *Miranda* right to counsel. Once an accused makes a clear indication that he wishes to consult with an attorney, police must accept that assertion and cease interrogation. Police cannot seek to undermine the clarity of the invocation by asking follow-up questions or by talking the suspect into changing his mind. An accused's post-request responses to further interrogation may not be used to cast doubt on the clarity of the initial request for counsel. *Smith v. Illinois*, 469 U.S. 91 (1984).

    When a suspect invokes the right to counsel, police must stop the interrogation. Here, after Dealer clearly invoked his Fifth Amendment right to counsel, the detective improperly initiated the discussion about the crime, leading Dealer to agree to further interrogation. Dealer's right to counsel was violated.

First Confession without Warnings

96. **Answer (C) is correct.** The first confession is inadmissible because the officer failed to comply with the *Miranda* requirements when Freddy was in custody (arrested) and interrogated (subject to police behavior reasonably likely to elicit an incriminating response). The second confession is admissible because it was taken at the police station, after two hours, by a different officer, and preceded by *Miranda* warnings and Freddy's waiver. The Supreme Court has said "that a suspect who has once responded to unwarned uncoercive questioning is not thereby disabled from waiving his rights and confessing after he has been given the requisite *Miranda* warnings." *Oregon v. Elstad*, 470 U.S. 298 (1985).

   Here, the trickery engaged in by the officer regarding the fingerprints would not likely lead to a finding that the first confession was involuntary under the Due Process Clause. Also, *Elstad* held that in such a situation a suspect need not be told that his first confession would likely be inadmissible.

   Answer (A) is incorrect. The first confession is inadmissible, but the second confession is likely admissible because for reasons noted above. The detective administered *Miranda* warnings before the second confession and there was a complete break between the first statement and the second.

   Answer (B) is incorrect. Freddy was under arrest and handcuffed at the time of the first confession, making the interrogation "custodial" despite occurring in Freddy's home. The first statement was given by Freddy in response to the arresting officer's falsehood that was reasonably likely to elicit an incriminating response. Even though the officer did not ask Freddy a question, his comment was the functional equivalent of interrogation because a reasonable officer should have known that his comment would provoke a possibly incriminating response. *Rhode Island v. Innis*, 446 U.S. 291 (1980). Thus, the first confession was inadmissible as a violation of *Miranda*. The second confession is admissible, as noted above.

   Answer (D) is incorrect. An incriminating statement secured in violation of *Miranda* requirements is rarely harmless error. The only time harmless error may become an issue is if there is other overwhelming evidence of guilt, and the reviewing court is convinced beyond a reasonable doubt that the confession did not play a role in the jury's determination of guilt. Here, there are no facts indicating that the first confession was harmless error.

97. Presuming Ramirez was in custody when he was at the police station, the next question would be whether he was interrogated by the two detectives. The answer would appear to be yes. Therefore, under *Oregon v. Elstad*, the first incriminating statement, provided by Ramirez without *Miranda* warnings or a waiver, would be inadmissible. What of the second, fuller in-

criminating statement? Here, we must consider whether the facts align with the police behavior condemned by the Court in *Missouri v. Seibert*, 542 U.S. 600 (2004).

The fact pattern raises concern that the second statement was the product of the "two-step interrogation" technique "used in a calculated way to undermine the *Miranda* warning" without any "curative measures." *Missouri v. Seibert*, 542 U.S. 600, 622 (2004) (Kennedy, J., concurring). Here, unlike in *Seibert*, there exists no demonstrable evidence that the police were intentionally evading *Miranda*. Also, unlike in *Seibert*, where only 20 minutes separated the first and second confessions, an hour passed; also, unlike in *Seibert*, a different detective took over. Yet, like in *Seibert*, the second interrogator made reference to the earlier incriminating statement. In short, it's a tough call, but the absence of evidence of calculated effort to evade *Miranda* makes it unlikely that the second statement — provided after a valid waiver — would be barred. *Elstad*.

Exercising *Miranda* Rights

98. Answer (C) is correct. A suspect who invokes the right to consult with a lawyer before interrogation must do so unequivocally. Only a clear invocation of the right imposes a duty upon the police to cease any attempt at questioning. Police are not required to ask any clarifying questions. *Davis v. United States*, 512 U.S. 452 (1994). Here, the suspect failed to effectively indicate that she wanted to see an attorney. The detective was not obligated to answer the suspect's question or pursue whether the suspect really wanted an attorney.

Answer (A) is incorrect. The Supreme Court has held that "waiver can be clearly inferred from the actions and words of the person interrogated." Here, the suspect's nod of the head in response to the detective's question would satisfy the waiver requirement. *Berghuis v. Thompkins*, 560 U.S. 370 (2010); *North Carolina v. Butler*, 441 U.S. 369 (1979).

Answer (B) is incorrect because a reviewing court would not interpret the suspect's statement and question as a clear invocation of the right to counsel.

Answer (D) is incorrect because the suspect never invoked her right to counsel. The suspect's comment that "Maybe I should talk with a lawyer?" followed by her question to the officer may have meant that she wanted to see a lawyer, but it would not satisfy the requirement of an unequivocal assertion of the right. If the reviewing court interpreted the suspect's statement as an assertion of the right to counsel, that assertion would not be revoked by her nod of the head in response to the detective's question whether she was ready to proceed with the interrogation. If a suspect asserts the right to counsel, all questioning must stop until the suspect has the opportunity to consult with a lawyer *or* the suspect initiates discussion about the crime. *Oregon v. Bradshaw*, 462 U.S. 1039 (1983); *Edwards v. Arizona*, 451 U.S. 477 (1981).

Invoking the Right to Remain Silent

99. **Answer (B) is correct.** The Supreme Court said that a suspect who has waived *Miranda* rights and agreed to questioning may stop the interrogation at any time. "Once warnings have been given, the subsequent procedure is clear. If the individual indicates in any manner, at any time prior to or during questioning, that he wishes to remain silent, the interrogation must cease. At this point he has shown that he intends to exercise his Fifth Amendment privilege; any statement taken after the person invokes his privilege cannot be other than the product of compulsion, subtle or otherwise. Without the right to cut off questioning, the setting of in-custody interrogation operates on the individual to overcome free choice in producing a statement after the privilege has been once invoked." *Miranda v. Arizona*, 384 U.S. 436, 473–74 (1966).

Allison unequivocally invoked her right to cut off questioning by her comment. An officer must "scrupulously honor" an invocation of the right to remain silent, and can only reinitiate questioning after a "cooling off" period, new *Miranda* warnings are provided, and a waiver is secured. *See Michigan v. Mosley*, 423 U.S. 96 (1975). The facts thus differ from those in *Berghuis v. Thompkis*, 560 U.S. 370 (2010), where the Court held that the defendant did not invoke his right to silence by remaining largely quiet for the just under three-hour interrogation.

Answer (A) is incorrect because Allison retained the right, following her waiver, to cut off questioning and invoke the right to remain silent, which occurred here.

Answer (C) is incorrect. Allison answered later questions because, notwithstanding her attempt to cut off interrogation, the questions kept coming. She may have felt that the officer could continue to ask her questions even though she had tried to stop the questioning. Her submission to authority is not an indication that she did not wish to cut off further interrogation. Questioning should have stopped after she invoked her right to remain silent.

Answer (D) is incorrect because exercising the right to remain silent does not also invoke the right to counsel. The exact words expressed by the suspect will control whether the suspect has invoked the right to remain silent or the right to counsel.

Resumption of Interrogation

100. Lewing's confession is likely inadmissible. The defendant signed a waiver of *Miranda* rights but then indicated that he did not want to talk the police any more. The detective cut off questioning at that point. A defendant who says he or she does not want to talk does not receive the same level of protection as a defendant who asks for an attorney. The defendant who exercises the right to remain silent can be subject to further interrogation under certain circumstances.

In *Michigan v. Mosley*, 423 U.S. 96 (1975), the Supreme Court said that *Miranda* requires police to stop questioning a suspect when he or she exercises the right to remain silent, but the exercise of the right does not insulate the suspect from later questioning. The defendant in *Mosley* was re-approached two hours after invoking his right to remain silent, by a different officer, in a different location, and questioned about a different, though related, crime. At the second interrogation, the defendant waived his rights after being given *Miranda* warnings again. The Court found the resumption of interrogation valid under these circumstances.

In this problem, the facts are very different: Lewing was kept in the same place, and then interrogated by the same detective about the same crime. Moreover, he was not given the warnings again prior to the second interrogation, and the short span of time between the interrogation sessions also makes the police behavior problematic.

101. Scott's statements are inadmissible because he was in custody and clearly invoked his right to counsel. Once a suspect unambiguously asserts the *Miranda* right to counsel, police can subject the suspect to custodial interrogation only under limited circumstances. Police may not resume interrogating the suspect except under certain circumstances. *Edwards v. Arizona*, 451 U.S. 477 (1981).

One such circumstance was addressed in *Oregon v. Bradshaw*, 462 U.S. 1039 (1983). There, the Supreme Court held that a suspect who had requested counsel, then initiated discussion about the crime as he was being moved from the police station to the jail, when he asked, "Well, what is going to happen to me now?" The Supreme Court said that a reviewing court must look to see whether the suspect's statement evidenced a willingness and a desire for a general discussion about the investigation — as opposed to "a request for a drink of water or a request to use a telephone that are so routine that they cannot be fairly said to represent a desire on the part of an accused to open up a more generalized discussion relating directly or indirectly to the investigation." The Supreme Court concluded that the defendant's inquiry as to what would happen to him, although ambiguous, "evinced a willingness and a desire for a generalized discussion about the investigation." *Id.* at 1045–46.

In the problem, the standard does not appear to be satisfied. Scott's expletive ("This is bull—") was a reaction to his predicament and cannot be construed as a willingness and desire for a generalized discussion about the investigation.

102. **Answer (C) is correct.** Following invocation of the *Miranda* right to counsel, police may not reinitiate interrogation without counsel present even though the accused has consulted with the requested attorney. *Minnick v. Mississippi*, 498 U.S. 146 (1990). *Minnick* held that a suspect who invokes the right need not only be allowed to consult with an attorney outside of the interrogation room, but also to the right to have counsel present in the interrogation room during custodial interrogation. *Minnick* was based on an understanding of *Miranda* that when an accused requests counsel, he is expressing the thought that he is unable personally to deal with the police interrogation and wishes to do so only through an attorney.

Answer (A) is incorrect because a suspect's right includes having the attorney present during interrogation.

Answer (B) is incorrect because the defendant's waiver was not knowingly, intelligently and voluntarily made. He acceded to the authority of the officer, who had no right to reapproach the defendant.

Answer (D) is incorrect. The officer should have read defendant the *Miranda* warnings prior to the second interrogation, but that would not have cured the error. The defendant had previously invoked his right to counsel and did not initiate the later discussion, and the defendant had the right to have his attorney present during any interrogation. *Minnick*.

Sixth Amendment Rights

103. **Answer (D) is correct.** *Miranda* rights only attach to custodial interrogation when a suspect knows that he is being questioned by a police officer or police agent. The *Miranda* rights are intended to alleviate the inherent coerciveness that attaches to official interrogation in a custodial setting, when a suspect presumably feels pressured by the questioner to respond to the questions. In the jail cell setting, Arthur did not know that the person questioning him was an undercover agent; therefore, he was not subject to those pressures. The agent was not required to administer the *Miranda* warnings prior to questioning. *Illinois v. Perkins*, 496 U.S. 292 (1990). Nor does the Sixth Amendment bar admission of the robbery and murder confession. This is because the Sixth Amendment is "offense-specific" and is triggered only when a "critical stage" is reached regarding an offense. *McNeil v. Wisconsin*, 501 U.S. 171 (1991). Here, a critical stage (e.g., an indictment) had not been reached regarding the robbery and murder of the bank guard, so no Sixth Amendment protection attached.

Answer (A) is incorrect. *Miranda* warnings are intended to alleviate the inherent coerciveness of custodial interrogation. Arthur was in custody, but he did not know that he was being interrogated by a police officer in his cell. Therefore, the conversation between two cellmates lacked the coercion that would attach when a suspect is questioned by police. The premise of *Miranda* is that danger of coercion results from the interaction of custody and official interrogation by a police officer who appears to control the suspect's fate. The Supreme Court has concluded that those pressures do not exist when the suspect is unaware that the person questioning him is not a police officer. *Perkins*.

Answer (B) is incorrect. The Sixth Amendment right to counsel only attaches when a "critical stage" in the adversarial process is reached. Such a stage was reached here when Arthur was charged with drunk driving. However, the Sixth Amendment right to counsel is a narrow right, compared to its *Miranda* counterpart, and is *offense-specific* in nature, meaning that Arthur only had Sixth Amendment protection with regard to the drunk driving case. Police could not have questioned him about that charge, absent a waiver. Police, however, used the undercover agent to secure information about other suspected criminal behavior — robbery and murder — as to which no critical stage had been reached. The Sixth Amendment right did not apply to the robbery and murder charges. *Texas v. Cobb*, 532 U.S. 162 (2001); *McNeil v. Wisconsin*, 501 U.S. 171 (1991).

Answer (C) is incorrect. There is no question that the defendant voluntarily confessed to the undercover agent. However, that is not the test under the Sixth Amendment. The Sixth Amendment prohibits the government from deliberately eliciting incriminating information from a defendant whose Sixth Amendment right has attached. It does not matter whether the defendant is directly questioned or indirectly questioned by someone who he does not know is a police officer or government agent. Here, the questioning would have met the Sixth Amendment test for interrogation, but the Sixth Amendment right is offense specific, and it had attached only to the drunk driving offense. *McNeil v. Wisconsin*, 501 U.S. 171 (1991); *Kuhlmann v. Wilson*, 477 U.S. 436 (1986); *Brewer v. Williams*, 430 U.S. 387 (1977).

104. Even though the undercover agent did not ask any questions about the pending drunk driving charge, Arthur's incriminating statement about the drunk driving charge will not admitted at the drunk driving trial. Arthur's Sixth Amendment right to counsel on the drunk driving charge attached at the first court appearance, which marked the commencement of formal judicial proceedings. The Sixth Amendment right is a trial right and following its attachment the state is not permitted to question the defendant without the defendant's attorney being present unless the defendant knowingly, intelligently, and voluntarily waives the right to counsel. *Brewer v. Williams.* In *Montejo v. Louisiana*, 556 U.S. 778 (2009), the Supreme Court said the formal attachment of the Sixth Amendment right does not preclude police from approaching an accused to seek a waiver and engage in questioning. However, a "knowing and voluntary waiver of Sixth Amendment rights does not apply in the context of communications with an undisclosed undercover agent." *United States v. Henry*, 447 U.S. 264, 273 (1980).

Even though the undercover agent did not directly question Arthur about the drunk driving charge, his incriminating statement about the pending drunk driving charge is inadmissible. *Kuhlman v. Wilson*, 477 U.S. 436 (1986). While police may question a formally charged suspect about uncharged crimes, the evidence secured may not be used on the pending charge. *Maine v. Moulton*, 474 U.S. 159 (1985).

Author's Note: The purpose of this and the previous question is to focus on the different rules applicable under *Miranda* and the Sixth Amendment right to counsel. It is important to note that the purposes, coverage and scope of the rules differ. You should be able to understand them and be able to apply them separately.

Interrogation and Confessions: Due Process (Voluntariness)

105. Answer (D) is correct. The voluntariness of a suspect's statement has long been the constitutional test for admissibility under the Due Process Clause of the Fourteenth Amendment. The test centers on whether a suspect's will has been "overborne," and a reviewing court will answer this question based on a totality of the circumstances, assessing the characteristics of the suspect and the behavior of police. *Colorado v. Connelly*, 479 U.S. 157 (1986). Police behaviors of particular concern to courts relate to the actual or threatened use of physical force, deprivation of food or water, and lengthy incommunicado interrogation. *Arizona v. Fulminante*, 499 U.S. 279 (1991); *Schneckloth v. Bustamonte*, 412 U.S. 218 (1973); *Payne v. Arkansas*, 356 U.S. 560 (1958).

In the problem, the defendant's will to resist the police was overborne by the prolonged, relentless incommunicado interrogation. Moreover, in *Spano v. New York*, 360 U.S. 315 (1959), the Court held that, among other factors, a reviewing court should consider the personal characteristics of the suspect when assessing voluntariness. Here, the fact that the defendant was a relatively young adult, had no prior arrests, and was unsophisticated about legal matters would be taken into account. A court would likely find that the confession was involuntary and inadmissible. This is so even though police falsely told the defendant that the victim had "unequivocally" identified him. Police can use falsehoods regarding the strength of their evidence. *See, e.g., Green v. Scully*, 850 F.2d 894 (2d Cir. 1988) (condoning police falsely telling the defendant that they had all the evidence they needed to convict).

Answer (A) is incorrect because waiver of *Miranda* rights is not totally dispositive. The due process voluntariness of a confession is a question that is independent of whether *Miranda* was or was not violated. Here the confession was involuntary, even though *Miranda* warnings were given.

Answer (B) is incorrect because even though the defendant waived *Miranda* rights, his will was overborne by the prolonged, relentless interrogation, causing his confession to be involuntary.

Answer (C) is incorrect because the officer properly read the *Miranda* warnings and then re-read them, and the defendant waived *Miranda* rights. However, waiver of *Miranda* rights, while persuasive, is not the end of the inquiry. The voluntariness of the confession, as noted above, is a distinct constitutional question.

106. Answer (C) is correct. The due process test for voluntariness is the constitutional standard for admissibility of a confession. A confession is voluntary if it is the product of a defendant's free choice rather than the result of police coercion. Whether a confession is voluntary is determined by assessing the totality of the circumstances.

In this question, the investigating officer adhered to the *Miranda* rules and engaged in no third-degree methods. However, it is likely that the police conduct will result in the confession being excluded from evidence because the confession was involuntary. The officer's behavior here is problematic in two respects. First, reviewing courts take a dim view of express statements by police that a lenient sentence will be secured if cooperation is forthcoming (broad assurances that they will "put in a good word" with the prosecutor are, however, usually permitted). Here, the interrogating officer clearly said Suzie would "definitely" get a probation sentence in juvenile court, which was not true.

Second, the officer's statement that Suzie (an adult) would be transferred to juvenile court rather than adult court is a misstatement of law. She is an adult and cannot be prosecuted in juvenile court. The misstatement of law likely had an enormous impact upon the defendant's willingness to cooperate and upon her admission, rendering the confession involuntary and inadmissible.

Answers (A) and (B) are incorrect. Although the police officer complied with the *Miranda* rules and the interrogation was not long or abusive, the voluntariness standard will be controlling in this problem based on the misstatements of law.

Answer (D) is incorrect. The defendant validly waived her *Miranda* rights and did not ask to consult with an attorney. The right to counsel under *Miranda* is not self-executing.

Eyewitness Identification

107. The evidence about the lineup identification is not admissible. Once adversary proceedings have begun, a defendant has the right to have an attorney present during a lineup. The defendant's Sixth Amendment right to counsel attached after she was indicted and arraigned on the indictment. *Kirby v. Illinois*, 406 U.S. 682 (1972).

The Supreme Court has held that counsel should be present at a lineup because it is "peculiarly riddled with innumerable dangers and variable factors which might seriously, even crucially, derogate from a fair trial." The Court said that eyewitness identification can be "untrustworthy" and a major factor contributing to miscarriages of justice because of "the degree of suggestion inherent in the manner in which the prosecution presents the suspect to witnesses for pretrial identification." *United States v. Wade*, 388 U.S. 218 (1967).

The defendant's right to counsel attached in this case, and there is no claim that the defendant waived counsel. The prosecutor was obligated to notify defendant's counsel of the lineup. Consequently, the witnesses may not testify regarding the pretrial lineup identification. *Gilbert v. California*, 388 U.S. 263 (1967); *United States v. Wade*, 388 U.S. 218 (1967).

108. The rule also bars in-court identifications that are the product of pretrial identifications in violation of the defendant's Sixth Amendment right to counsel. However, the rule does not mandate exclusion of in-court identification testimony when an in-court identification does not amount to exploitation of the tainted lineup. The in-court identification may be admissible despite the tainted lineup if the in-court identification was premised on solid observations of the accused at the time of the alleged criminal act, which would be an adequate independent source to overcome the constitutional failure to have counsel present at the lineup. The prosecution must demonstrate by clear and convincing evidence that the in-court identification is derived from an independent source and not the product of the tainted confrontation. *United States v. Wade*, 388 U.S. 218 (1967). Whether the witnesses who identified the defendant at the tainted lineup may be able to identify her in court will turn on the strength of their testimony about their prior encounters with the accused.

109. Answer (A) is the correct answer. Even though the defendant's Sixth Amendment right to counsel had attached, the right to counsel is not applicable to photographic displays conducted by police for the purpose of allowing a witness to attempt an identification of an offender. The Supreme Court said that a photographic identification differs from a lineup because there are substantially fewer possibilities of suggestion and any unfairness in the composition of the array can be readily reconstructed at trial. *United States v. Ash*, 413 U.S. 300 (1973).

Answer (B) is incorrect because the witness may testify about his or her pretrial identification from the photo array. The witness may also identify the defendant in court as the person who committed fraud.

Answer (C) is incorrect because the Sixth Amendment right to counsel does not attach to photographic displays even after the defendant has counsel and has been charged formally with a crime.

Answer (D) is incorrect because there is nothing in the facts to indicate that the photo array was unnecessarily suggestive to require exclusion of the testimony. The photos depicted women who resembled the defendant. The defense may attempt to undermine the witnesses' credibility, and the jury will decide whether or not to believe the witnesses.

110. **Answer (D) is the correct answer.** To establish a due process violation, a defendant must prove that the out-of-court identification challenged was "unnecessarily suggestive and conducive to irreparable mistaken identification." *Stovall v. Denno*, 388 U.S. 293 (1967). In evaluating whether a particular identification is improper, a court considers several factors: "includ[ing] the opportunity of the witness to view the criminal at the time of the crime, the witness' degree of attention, the accuracy of the witness' prior description of the criminal, the level of certainty demonstrated by the witness at the confrontation, and the length of time between the crime and the confrontation." *Neil v. Biggers*, 409 U.S. 188, 199 (1972). Reliability, the Court has since instructed, is the "lynchpin" of the due process analysis. *Manson v. Brathwaite*, 432 U.S. 98 (1977).

Here, Tina had only a brief view of the suspect. Her view lasted less than a minute, it was dusk, and she had only a three-quarter view of the suspect's face. Moreover, the photo array was unduly suggestive, because only the defendant matched her description, and the police allowed her to reread her description before she was shown the photos.

Answer (A) is incorrect. For Sixth Amendment purposes, a photo array is permissible both before and after a defendant's Sixth Amendment right to counsel attaches. *United States v. Ash*, 413 U.S. 300 (1973). A due process challenge can exist independently of the right to counsel.

Answer (B) is incorrect. Tina had no reason to lie. However, as noted *supra*, she selected the defendant from a photo array that was unnecessarily suggestive and conducive to irreparable mistaken identification. There is no basis to conclude that her trial identification was not affected by the tainted photo array.

Answer (C) is incorrect. As noted, a photo array does not implicate the Sixth Amendment right to counsel. Police need not contact defense counsel in advance of conducting a photo array.

111. **Answer (B) is correct.** In *Perry v. New Hampshire*, 565 U.S. 228 (2012), the Court held that the goal of deterring unnecessarily suggestive police identification techniques is only served if police actually arrange the identification that is challenged. In *Perry*, the Court held that the requirement was not satisfied when a witness, on her own initiative and without police prompting, looked out a window and identified the suspect. Under the facts here, we have a closer case, as the suspect was brought to the police station, but the facts state that police

bringing the suspect to the station was "coincidental[]," suggesting that the identification was not arranged.

Answer (A) is incorrect. The fact that the identification occurred in the hallway of a busy police station is irrelevant.

Answer (C) is incorrect. The motivations of witnesses are not determinative of admissibility.

Answer (D) is incorrect. Whether the suspect was in custody, for *Miranda* and Fifth Amendment purposes, is irrelevant because eyewitness identification is not "testimonial."

Standing

112. Answer (A) is the correct answer. The defendant had an expectation of privacy in his backpack (branded with his name), even though it was located in the car's trunk, and therefore has standing to challenge the officer's unlawful entry into and search of the car trunk. *Rakas v. Illinois*, 439 U.S. 128 (1978). *See also, e.g., United States v. Trejo*, 135 F. Supp. 3d 1023, 1031–32 (D. S. Dakota 2015) (citing cases finding that while passenger-defendant lacked standing to challenge the search of car, he had standing to challenge the search of his luggage inside the car's trunk).The entry and search of the trunk are unlawful because there was no consent and the officer lacked probable cause to believe contraband (*e.g.*, illegal drugs) was inside. *Wyoming v. Houghton*, 526 U.S. 295 (1999).

Answer (B) is incorrect. Incident to a lawful traffic stop, an officer, for safety reasons, can order the driver and any passengers out of the vehicle. *Maryland v. Wilson*, 519 U.S. 408 (1997) (passengers); *Pennsylvania v. Mimms*, 434 U.S. 106 (1977) (drivers).

Answer (C) is incorrect. Although the officer was justified in stopping the vehicle because of the traffic violation, despite the apparent presence of pretext (*see Whren v. United States*, 517 U.S. 806 (1996)), her hunch that the two teenagers "were up to no good" does not constitute probable cause to believe that contraband was in the trunk.

Answer (D) is incorrect. This is because no probable cause existed to support an arrest (before the drugs were discovered in the backpack) and, even if a lawful arrest occurred, the search incident to arrest exception does not apply because police cannot enter and search a car's trunk. *New York v. Belton*, 453 U.S. 454 (1981).

113. Answer (B) is the correct answer. A police stop of a vehicle constitutes a Fourth Amendment seizure of both the driver and any passengers in the vehicle. Jeremy can bring a Fourth Amendment claim because he received permission to drive from Laura, and could even bring a claim if he were a passenger. "A traffic stop necessarily curtails the travel a passenger has chosen just as much as it halts the driver, diverting both from the stream of traffic to the side of the road, and the police activity that normally amounts to intrusion on 'privacy and personal security' does not normally (and did not here) distinguish between passenger and driver." *Brendlin v. California*, 551 U.S. 249 (2007).

The officer had neither probable cause nor reasonable suspicion to stop the vehicle, making the stop improper. Because the search of Jeremy's body, as to which he has a reasonable expectation of privacy, stemmed from the illegal stop, it too was unlawful. As an aside, the fact that Jeremy is not an authorized driver of the Cadillac, based on the rental agreement, is irrelevant. The Court in *Byrd v. United States*, 138 S. Ct. 1518 (2018) held that a defendant who violated a rental car agreement signed by a third party, but had her permission to drive the car, did not eliminate any reasonable expectation of privacy the defendant had in the vehicle.

Answer (A) is incorrect. The subjective motivation of the officer is irrelevant.

Answer (C) is incorrect. As noted above, Jeremy has standing to challenge the unlawful stop, and he has standing to contest the search because it is his body.

Answer (D) is incorrect. As noted, in *Byrd*, the Court held that violation of a rental contract, in itself, does not preclude an expectation of privacy in the vehicle. Furthermore, Jeremy has an expectation of privacy in his body, which was searched by the officer.

114. The question turns on whether a party guest has standing to challenge the illegal search of his date's purse. Here, standing is unlikely absent more information about the defendant's relationship to the purse.

The Supreme Court has held that police cannot search the bodies of bar patrons simply because the bar they are visiting is the subject of a lawful search warrant. *Ybarra v. Illinois*, 444 U.S. 85 (1979). Here, however, question exists over whether the defendant has standing to challenge what appears to be an unlawful search. To establish standing, a defendant must demonstrate a privacy interest in the place searched and the objects seized. In other words, he must convince the court that his personal, constitutional rights were violated.

In a case with similar facts, the Supreme Court held that a defendant lacked standing to challenge the search of his girlfriend's purse. He did not have a protected privacy interest in his girlfriend's purse because their relationship was casual (even though they had spent the previous 48 hours together), the defendant did not have authority to prevent others from access to the girlfriend's purse (the girlfriend had permitted her girlfriend to store her hairbrush in the purse along with the defendant's marijuana), and the defendant had never sought or been given a possessory interest in the purse. *Rawlings v. Kentucky*, 448 U.S. 98 (1980).

115. **Answer (C) is the best answer.** The Supreme Court has said that an overnight guest at a home has standing to challenge an illegal search of the home. *Minnesota v. Olson*, 495 U.S. 91 (1990). The Court made it clear that a place need not be a defendant's home in order for there to be a legitimate expectation of privacy. However, there is no mention in the facts whether Carter was an overnight guest. Later, in *Minnesota v. Carter*, 525 U.S. 83 (1991), the Court held that a defendant did not have a legitimate expectation of privacy in an apartment used for a short time for a purely illegal commercial purpose (preparing illegal drugs for sale) and, thus, did not have standing to challenge the search. The *Carter* facts are similar to those here.

Answer (A) is incorrect because it too broadly casts the standing inquiry. It is simply inaccurate to say anyone in a home has standing to contest the search. Before the court rules on the legality of the entry and search, the court first would have to determine whether the defendant has standing to raise the Fourth Amendment issue. This involves looking at the relationship between the defendant and the home and the people who live there.

Answer (B) is incorrect. It is difficult to justify the police decision not to seek a warrant when there is no evidence leading them to believe that the defendant knew that they were on to him or that evidence may be destroyed. Therefore, there is no applicable exception to the requirement of a warrant prior to search of a home. The entry and search were unlawful.

Answer (D) is incorrect for reasons already noted.

Appellate Review of a Motion to Suppress

116. Answer (C) is correct. A trial court's finding of fact is entitled to great deference on appeal. The hearing judge saw the witnesses and heard their testimony. The appellate court may not substitute its own judgment for that of the trial judge on a question of fact as long as there is any evidence in the record to support the finding.

Answer (A) is incorrect. Issues of credibility are questions of fact to be decided by the trier of fact. Credibility is not merely how many witnesses appeared on each side.

Answer (B) is incorrect. The appellate court may not substitute its judgment for that of the trial court on a question of fact, even if the appellate court would have decided the matter differently.

Answer (D) is incorrect. A trial court's finding of fact will generally stand on appeal, provided there is some evidence in the record to support the trial court's finding. The answer is incorrect because the trial judge's findings of fact are subject to review on appeal. The appellate court, however, may not substitute its own conclusion for that of the trial judge.

117. Answer (B) is correct. Unlike decisions based upon questions of fact, the trial judge's conclusions of law are not entitled to any deference. The court of appeals is entitled to substitute its own judgment on matters of law. A search conducted with a warrant is presumptively legal because the police have followed the preferred constitutional procedure by seeking prior judicial authority to conduct the search. Consequently, a defendant challenging a search conducted with a warrant has the burden of proof on a motion to suppress.

A search conducted without a warrant carries no presumption of regularity and correctness. The burden falls upon the prosecution to prove the legality of such a warrantless search by a preponderance of the evidence. *United States v. Matlock*, 415 U.S. 164 (1974). Therefore, in this case, the prosecution had the burden to prove that the search was voluntary. The trial court erred in its assignment of the burden of proof to the defendant.

Answer (A) is incorrect. The finding of fact will stand, but the error is based upon the court's erroneous assignment of the burden of proof, a matter of law.

Answer (C) is incorrect. The trial court's decisions on a legal issue are entitled to no deference. The court of appeals may substitute its own conclusion of law for that of the trial judge's.

Answer (D) is incorrect. The trial court erroneously assigned the burden of proof to the defendant on the issue of law. The burden rests upon the state to prove that the consent to search was voluntary. *See, e.g., United States v. Hurtado*, 905 F.2d 74 (5th Cir. 1990) (government must prove voluntariness by preponderance of evidence).

Author's Note: The prosecution has the burden of proving that a confession is voluntary, *Lego v. Twomey*, 404 U.S. 477 (1972), or was secured in compliance with *Miranda* requirements. *Fare v. Michael C.*, 442 U.S. 707 (1979). When identification evidence is challenged, the defendant has the burden of proving that the identification violated the right to counsel, but the prosecution has the burden of proving an independent source for that identification. *United States v. Wade*, 388 U.S. 218 (1967). The defendant has the burden of showing that an identification procedure violates due process because it was so suggestive as to create a likelihood of misidentification. *Stovall v. Denno*, 388 U.S. 293 (1967).

118. A trial judge's determination that probable cause or reasonable suspicion exists, even though based on factual conclusions, is a matter of law. A trial court's conclusions of law on constitutional issues are entitled to no deference. Those issues of law are subject to a *de novo* review in an appellate court. *Ornelas v. United States*, 517 U.S. 690 (1996).

Here, the trial court's decision that probable cause existed to arrest the young man was erroneous. A weak argument is that the police officer had reasonable suspicion to stop and question the suspect to confirm or dispel his suspicion that the defendant was on the corner dealing drugs. However, standing on a street corner, without more, does not rise to the level of reasonable suspicion allowing for a *Terry* stop. Nor does walking away from an officer, although the Court has held that flight from police in a "high crime" area can be a basis for reasonable suspicion. *Illinois v. Wardlow*, 528 U.S. 119 (2000).

In this case, the defendant walked away from the corner when he saw the police officer heading in his direction; he did not run. Moreover, he stopped immediately when the officer ordered him to stop. Even if the court had found that reasonable suspicion existed to stop the defendant, the police officer only could at most only do a pat down of the defendant's clothing to determine whether the defendant had a weapon (i.e., conduct a *Terry* "frisk"). The defendant's dress, however, might not even allow for a pat down for weapons if the officer could have seen a weapon without a pat down. Moreover, the officer lacked reasonable suspicion to believe the defendant was armed and dangerous, thereby rendering even a pat down for weapons unconstitutional.

But here the officer did not frisk for weapons; he reached into the defendant's shorts and removed the evidence. A full search incident to arrest is permitted only following a lawful arrest. Since the officer did not have probable cause to arrest, this was not a lawful arrest, and the search was therefore illegal. The evidence should have been suppressed.

119. In most state and federal jurisdictions, the appellate court will consider the state's appeal from the ruling to suppress the government's evidence. Ordinarily, a party to a law suit (including a criminal case) may not appeal a trial judge's preliminary or trial ruling. For

example, in a criminal case a *defendant* may not appeal from an adverse ruling on her motion to suppress government evidence. The principal reason for that rule is that the defendant may yet prevail at trial and will no longer need to appeal from the adverse ruling. Also, if the defendant is convicted at trial, he or she may appeal the trial court's erroneous suppression of defense evidence or erroneous admission of government evidence.

However, to conserve time and resources, federal courts and many state jurisdictions do not require the defendant to go trial to preserve a right to appeal an adverse ruling on a motion to suppress. The defendant may preserve the right to appeal from the pretrial ruling denying her motion to suppress by entering a conditional plea. This means the defendant essentially pleads guilty but reserves the right to appeal the evidence ruling. The plea can be withdrawn if the appellate court rules favorably on the appeal on the evidence issue.

However, if the trial court grants the defendant's motion to suppress evidence, the prosecution may not have any additional evidence to proceed to trial. Consequently, many jurisdictions, including federal courts, allow the prosecution a limited interlocutory appeal from an adverse ruling by the trial court on a defense motion to suppress government proof. *See, e.g.,* 18 U.S.C. §3731. The justification for allowing the prosecution to appeal, while not allowing the defense the same appeal, is that the prosecution may lose its right to prosecute the case altogether based upon an erroneous decision suppressing evidence. If the state proceeds to trial without the evidence and the defendant is acquitted, the double jeopardy prohibition precludes the state from appealing from an acquittal.

Some jurisdictions require the state to seek leave to appeal from the appellate court, and some jurisdictions also require the prosecutor to claim that the state will be unable to proceed to trial if the pretrial decision to suppress evidence is not overturned. Federal law mandates the U.S. Attorney certifies that the appeal is not taken for purposes of delay and the evidence is substantial proof of a material fact in the case. 18 U.S.C. §3731.

Derivative Evidence

120. The exclusionary rule reaches not only primary evidence obtained as a direct result of an illegal search or seizure, but also evidence later discovered and found to be derivative of an illegality, or "fruit of the poisonous tree." The reason is if derivative evidence were not suppressed, police would have an incentive to violate constitutional rights in order to secure admissible derivative evidence even though the primary evidence secured as a result of the constitutional violation would be inadmissible.

At the very most, Officer Lowe was permitted to conduct a *Terry* stop of the vehicle to confirm or dispel his suspicion of illegal activity. The police, however, executed an arrest and vehicle search even though they lacked probable cause to do either. Because the arrest was invalid, the search of the vehicle's passenger compartment would be invalid.

The evidence found in the car as a result of the illegal search provided the evidence for probable cause to secure a search warrant for the house and garage. While the search warrant was valid based upon probable cause, the probable cause obtained during the illegal search was the fruit of the illegal search and, therefore, tainted. The evidence found during the execution of the search warrant is the fruit of the "poisonous tree" because of the original illegal search.

In order to undo the taint of the original illegality, the state would have to demonstrate that the evidence obtained with the search warrant was not the result of the search of the Bronco. Had the judge who issued the search warrant not been provided with the evidence of the cocaine found in the Bronco as a result of a violation of the Fourth Amendment, the search warrant would not have been issued. Therefore, evidence obtained in the execution of the search warrant must likewise be suppressed. Moreover, the good faith exception to the exclusionary rule does not apply where a search warrant is issued on the basis of evidence obtained as a result of an illegal search. *United States v. Scales*, 903 F.2d 765 (10th Cir. 1990); *United States v. Vasey*, 834 F.2d 782 (9th Cir. 1987).

Derivative Evidence:
Miranda Violation

121. Answer (C) is correct. The statement of the defendant was the product of custodial interrogation. The police should have given *Miranda* warnings to the defendant because he was in custody (arrested) and subject to interrogation. The failure to *Mirandize* the defendant renders the statement inadmissible. However, *Miranda* violations do not taint physical evidence obtained as a result of the violation. Physical fruit (here jewelry) of a suspect's "unwarned but voluntary" statement need not be suppressed. *United States v. Patane*, 542 U.S. 630 (2004).

A statement taken without *Miranda* warnings will not serve as a poisonous tree and will not taint the evidence that is discovered as a result of that statement, provided that the statement is voluntary. An involuntary statement violates the defendant's due process right, and the physical evidence secured as a result would be inadmissible.

Answer (A) is incorrect. There was a *Miranda* violation, and the jewelry is derivative of that violation. However, a statement taken without *Miranda* warnings will not serve as a poisonous tree and will not taint the physical evidence that is discovered as a result of that statement, provided that the statement is voluntary.

Answer (B) is incorrect. There was no public safety emergency once the defendant was disarmed. A reasonable police officer would not have believed that finding the jewelry was part of such an emergency. Therefore, that exception to the *Miranda* rules does not apply.

Answer (D) is incorrect. A violation of the *Miranda* rules does not automatically render the statement involuntary. The Supreme Court treats *Miranda* violations differently than due process violations (*i.e.*, involuntarily secured). Evidence secured as the result of a statement secured in violation of due process voluntariness requirement is suppressed, whereas a "mere" Miranda violation is not. *United States v. Patane*, 542 U.S. 630 (2004); *Oregon v. Elstad*, 470 U.S. 298 (1985). Here, it does not appear that the due process voluntariness standard, which is demanding, was met.

Derivative Evidence: Causal Connection

122. **Answer (D) is the correct answer.** The warrantless entry of the defendant's home studio to search and make the arrest violated the defendant's Fourth Amendment rights. A search warrant is ordinarily needed to enter and search a home and an arrest warrant to make an arrest inside a home, absent consent or exigent circumstances. However, the Supreme Court has held that such an illegal arrest, provided there is probable cause, is not a poisonous tree once the arrestee is removed from the residence. If there is probable cause to justify the arrest, the detention is lawful once the defendant is taken from the house. *New York v. Harris*, 495 U.S. 14 (1990). Here, Gaston was removed from the home after the illegal arrest and given *Miranda* warnings prior to his confession. Therefore, the confession is not suppressed as the fruit of the poisonous tree.

Answer (A) is incorrect. There were no articulated exigent circumstances to justify the warrantless entry to arrest or search. The police had probable cause to arrest and to search and could have obtained arrest and search warrants, but they did not.

Answer (B) is incorrect. The entry of the home studio was illegal. However, *New York v. Harris*, 495 U.S. 14 (1990), stands for the proposition that even though a constitutional violation is established, evidence will not be excluded unless it is obtained as a direct consequence of the illegal act. The rule separates the confession from the constitutional violation, once the violation ends.

Answer (C) is incorrect. Police had probable cause to search the home studio and arrest Gaston, but they should have obtained the necessary warrants. Based on the totality of the circumstances, probable cause existed to believe that the defendant was the source of the fake "original" paintings.

Derivative Evidence: What May Be Suppressed

123. **Answer (A) is correct.** The facts are clear that the defendant's in-court presence and identification followed an illegal arrest and a lineup identification derivative of the illegal arrest. However, the power of the court to try a person for a crime is not impaired by the fact of an illegal arrest. *Frisbie v. Collins*, 342 U.S. 519 (1952). Even if the defendant is in court as a result of an illegal arrest, he cannot have his face suppressed as the fruit of an illegal arrest to prevent an in-court identification. *United States v. Crews*, 445 U.S. 463 (1980).

Answer (B) is incorrect. The arrest following the lineup was derivative of the earlier illegal street arrest and the lineup identification. However, the illegal arrest and subsequent lineup do not affect the legality of the in-court identification provided that the prosecution establishes that the witness's in-court identification is based upon prior contact (the crime) and not based upon the tainted lineup. *United States v. Wade*, 388 U.S. 218 (1967).

Answer (C) is incorrect. Even if the defendant is in court as a result of an illegal arrest, he cannot have his face suppressed as the fruit of an illegal arrest to prevent an in-court identification. *United States v. Crews*, 445 U.S. 463 (1980).

Answer (D) is incorrect. The witness's in-court identification is admissible if the prosecution establishes that there was an independent source for the in-court identification. When the witness testified that she was able to identify the defendant as the burglar based upon her observation of him at the time of his exit from the burglarized house, the prosecution argued successfully that the in-court identification was independent of the tainted lineup.

124. **Answer (B) is correct.** The knock-and-announce-and-wait rule is part of the Fourth Amendment's requirements. *Wilson v. Arkansas*, 514 U.S. 927 (1995). However, evidence seized during execution of a lawful search warrant is admissible even though police violated the knock and announce rule. *Hudson v. Michigan*, 547 U.S. 586 (2006). In refusing to extend the exclusionary rule to violations of knock and announce, the Supreme Court said that "interests that were violated ... have nothing to do with the seizure of evidence."

Answer (A) is incorrect. Police may request a no-knock authorization in a search warrant. But with or without this authorization, the exclusionary rule does not bar evidence obtained in violation of the knock and announce requirement.

Answer (C) is incorrect. The answer is correct in suggesting that there was no evidence of exigency to justify the no knock entry. However, evidence seized during execution of a lawful search warrant is admissible even though police violated the knock and announce rule. *Hudson v. Michigan*, 547 U.S. 586 (2006) (exclusionary rule not extended to violation of knock and announce regarding a lawful search warrant).

Answer (D) is incorrect. The Fourth Amendment does require police to knock and identify themselves and wait before entering a dwelling to execute a search warrant. *Wilson v. Arkansas*, 514 U.S. 927 (1995). However, any such violation will not result in exclusion of evidence secured; rather, as envisioned by the Court in *Hudson v. Michigan*, the defendant can seek redress based on a civil rights lawsuit pursuant to 42 U.S.C. § 1983.

Derivative Evidence: Exceptions

125. Justice Oliver Wendell Holmes, in *Silverthorne Lumber Co. v. United States*, 251 U.S. 385 (1920), allowed that if knowledge of the derivative evidence is gained from an independent source, rather than from the government's own illegality, the derivative evidence may be used. In actuality, the independent source exception is not an exception at all. The secondary evidence is not derivative because it was not obtained as a result of the initial police illegality. In *Segura v. United States*, 468 U.S. 796 (1984), the Supreme Court held admissible items not discovered during the illegal entry "and first discovered … the day after the entry, under an admittedly valid search warrant" for which there was an independent source. The independent source rule has been significantly expanded in recent years so that the independence of the source is not quite as clear as it once was.

In *Murray v. United States*, 487 U.S. 533 (1988), the Supreme Court held that evidence observed by police during an illegal entry need not be excluded if such evidence is later discovered during the execution of a valid search warrant issued on information wholly unconnected to the prior entry. The Court said the government must establish that: (1) information seen during the illegal entry and presented in the affidavit did not "affect" the magistrate's decision to issue the warrant; and (2) the agents' decision to seek the warrant was not prompted by what they had seen during the initial entry.

The problem case is very similar to *Murray*. The police had ample probable cause to obtain a search warrant for the Washington Street house independent of and prior to the officer's break-in, yet the facts do not suggest that knowledge gained by the unlawful entry affected the probable cause analysis of the court. While it could be challenging to meet the Court's second condition in *Murray* (decision to seek the warrant was not prompted by the illegal entry), it is likely that the court, in reliance on *Murray*, would deny the motion to suppress. Because of the dangerous nature of providing weapons to violent gang members and the information obtained from several pre-illegal entry sources, police very likely would have sought and obtained the warrant irrespective of the illegal entry by the officer.

126. Answer (C) is correct. Inevitable discovery is a limitation on the derivative or fruit-of-the-poisonous-tree evidence rule; some courts even treat it as an exception to the exclusionary rule, itself. The inevitable discovery limitation seeks to put the prosecution in the same position, not a worse position, than it would have been if no police error or misconduct had occurred. Under the limitation, evidence that was obtained illegally is admitted, nonetheless, if it would have been obtained lawfully without the constitutional violation. *Nix v. Williams*, 467 U.S. 431 (1984).

In the problem, the room search was illegal since there was no warrant and no exigent circumstances. Indeed, the police had seen Watson leave the room shortly before the search, giving time to try to obtain a search warrant. However, the maid would have cleaned the room in a few minutes and, consistent with hotel policy, would have alerted the police to the huge quantity of marijuana. This would satisfy the inevitable discovery rule.

Answer (A) is incorrect. Even though there was no warrant or exigent circumstances or possibly probable cause, the marijuana would have been discovered in a few minutes anyway by the maid who would have alerted the police. Thus, the suppression motion should not be granted.

Answer (B) is incorrect. The facts of this question do not provide evidence for any of the exceptions allowing a warrantless search of a motel room. More particularly, there was no information that anyone was left in the room after Watson drove away.

Answer (D) is incorrect. The search was illegal since Watson did not consent. The fact that the police complied with their responsibility to knock and announce their presence does not turn an illegal search into a legal one. However, the inevitable discovery rule applies, and the motion should be denied for this reason.

127. **Answer (C) is correct.** The answer turns on whether discovery of the heroin, based on a search incident to an arrest based on the discovery of a valid arrest warrant, is attenuated from the initial wrongdoing of police. In *Utah v. Strieff*, 136 S. Ct. 2056 (2016), the Court addressed a similar factual situation. In *Strieff*, an officer observed the defendant leaving a suspected drug location and, without reasonable suspicion or probable cause of wrongdoing, detained the defendant, asked for identification, and ran a warrants check. The check revealed that the defendant had an outstanding arrest warrant. In the ensuing search incident to arrest, the officer found methamphetamine in the defendant's pocket. Under the attenuation doctrine, a court assesses three factors: (1) the amount of time elapsed between the police misconduct and the discovery of evidence; (2) the occurrence of any intervening circumstance(s); and (3) "particularly, the purpose and flagrancy of the [initial police] misconduct." *Brown v. Illinois*, 422 U.S. 590, 604 (1975). In *Strieff*, the Court concluded that although little time elapsed, the discovery of the warrant was an intervening circumstance and that the officer's seizure of the defendant, while lacking in legal basis, was not flagrant or purposeful. Here, the police acted unlawfully in detaining Loser and retaining his identification after twice determining that he was not the subject of the Bobo arrest warrant. As in *Strieff*, little time elapsed between the police wrongdoing and the discovery of heroin, and there was an intervening circumstance (discovery of a valid arrest warrant), but the officers' behavior here is more problematic than in *Strieff*, militating against application of the attenuation doctrine.

Answer (A) is incorrect. Although police can run a database check, they cannot do so by means of unlawfully restraining an individual. That the warrant was valid is not dispositive in attenuation analysis.

Answer (B) is incorrect. Even though Loser might have possessed heroin if and when he would have been arrested, absent the instant police wrongdoing, the possibility has no bearing on whether the heroin should be admitted in this instance.

Answer (D) is incorrect. The statement is incorrect because police in fact can ask for identification without a legal basis, for instance, during a police-citizen encounter.

Impeachment

128. Answer (A) is the best answer. At one time, evidence seized as a result of a Fourth Amendment violation could not be used by the government for any purpose. However, the Supreme Court now supports the view that the exclusionary rule should only be used as a "shield," preventing the government from using the evidence in its case-in-chief, and may not be used by the defendant as a "sword" to commit perjury. Therefore, when the defendant was called as a witness and testified that she never had a weapon in her Hummer, the prosecution could impeach the defendant's testimony during cross-examination by asking her about the evidence seized during the illegal search. The jury must be instructed that it only may consider that evidence in determining the defendant's credibility as a witness (*i.e.*, for impeachment) and not in determining whether the prosecution has proven its case beyond a reasonable doubt.

Answer (B) is incorrect. The stop and search violated the Fourth Amendment since neither was based on current probable cause or even reasonable suspicion. The legitimate rationale of controlling gang activity does not authorize a search and seizure in violation of the Fourth Amendment.

Answer (C) is incorrect. It is true that allowing the prosecutor to inquire about evidence discovered during the illegal search permits the government to profit by the illegal conduct of the police officer. Moreover, it puts the defense in the very difficult position of having to decide whether to call the defendant as a witness or to keep him or her off the witness stand altogether. But since the Supreme Court has clearly upheld the use of suppressed evidence to impeach an accused, answer (C) has been rejected by the federal courts. This is true even when the suppressed evidence is introduced to rebut a statement made in response to government questioning during cross examination. *United States v. Havens*, 446 U.S. 620 (1980).

Answer (D) is not the best answer. The suppression of the evidence from the prosecution's case-in-chief does not determine whether it may be used on cross-examination for impeachment when the defendant elects to testify in his or her own behalf. *United States v. Havens*, 446 U.S. 620 (1980).

129. Answer (C) is the correct answer. The Supreme Court in *Miranda* said that a confession secured without compliance with the warnings is not admissible for any purpose. Later cases have distinguished between use of the confession in the prosecution's case-in-chief and in use during cross-examination of a defendant who elects to testify. Consequently, statements secured in violation of the *Miranda* rules may be used by the prosecution to impeach the defendant's credibility as a witness. *Harris v. New York*, 401 U.S. 222 (1971).

Answer (A) is incorrect. A confession, although inadmissible to prove the charge because of the *Miranda* violation, may be used during cross-examination to impeach the credibility of a defendant who elects to testify.

Answer (B) is incorrect. The statement is backwards. The impeachment exception to the exclusionary rules may not be used to impeach the testimony of defense witnesses other than the defendant. Here, it was used only to impeach the defendant and therefore the conviction should not be overturned for this reason.

Answer (D) is incorrect. The confession may be used during the criminal trial to impeach a defendant who testifies inconsistent with his or her earlier confession, irrespective of the *Miranda* violation.

130. **Answer (B) is correct.** Fulton's confession is involuntary and may not be used for any purpose. The Supreme Court has distinguished between the impeachment use of statements secured in violation of *Miranda* and involuntary statements that violate due process. The latter may not be used for any purpose. *Mincey v. Arizona*, 437 U.S. 385 (1978). Here, the detective shouted at Fulton, interrogated him for 13 hours, slapped him, denied him food and water for the entire time, and then lied about the existence of an eyewitness to the shooting. The officer's conduct violated Fulton's due process rights and the confession is inadmissible for any purpose.

Answer (A) is incorrect. The confession may not be used to impeach the defendant's testimony because the statement was the product of actual coercion, violating the defendant's due process rights. If the statement was voluntary but secured without compliance with the *Miranda* rules, the statement could be used on cross-examination for the limited purpose of impeaching Fulton's credibility.

Answer (C) is incorrect. When Fulton elected to take the witness stand and deny involvement in the illegal enterprise, the prosecutor could use his statement, if it were voluntary, for the limited purpose of impeaching his credibility. It could not be used in the prosecution's case-in-chief. In the problem, however, the statement was involuntary and may not be used for any purpose.

Answer (D) is incorrect. Coerced statements may not be used for any purpose. *Mincey v. Arizona*, 437 U.S. 385 (1978). The statement may not be used even for the limited purpose of impeaching Fulton's credibility.

131. **Answer (D) is correct.** It is permissible for the prosecutor at trial to ask the defendant about his failure to come forward and tell police that he shot in self-defense, whether such silence occurs before or after arrest. *Fletcher v. Weir*, 455 U.S. 603 (1982); *Jenkins v. Anderson*, 447 U.S. 231 (1980). However, once the defendant is given *Miranda* warnings, and the defendant conveys that he does not wish to speak to police, the government cannot use his silence to

impeach his testimony on cross-examination. The Supreme Court has held that it is fundamentally unfair and thus a violation of the Due Process Clause (as opposed to *Miranda*) to in effect penalize a defendant for invoking his *Miranda* right. *Doyle v. Ohio*, 426 U.S. 610 (1976). Any reference to a defendant's silence following issuance of *Miranda* warnings requires reversal unless the state can show that the error was harmless.

Answer (A) is incorrect. As just noted, whether a defendant's silence, which may be inconsistent with his in-court explanation, may be used for impeachment purposes depends on whether the accused was given *Miranda* warnings. Contrary to the answer, the government cannot use post-*Miranda* silence for impeachment purposes.

Answer (B) is incorrect. A defendant's silence at the time of an arrest may be used for impeachment purposes. The state also may use the defendant's silence following the formal arrest, until such time as he is read the *Miranda* warnings.

Answer (C) is incorrect. A defendant's silence at the time of arrest and at the police station following an arrest may be used for impeachment purposes. The location is not the critical factor. The cut-off is the reading of *Miranda* rights: "It is fundamentally unfair to promise an arrested person that his silence will not be used against him and thereafter to breach that promise by using the silence to impeach his trial testimony." *Wainwright v. Greenfield*, 474 U.S. 284 (1986).

Answers

Practice Final Exam

Part I

132. In the past, courts found a hallway dog sniff not to be a search. *See, e.g., United States v. Scott*, 610 F.3d 1009 (8th Cir. 2010). Today, this question requires application of the Supreme Court's decision in *Florida v. Jardines*, 569 U.S. 1 (2013). In *Jardines*, the Court concluded that police, acting without a search warrant, violated the Fourth Amendment when they brought a drug dog to the front porch of a residence and the dog alerted to the presence of drugs inside the residence. This was so even though the Court previously held that a dog sniff, at least of a lawfully stopped car, does not constitute a search because a properly trained dog can only detect illegal drugs and not items deserving of Fourth Amendment protection.

The question pits a black letter rule against the fundamental Fourth Amendment principle that our homes are entitled to the highest protection of Fourth Amendment privacy interests. *Kyllo v. United States*, 533 U.S. 27 (2001). The black letter rule is that a dog sniff in a public place that alerts police to the presence of drugs is not a search. *Illinois v. Caballes*, 543 U.S. 405 (2005); *United States v. Place*, 462 U.S. 696 (1983). The Court's reasoning in exempting a dog sniff from the reasonableness standard of the Fourth Amendment was based upon three factors: a dog sniff is a minimal intrusion, a dog only sniffs for the presence of contraband, and a well-trained drug dog is highly accurate. If the dog sniff here is not a search, the dog's positive alert provided probable cause to secure the search warrant. A key difference in *Jardines* was that the dog sniffed on the porch of a home, a physical space deserving of paramount privacy protection.

Here, the dog sniff did not involve the front porch of a stand-alone home, as in *Jardines*, but rather the common hallway of a multi-dwelling apartment building, as to which fellow residents and others presumably had ready access. While an apartment itself is a residence, and its interior is surely deserving of privacy protection, the common hallway that lies outside arguably enjoys less protection. *State v. Williams*, 862 N.W.2d 831, 838 (N. Dakota 2015). Be aware, however, that this view is not universally held. *See, e.g., State v. Kono*, 152 A.3d 1 (Conn. 2016).

133. **Answer (A) is correct.** The solution to this question lies along the divisions of power in the criminal justice system. The judge's authority is to issue the search warrant or deny the application. The prosecutor determines what type and how much evidence to present in the

affidavit to the issuing judge. The judge may demand additional evidence, including information about the informant, as a condition of issuing the warrant. At that point, the prosecutor must decide whether to produce the additional evidence or forgo the warrant.

Answers (B) and (C) are incorrect. There is an "informant's privilege" that allows the prosecutor to use information from an informant without disclosing the informant's identity. The justification for the privilege is two-fold. Certain crimes cannot be prosecuted without inside information. Such information is usually supplied by someone involved in the illegal enterprise or a purchaser of contraband offered for sale by the illegal enterprise. The lives of informants would be placed in danger if the source of the information becomes known. The safety concerns of ordinary witnesses who are not involved in the enterprise also may need to be protected.

While the privilege may allow the prosecution not to disclose the identity of the informant, it does not require a judge to issue a warrant without such disclosure. Therefore, it is up to the prosecutor to produce the witness, or in some cases provide just the informant's identity, or not pursue the warrant. *McCray v. Illinois*, 386 U.S. 300 (1967). The informant's privilege is not absolute. If the informant's testimony is relevant to questions of guilt or innocence at trial, the defendant has the right to know the identity of the informant and have the opportunity to cross-examine the informant at trial. *Roviaro v. United States*, 353 U.S. 53 (1957). In most cases where an informant's information is used to obtain a search warrant, the subsequent prosecution will be based on evidence found during the execution of the search warrant, and the informant will never have to testify, nor will the informant's identity have to be disclosed.

Answer (D) is incorrect. In most jurisdictions, the prosecutor's office could submit the application to another judge (judge shopping). The judge, an independent decisionmaker, does have the right to demand the information and can enforce the order by refusing to issue the warrant if the information is not forthcoming.

134. **Answer (C) is correct.** A warrant must specify the place to be searched. Where the search involves a multi-unit building, the warrant must describe the specific unit to be searched. The specificity required in a warrant must control police during execution of the warrant. Although there was an error in the description of the apartment to be searched, the warrant contained sufficient specificity to direct police to the correct unit. The warrant correctly specified a unit on the second floor belonging to Angel Smith whose name was on the door plate. The error—front or back unit—did not lead police to the wrong unit. A requirement of greater specificity would exceed the constitutional standard of reasonableness. The federal constitutional requirement is satisfied "if the description is such that an officer with a search warrant can, with reasonable effort, ascertain and identify the place to be searched." *Steele v. United States*, 267 U.S. 498 (1925).

Answer (D) is also a correct answer though not the best approach. If the error in the description of the place to be searched proved to be sufficient to invalidate the warrant, the good faith exception to the warrant requirement would still probably save the evidence and insure its admissibility. *United States v. Leon*, 468 U.S. 897 (1984). Indeed, the court could skip an assessment of the validity of the warrant and simply apply the good faith exception without first determining the validity of the search warrant. Here, the police officers executing the warrant acted in an objectively reasonable manner in executing the warrant. Common sense told them which apartment was the proper one to search. *See Leon.*

However, the best approach is for the judge to rule on the search warrant first without deciding whether the good faith rule in *Leon* applies; otherwise, there is no future guidance for police and magistrates about warrant requirements.

Answers (A) and (B) are incorrect. The purpose of the specificity requirement is to limit the discretion of officers executing a warrant and to ensure that the search is limited to the place where probable cause existed to believe that evidence would be found. A minor error in the number of the house or apartment will not necessarily be fatal to the search, if the place to be searched is otherwise sufficiently described in the warrant and readily identifiable.

The Fourth Amendment standard is reasonableness. A mistake in the identification of the premises to be searched will not necessarily invalidate the warrant so long as the mistake is reasonable. In another case, the Supreme Court held that even when an investigation led police to believe that the entire third floor of a house was one apartment and this belief continued during execution of the warrant until they discovered incriminating evidence in a second apartment, not occupied by the targeted original suspect, the mistake was held to be reasonable and the search upheld. *Maryland v. Garrison*, 480 U.S. 79 (1987).

135. The motion to suppress should be denied in part and granted in part; the drugs and the necklace are admissible, while the gun would not be admissible. A search warrant is more than just an admission ticket; it also regulates the scope of the search. During the execution of a lawful search warrant, police may seize other objects in plain view in the course of a lawful search. Those objects must be found while the police are lawfully searching in a place where the specified target of the search might be found.

Here, police discovered drugs while searching for the necklace. The fact that police had probable cause to look for drugs does not expand the lawful scope of the search. The failure to include that evidence in the affidavit and its absence from the warrant precluded them from searching for anything beyond the necklace listed in the warrant. However, as long as the police were searching for the necklace, what they discovered in "plain view" may be admissible. For the plain view exception to the warrant requirement to apply, it must be established that police (1) are in a lawful vantage point when the item is discovered and (2) have a right to physical access to the item; it must also be the case that (3) the "incriminating nature" is "immediately apparent," constituting contraband, or the fruit, instrumentality or evidence of a crime. *Horton v. California*, 496 U.S. 128 (1990).

Here, requirements one and two are satisfied for the drugs, based on what appears to be a lawful warrant to search the home for a necklace. Requirement three is also satisfied — if police can establish that it was "immediately apparent" that the drugs are contraband, which should not pose difficulty. Because police were searching where the necklace could be found (a walk-in closet), the drugs they ran across would be admissible. It is immaterial that the police had the subjective desire to also look for drugs, which were not specified in the warrant. The Supreme Court has held that finding contraband, etc., need not be inadvertent — police can operate based on a desire to find items not specified in a warrant. *Id.*

Getting the gun admitted into evidence, however, would be another matter. A warrant in effect functions as a roadmap, and when police found the necklace, their search should have concluded. If the police had discovered the necklace early in the search, they would have had to terminate the search immediately, even though they had probable cause to look for drugs. Since a necklace could be hidden almost anywhere, the search for the necklace could extend to most any area, room, and container within the house. However, once they secured the item specified in the warrant, they had no authority to search for anything else. Here, the police lucked out because the necklace was not discovered until they had completed the search of the first floor. *Horton v. California*, 496 U.S. 128 (1990). But their good fortune ended when the gun was discovered after the necklace was found.

136. **Answer (A) is the best answer.** The illegal entry of the girlfriend's home does not render Tom's arrest illegal. A magistrate issued an arrest warrant based upon probable cause, and the arrest in the girlfriend's apartment was legal because an arrest warrant allows police to detain an individual anywhere. *Payton v. New York*, 445 U.S. 573 (1980). Even if the entry tainted the arrest, based upon probable cause, the arrest would become legal as soon as the police removed Tom from his girlfriend's home. *New York v. Harris*, 495 U.S. 14 (1990). If police found contraband in the girlfriend's home, and charged her, she would have a basis to challenge the police entry, arguing that they needed a search warrant. *Steagald v. United States*, 451 U.S. 204 (1981).

Answer (B) is not the best answer. Even if Tom's mother had warned him that the police were on the way, there are no facts to support a reasonable belief that Tom, charged with the nonviolent crime of embezzlement, is armed or dangerous or a flight risk. Consequently, exigent circumstances did not exist to justify an entry without a search warrant. However, here there was an arrest warrant which makes the arrest legal, and Tom has no standing to object to the search of his girlfriend's house (absent additional facts such as he lived there part of the time).

Answers (C) and (D) are not the best answers. Ordinarily, entry of a home to arrest a nonresident without a search warrant and without consent or exigent circumstances violates the Fourth Amendment. However, the entry does not make the arrest illegal, presuming existence of probable cause. Here, a magistrate issued an arrest warrant based on probable cause. The police violated the girlfriend's privacy, not the defendant's privacy. Even if the entry tainted the arrest, the arrest would become legal as soon as the police removed Tom from his girlfriend's home.

137. **Answer (A) is correct.** In *Florence v. Board of Chosen Freeholders of the County of Burlington*, 566 U.S. 318 (2012), the Court held that a strip search at intake by county jail officials is permissible even when there is no reason to think that an arrestee is armed or possesses contraband. The Court reasoned that individuals arrested for even minor offenses can present security concerns and that jail officials act in a constitutional manner when they employ a standardized search protocol before an arrestee is admitted into the general population.

Florence would likely control, resulting in admission of the marijuana. The Fourth Amendment standard governing the scope of an intrusion following a custodial arrest is reasonableness. In order to determine the reasonableness of such an invasive procedure as a strip search, the court balances the need against the invasion that the search entails. Presumably, the governmental interest is serious — to prevent smuggling of contraband and weapons into the jail.

Answer (B) is incorrect as there is no evidence of an exigency. Incident to a custodial arrest, police may conduct a full search of an arrestee's person. However, strip searches are not treated like ordinary incidental searches. But if the arrestee is taken to jail as here, a routine strip search is permitted. *Florence.*

Answer (C) is incorrect. The scope of a search incident to incarceration is not limited by the offense for which the person is arrested. Because of security concerns, a strip search is permissible irrespective of the charge. *Florence.*

Answer (D) is incorrect because, as *Florence* held, a strip search at jail intake is permissible even when jail officials lack an individualized suspicion or probable cause that the arrestee possesses contraband or a weapon.

138. The statute authorizing warrantless record inspections will be upheld. The Supreme Court upheld a statute authorizing warrantless administrative searches of automobile junkyards. The Court found that junkyards are pervasively regulated businesses. Those businesses are regulated because of the societal interest in tracking down stolen vehicles. The same interest justifies regulation of second-hand car dealers that may serve as a market for stolen goods. Even though administrative searches originally focused on health and safety issues, expansion to other public interests did not cause the Supreme Court even to hesitate. *New York v. Burger*, 482 U.S. 691 (1987).

The issue turns on the lawfulness of warrantless inspections of such records. The thrust for warrantless inspection systems has focused on regulated businesses. The Supreme Court in *See v. City of Seattle*, 387 U.S. 541 (1967), stated that challenges to such programs could only be resolved on a case-by-case basis under the Fourth Amendment standard of reasonableness.

In *Burger*, the Supreme Court majority upheld the warrantless inspection scheme because junkyards are a closely regulated business. Thus, police do not need exigent circumstances to excuse the normal warrant requirement when inspecting a closely regulated business. A closely regulated business is apparently any business that has a long history of governmental regulation in a number of states.

The statutory scheme here is aimed specifically at finding evidence of criminal violations. The whole concept of administrative searches focused on the existence of a critical governmental interest, such as health and safety, which justified excusing traditional Fourth Amendment requirements such as a warrant and probable cause. Thus, historically, even though criminal prosecution could result from an administrative search, the primary purpose for the administrative search served a different governmental non-criminal interest. However, in *Burger*, the Court upheld a state regulatory inspection scheme, like the statute in this Question, that was intended solely to uncover evidence of criminal acts. This statute falls within the *Burger* holding expanding the scope of warrantless administrative searches to closely regulated businesses.

139. **Answer (C) is correct.** A thorny issue arises when a third person holds out to police that he has authority to consent when in fact he never did or no longer has such authority. The doctrine of apparent consent allows police to rely on third party consent when they erroneously, but reasonably, believe that the third party possesses common authority over the premises. An objective standard is used when testing whether facts available at the moment would warrant a reasonably cautious police officer to believe that the consenting party had authority. *Illinois v. Rodriguez*, 497 U.S. 177 (1990).

The issue often arises when police rely on the consent of a temporary worker in a home, such as a babysitter, to enter and conduct a search. Ordinarily, one would not expect such persons to have authority over the premises to grant consent to search. Even though the temporary worker may have the run of the house, that authority does not generally extend to allowing strangers into the house, including the police, except in emergency situations.

The rules pertaining to apparent authority provide that police may not rely on the consent of a third person when facts and circumstances would alert the reasonable person to question the third-party's authority. *See, e.g., United States v. Dearing*, 9 F.3d 1428 (9th Cir. 1993) (holding that a live-in babysitter lacked apparent authority to consent to search of employer's bedroom). Here, the facts should have put the police on notice that Craig, whom they knew to be a handyman, did not have unlimited access to every room in the house, except for the very limited purpose of making repairs. Craig's consent does not qualify as legal (apparent) consent for Fourth Amendment purposes. The police violated the Fourth Amendment when they searched the locked bedroom, and the pictures are inadmissible against the daughter.

Answer (A) is incorrect. The issue surrounding consent by a third person is to be resolved by determining the authority of the consenting person. The question should not be resolved under an agency theory. A third person may not waive another person's Fourth Amendment rights. The question comes down to whether Craig had sufficient access to the house and the daughter's bedroom to waive the owner's Fourth Amendment rights. Here, he did not have unlimited authority; his authority was limited to making necessary repairs.

Answer (B) is incorrect. Although police were investigating a potentially serious threat to public safety, the facts (involving a threat to classmates at school, not known to involve powerful weapons) do not present the type of urgency and immediate need that would qualify under exigent circumstances. Their investigation might have sufficiently ripened, given public concern with school shootings, to allow a judge to issue a search warrant to investigate the potential threat to public safety. The claim of exigency would fail.

Answer (D) is incorrect. Police may seek third-party consent, but they do not have to seek the consent of the target of the search. They may even seek third-party consent, in certain circumstances, after the target has refused consent. *Fernandez v. California*, 571 U.S. 292 (2014).

140. **Answer (C) is correct.** The search warrant was valid because it was based on the personal observations of Officer 2 in the open fields rather than from information from the anonymous tipster. The Supreme Court has held that so-called "open fields" are not subject to the same protection as the home or curtilage, even where the field is fenced, locked and posted with No Trespassing signs. *Oliver v. United States*, 466 U.S. 170 (1984).

Here, Officer 2 intruded on an "open field" and viewed the 100 marijuana plants. His discovery served as a proper basis for the later issuance of a search warrant based on probable cause. There were two simultaneous searches, one (of the porch) was unlawful (by Officer 1) and the other (of the open fields) lawful (by Officer 2). Because the unlawful search was not relied on in obtaining the search warrant, the lawful search served as an "independent source" for issuance of a valid search warrant. *Murray v. United States*, 487 U.S. 533 (1988).

Answer (A) is incorrect. While an anonymous tip ordinarily cannot by itself provide probable cause, police are free to investigate such tips. Entry onto an "open field" by Officer 2 requires no factual predicate, whether probable cause or reasonable suspicion. Here, the search warrant was based on Officer 2's personal observations in the open field and was not based on the anonymous tip. The warrant and ensuing searches are valid.

Answer (B) is incorrect. Officer 2 did not violate Glass's protected privacy interest by entering the open field and walking around. However, Officer 1 did violate Glass's Fourth Amendment rights by entering the patio attached to Glass' house. The issue is irrelevant, however, since there was a valid search warrant based solely on probable cause obtained by Officer 2's personal observations in the open fields. *Murray.*

Answer (D) is incorrect because ultimately, as discussed, all of the marijuana is admissible pursuant to the lawful search warrant that was issued based only on the legal observations of Officer 2.

141. **Answer (D) is correct.** The Supreme Court has held that police can conduct a search incident to an arrest only when they actually arrest, not when they merely issue a ticket or summons. *Knowles v. Iowa*, 525 U.S. 113 (1998). Here, the officer issued a ticket and then conducted an illegal search, requiring that the contraband be suppressed.

Answers (A) and (C) are incorrect. Whether or not speeding is an arrestable offense in the jurisdiction, the officer had already issued a traffic citation and did not arrest the defendant. Again, an officer may not conduct a warrantless search incident to the issuance of a traffic citation whether or not state law authorizes an arrest in the situation. *Knowles.*

Answer (B) is incorrect. Incident to any lawful stop of a motor vehicle, a police officer may order the motorist and any other occupants of the vehicle out of the car. The officer need not articulate any reason for ordering the occupant out of the vehicle. *Maryland v. Wilson,* 519 U.S. 408 (1997); *Pennsylvania v. Mimms,* 434 U.S. 106 (1977). However, absent an arrest, the authority over the motorist does not extend beyond ordering the motorist to get out or stay inside the vehicle. Any further intrusion, such as a limited search of the car's passenger compartment for weapons, must be based on articulable facts and circumstances creating a reasonable suspicion that the motorist is armed or otherwise poses a danger to the police officer. *Michigan v. Long,* 463 U.S. 1032 (1983). No such factual basis was presented in this case.

142. **Answer (B) is correct.** Incident to a valid non-custodial traffic stop, a police officer may order the motorist out of the car and may conduct a limited search — frisk — of the motorist's outer clothing for a weapon if facts support a reasonable suspicion that the motorist is armed and poses a threat to the officer. The supplemental facts in the question support such an inference. *Terry v. Ohio,* 392 U.S. 1 (1968). In fact, Abby's conduct justified the officer's decision to have her sit in the police car so that she would be under control. Moreover, a police officer may conduct a limited search of the interior of a vehicle for weapons under the same justification that gives rise to a frisk of the motorist's person. *Michigan v. Long,* 463 U.S. 1032 (1983). The gun was found during such a limited search as Abby was being given access to her car.

Answer (A) is incorrect. Although the motorist was validly stopped for speeding, there was no custodial arrest until after the officer found the gun under the driver's seat in the vehicle. Therefore, this was not a search incident to an arrest. Abby was being released at the time of the search.

Answer (C) is incorrect. Reasonable suspicion that the motorist is armed or dangerous will support a limited search of a vehicle for weapons. Probable cause is not required. Here there was reasonable suspicion but not probable cause.

Answer (D) is incorrect. The decision to issue the traffic citation and release the motorist does not negate the authority to conduct a limited *Terry*-type search for weapons to protect the safety of the officer as the defendant is being released. *Michigan v. Long.*

143. **Answer (C) is correct.** The evidence is inadmissible. The bullet would not have been lost if the procedure were delayed while a court order or warrant was sought. Therefore, there was no justification for the warrantless intrusion. If the object sought was transient and might have dissipated if the procedure were delayed, exigent circumstances could justify a warrantless intrusion.

Even if one could imagine such a procedure that might have been necessary to proceed without judicial authorization, the facts of this case do not come close to creating exigent circumstances to justify bypassing prior judicial authorization for a Fourth Amendment search and seizure. But prior judicial authorization is not required if the procedure is medically necessary for Dunn's health and safety. Here, the surgery was done at the request of the police and does not appear to be medically necessary. Moreover, the bullet was not going anywhere. Therefore, a court order should have been obtained in order to extract the bullet.

Answer (A) is incorrect. While the state's need for the evidence in this particular case would weigh heavily in favor of allowing such a procedure, there was no exigency to justify bypassing prior judicial authorization. The Fourth Amendment requires more than the evidence being important justify a search.

Answer (B) is incorrect. Incident to arrest, a defendant is subject to a full search of his or her person. However, the authority to conduct a warrantless search incident to arrest does not extend to surgical procedures, especially one that involves administration of a general anesthetic. For a surgical intrusion, even a warrant is probably insufficient. Whether a court will order a surgical intrusion must be decided by balancing the state's need for the evidence versus the nature of the intrusion and the risk it poses to the defendant. *Winston v. Lee*, 470 U.S. 753 (1985).

Answer (D) is incorrect. The United States Supreme Court has held that the Fifth Amendment privilege against compelled self-incrimination applies only to testimonial evidence, not physical evidence such as the bullet at issue here. *Schmerber v. California*, 384 U.S. 757 (1966). In this case, the issue comes down solely to whether the surgical intrusion to retrieve the bullet complied with the reasonableness command of the Fourth Amendment.

144. Both are admissible. There are several exceptions to the warrant requirement that allow for a search of an automobile without a search warrant. Here, the warrantless searches under the driver's seat and in the trunk were legal.

Search incident to an arrest. Incident to the arrest of a "recent occupant" of a vehicle, a police officer may search the interior compartment of the vehicle and any containers within it. *New York v. Belton*, 453 U.S. 454 (1981). Although *Arizona v. Gant*, 556 U.S. 332 (2009) limited the ability of the police to search a car incident to an arrest, this case is within the arena of permissible searches under *Gant*. Anderson was near the car and could access the interior at the time of the search. He was not handcuffed. *Gant* does not require some specific degree of certainty that Anderson could or would reach into the interior of the car; it only requires that the person be unsecured and within reaching distance of the car at the time of the search.

Gant also authorized search of the car's passenger compartment when it is "reasonable to believe evidence relevant to the crime of arrest might be found in the vehicle." Here, the defendant was arrested for driving while impaired and the officer reasonably searched the passenger compartment of the car for intoxicants such as liquor bottles or drugs. This would justify the search under the driver's seat that found the credit cards. However, *Belton* does not allow for the search of the trunk, which revealed the vase.

Automobile exception. A police officer may search the entire vehicle, including the trunk, under the automobile exception. However, the automobile exception requires independent probable cause to believe that contraband or evidence is located in the vehicle. *Carroll v. United States*, 267 U.S. 132 (1925). Here there may have been probable cause to search the car for evidence of intoxication, such as alcohol or drugs. And the credit cards, bearing various names, may be admissible under the plain view exception to the search warrant requirement. It is questionable whether the auto exception would allow for the search of the trunk, as the facts do not suggest a basis to infer probable cause that it contains evidence or contraband. *California v. Acevedo*, 500 U.S. 565 (1991).

Automobile frisk. Police may search the area around the driver's seat for a weapon if there is reasonable suspicion to believe that the motorist is armed or dangerous. *Michigan v. Long*, 463 U.S. 1032 (1983). However, a "frisk" of the vehicle is not permitted absent reasonable suspicion. Here there is no reason to believe Anderson was armed and dangerous, so a car search on this basis is not legal.

Inventory search. An alternative theory that would allow for discovery of the credit cards and vase is the search at the impound lot, which appears to comply with the inventory exception to the warrant requirement. An inventory search is not a search for evidence; it is an administrative procedure, comparable to booking at the police station, that permits police to inventory the contents of a vehicle in order to protect the owner's property, remove any weapons that might pose a threat, and insulate police from false claims of loss. *Colorado v. Bertine*, 479 U.S. 367 (1987); *South Dakota v. Opperman*, 428 U.S. 364 (1976).

Authorization to conduct an inventory search, however, requires a lawful impoundment. If the car is impounded, police may conduct an inventory of its contents and inventory the contents of closed containers provided it is part of the standardized procedure. *Florida v. Wells*, 495 U.S. 1 (1990). Anderson's car was lawfully impounded (he was arrested and taken to jail and no one was present to safeguard the car left in a public parking lot in the middle of the night) and a routine inventory search was permissible, making the vase admissible evidence as the product of a lawful search. Once the vase was inventoried, police consulted a list of stolen property and identified the vase as having been stolen.

145. **Answer (D) is correct.** An ordinary traffic stop does not trigger the need for *Miranda* warnings. It is short in duration, and its purpose is the issuance of a traffic citation. Moreover, it is done in full view of the public, and police are thus naturally restrained. *Berkemer v. Mc-Carty*, 468 U.S. 420 (1984). The test for whether a police-citizen encounter is custodial is an objective one: whether a reasonable person in the suspect's position would have believed that he was in custody. Here, the detention was lengthy, the officer had his hand on his service weapon, backup officers were present, Deputy Dodge had his hand on Stout's elbow, and Stout was being escorted to the police car. These factors in combination show that Stout likely was in custody when Officer Dogood asked him how much he had consumed that evening. Stout should have been advised of his *Miranda* rights before being asked the question.

Answer (A) is incorrect. This was not an ordinary traffic stop for the purpose of issuing a citation. It matured into a custodial arrest fairly quickly, requiring warnings prior to any questioning.

Answer (B) in incorrect. Stout was in custody before he was told he was under arrest. The police do not have to utter the magic words "you are under arrest" before a person is arrested. The issue is whether the person's freedom to leave has been curtailed. It is clear that Stout could not leave when asked about his drinking.

Answer (C) is incorrect. Ordinarily a traffic stop is not custodial and does not require police to administer *Miranda* warnings prior to questioning a suspect. However, traffic stops, like all *Terry* stops, can be custodial depending on the conduct of the officers. At the time the question was asked, the interaction had changed from a *Terry* stop to a custodial arrest.

146. **Answer (B) is the correct answer.** There was no valid reason for the state to have the pretrial holding cell identification take place outside the presence of defendant's attorney. It was the day of trial and counsel was present in the courtroom. The final out-of-court identification in the holding cell took place for either or both of two reasons: a final check to make sure that the defendant was the right one or an effort to bolster the victim/witness's testimony and provide her with a live opportunity to see the defendant in order to make her in-court identification more certain. Considering there was no reason whatsoever for excluding the defense attorney from the holding cell identification, the state raised unnecessary uncertainty about its own witness' testimony.

However, courts will hold that the victim/witness's in-court identification was admissible and did not violate due process. It was reliable and independent of the tainted holding cell viewing because of the victim's hour-long opportunity to observe the offender, her detailed description of him, the description's resemblance to Big, and her ability earlier on two occasions to identify him. Because of these factors, there was little likelihood that the in-court identification was so tainted by the holding cell identification that there was a very substantial likelihood of irreparable misidentification. *Manson v. Brathwaite*, 432 U.S. 98 (1977).

Answer (A) is incorrect. Big's Sixth Amendment right to counsel was violated when his attorney, who was nearby, was excluded from the holding cell viewing. While this violation may exclude testimony about the holding cell identification, the prosecution may still demonstrate that the in-court identification is not the fruit of the constitutional violation. Here, the victim/witness had extensive exposure to the rapist, gave a strong description of the defendant shortly after the crime and identified him twice before the tainted holding cell viewing. *United States v. Wade*, 388 U.S. 218 (1967).

Answer (C) is incorrect. The violation of the defendant's Sixth Amendment right to counsel was purposeful. However, that is not the end of the inquiry. The victim/witness may still identify the defendant in court if the state proves that the in-court identification is not the result of the tainted identification. The in-court identification is likely permissible here.

Answer (D) is incorrect. Although it could be argued that the holding cell show-up was a lineup, it does not matter. The Sixth Amendment right to counsel is equally applicable to show-ups and confrontations where the accused is not in a lineup but presented individually in a pretrial court appearance or out of court. *Moore v. Illinois*, 434 U.S. 220 (1977).

Part II

147. The information initially obtained by the police from the informant was insufficient to create probable cause. However, the police did not conduct a search or seizure based on this information. Ram and Smith's challenge to the surveillance and tracking will fail. The surveillance took place from a place the police were allowed to be, in public, and the police simply observed public activities of Ram and Smith. There is no expectation of privacy in activity one knowingly exposes to the public. *California v. Greenwood*, 486 U.S. 35 (1988); *United States v. Knotts*, 460 U.S. 276 (1983). The tracking of the car simply involved following Ram and Smith as they drove around town. This surveillance was not so extensive as to implicate an expectation of privacy. *See United States v. Jones*, 565 U.S. 400 (2012) (Alito, J., concurring). The tracking was limited in time and place and did not intrude on the interior of a home, which is deserving of particular privacy protection. Additionally, there was no trespass on the car because the police did not place a tracking device on the car, as in *Jones*. The surveillance and tracking were well within constitutional constraints and any information the police obtained can be used in the investigation or trial.

148. This question turns on the constitutionality of the traffic stop and search of Arnold's car. By the morning of June 2, the police investigation provided significant detailed corroboration of the informant's information. Although the informant is anonymous and of unknown reliability, the police investigation coupled with the tip constitute at least reasonable articulable suspicion and perhaps probable cause to believe a drug deal was happening. The police observed Arnold leaving the hotel room 45 minutes after entering. They could not tell whether he was still carrying the plastic bag. Although there could be a plethora of non-criminal explanations for Arnold's actions, this is not the constitutional test. Rather, the question is whether the police had reasonable suspicion or probable cause of Arnold's involvement in illegal drug activity. *Illinois v. Gates*, 462 U.S. 213 (1983).

Once Arnold entered the car possibly carrying the plastic bag, the police could lawfully stop the car. *California v. Acevedo*, 500 U.S. 565 (1991). The stop of the car was appropriate because, again, the police had reasonable suspicion or probable cause that a drug deal was underway.

Alternatively, the police had an independent legal basis to stop the car — the purported fog line violation. The particular question added the information that the officer was wrong, as a legal matter, in believing that crossing the fog line was a legal violation. In *Heien v. North Carolina*, 574 U.S. 54 (2014), the Court addressed whether an automobile stop can be deemed reasonable under the Fourth Amendment if the justification for the stop is based on the officer's misunderstanding of the law. Police, the Court held, can make reasonable mistakes of law. Here, the facts do not provide sufficient information about the specifics of the fog line statute but, presuming the officer's mistake was reasonable, the stop was lawful, and therefore, so too was the consent-based search (which appeared voluntary) resulting in discovery of the shotgun.

149. The stop of Ram and Smith is reviewable under two different Fourth Amendment constructs. First, was there probable cause to stop and arrest Ram and Smith? The totality of the circumstances seemingly supports probable cause to stop and arrest the men. A major factor is the informant's detailed information coupled with the independent investigation by the police. Also, the stop and search of Arnold's car supports a determination that, because the drugs were not in Arnold's car, there arguably was probable cause to believe the drugs could be in Ram's car and that Ram and Smith were involved in a drug transaction.

Even if the stop is not justified under probable cause, there was reasonable articulable suspicion to stop the car and investigate possible criminal activity. *Terry* permits stops of vehicles based on reasonable articulable suspicion. *Navarette v. California*, 572 U.S. 393 (2014); *Alabama v. White*, 496 U.S. 325 (1990). The totality of the circumstances supports a conclusion that Ram and Smith were involved in illegal activity. This permitted the stop of the vehicle and a brief questioning by agents.

Though a *Terry* stop is not a custodial arrest, this does not prevent the police from taking protective measures such as moving to a secure location or even handcuffing the people. *See Florida v. Royer*, 460 U.S. 491 (1983); *Pennsylvania v. Mimms*, 434 U.S. 106 (1977). The use of force in an investigatory stop is reviewed under a reasonableness standard. *United States v. Sharpe*, 470 U.S. 675 (1985). The lower courts have consistently held that the use of handcuffs does not necessarily transform a *Terry* stop into a custodial arrest (requiring probable cause). *See United States v. Hood*, 774 F.3d 638 (10th Cir. 2014); *Matz v. Klotka*, 769 F.3d 517 (7th Cir. 2014).

However, here, there was likely a custodial arrest. The police drew their weapons, handcuffed Ram and Smith, placed them in separate police vehicles, took them to another location, and provided *Miranda* warnings.

150. There are two possible justifications for the search of Smith. If the detention of Smith was an arrest as outlined in the previous question, then the search of his pocket was a valid search incident to arrest. *United States v. Robinson*, 414 U.S. 218 (1973). There is no need for any suspicion or probable cause to do the search.

Second, if the detention was a valid *Terry* stop, then the removal of the motel key would likely remain valid. The police suspected Ram and Smith to be involved in a drug transaction, which often involve weapons. The facts reveal that the officer did a pat down of Smith and only removed the key and the attached metal plate after feeling it during the pat down. If the reviewing court believes the officer reasonably thought it was a weapon, the key and its metal attachment could be lawfully removed. *Minnesota v. Dickerson*, 508 U.S. 366 (1993).

151. Smith's consent to the search of Room 17 appears to be valid. He had a key to the room, claimed the room was in his name, the police had confirmed the room was in his name, and he was seen entering and leaving the room over a few days. This was actual authority consent. *United States v. Matlock*, 415 U.S. 164 (1974). In addition, apparent authority consent would be reasonable. *Illinois v. Rodriguez*, 497 U.S. 177 (1990).

Another issue is whether Smith's consent was voluntary. Although the nature of the detention is a factor in determining whether Smith voluntarily agreed to the search, the conduct of the officers was well within constitutional limits. Nor is there any indication of police overreaching or coercion in obtaining consent. *Bumper v. North Carolina*, 391 U.S. 543 (1968). People under arrest may voluntarily consent to a search.

Even if Smith's consent is somehow invalid, the police could rely on Ram's consent, as well, because he was staying with Smith in Room 17 and had a key to it. At the least, he may have had apparent consent. *Rodriguez.*

Index

Topic	Question
Appellate Review (of Motion to Dismiss)	116–119
Arrest	34–39, 84, 136, 149
Automobile Exception	56–58, 60, 63, 144
Blood Testing	22
Community Caretaking (Police Function)	53
Confessions (see Miranda, Due process, Sixth Amendment)	
Consent Searches	74–79, 139, 151
Due Process — Confessions	105, 106
Electronic Eavesdropping	80
Exclusionary Rule (Fourth Amendment)	81–84, 112–115, 120, 122–128, 136
Exigent Circumstances (Excusing Warrant)	36, 49, 50, 52
Eyewitness Identification	107–111, 123, 146
Frisk (Protective Search for Weapons)	18, 64–68, 142, 150
Incorporation	1, 2
Inventory Searches	61–63, 144
Miranda — Confessions	85–95, 102, 121, 129–131, 145
Motion to Dismiss	12
Plain View	31–33, 53, 135
Pretextual Stops and Arrests	40
Privacy, Right of (What Qualifies as a Search)	5–10, 23, 132, 140, 147, 148

Topic	Question
Private Person Search	11
Protective Sweep (per *Maryland v. Buie*)	41, 42
Right to Privacy (see Privacy, Right of)	
Search Incident to Arrest	
Automobile	21, 54, 55, 65, 141, 144
Homes	46–48
Persons and Possessions	19–20, 43–45, 59
Search Warrants	13–17, 22, 24–30, 133–135, 143
Securing a Home to Secure a Search Warrant	51
Sixth Amendment — Confessions	103, 104
Special Needs/Administrative Searches	69, 71–73, 119, 138
Standing	112–115
State Constitutional Law	3, 4
Stops by Police (Traffic and per *Terry v. Ohio*)	70, 149
Strip Search	137